The Complete Plain Words

The Complete Plain Words

by Sir Ernest Gowers

REVISED BY
SIDNEY GREENBAUM & JANET WHITCUT

INTRODUCTION BY JOSEPH EPSTEIN

David R. Godine · Publisher · Boston

As if plain words, useful and intelligible instructions, were not as
good for an esquire, or one that is in commission from the King,
as for him that holds the plough.
John Eachard

The Grounds and Occasions of the Contempt of the
Clergy and Religion enquired into. 1670

First U.S. edition published in 1988 by
David R. Godine, Publisher, Inc.
Horticultural Hall
300 Massachusetts Avenue
Boston, Massachusetts 02115

Library of Congress Cataloging-in-Publication Data
Gowers, Ernest, Sir, 1880–1966.
  The complete plain words.
  Includes index.
  1. English language—Style. 2. English language—
Errors of usage. 3. English language—Terms and phrases.
I. Greenbaum, Sidney. II. Whitcut, Janet. III. Title.
PE1421.G592 1988   428   87-46281
ISBN 0-87923-733-3

First printing
Printed in the United States of America

What's the Usage?

In the preface to a small but impressively lucid book on punctuation written in 1939 and entitled *Mind the Stop*, the author, an Englishman named G. V. Carey, reserved his last sentences for "a spasm of self-consciousness" in which, given the year of publication, he felt he ought to register the fact that "the mind of one who happens to have an eye for a comma is not necessarily incapable of comprehending larger issues or embracing wider interests." Yet perhaps no disclaimer, however mild, needed to be entered. One of the reasons that nations go to war is so that men like G. V. Carey, in immaculately setting out the subtleties of the semicolon, can carry on the work of civilization. Today, nearly fifty years later, when the art of careful punctuation threatens among the young to become as widespread as that of intaglio, a book such as Carey's seems rather more significant. But then those who have taken it upon themselves to be guardians of the language must alternate hourly in their feeling about their work between certainty of its fundamental importance and an at least equal certainty about its utter hopelessness.

All guardians of the language resemble a little the village idiot in the *shtetl* of Frampol, who was given the job of standing at the village gates to wait for the coming of the Messiah. The pay is not high, he was told, but he didn't have to worry about running out of work. The guardians of the language need similarly never worry about running out of work. Like Heraclitus's famous river—"Upon those who step into the same river different and ever different waters flow down"—the river of language continues to flow along, never remaining the same, changing every foot of the way. Heraclitus spoke of his river being in perpetual flux but never of its muddying, whereas in the river of language flux frequently does issue in mud, garbage, and other detritus. To change classical references, the task of the guardian of language can be likened to that of cleaning out the Augean stables with the horses still in them. This, for reasons needing no explanation, is not everybody's idea of a good time.

What may need explanation is the motivation of those who go in for it. As a university teacher, I find myself, among my students, from time to time wielding a small Augean broom. Why do I bother? It won't do to say, *à la* John Wayne in the role of federal marshal, "Cause it's my job, ma'am." It is closer to the truth to say that woolly circumlocutions, psychobabblous phrasing and sentiments, and language used as if it were a game of horseshoes (in which one expects points for being close) offends me. What it offends is my sense of decorum. When a student, asked about the quality of the character Verloc's relationship with his wife Winnie in Joseph Conrad's *The Secret Agent,* answers, "At this point in time, a caring person would not consider it meaningful, at least hopefully not," I find I cannot let it pass—especially at these prices. It offends me that such wobbly language is being tossed around by a high-IQ kid in a hall of learning where the cover charge is roughly $15,000 a head. Such language also makes it impossible, of course, to talk about literature or anything else above the level of yogurt.

I go directly into my gentle crank act. "Meaningful?" I ask. "What can 'meaningful' possibly *mean?* And 'caring'—caring for or about what, exactly? Does time, I must inquire, truly have 'points'? I note, too, that you say 'hopefully.' Who precisely is doing the hoping in that sentence?" An amusing old guy, they must think, as I rocket off on one of these brief tirades, but with kind of a short fuse. I recall, too, an occasion on which one of my students asked me why I spoke so slowly. I hadn't been aware that I did. Then it occurred to me that, in my speech, at least before a classroom, I take pains to form complete sentences. For the majority of my students, most of whom come from homes where their parents attended university, and even though they themselves are enrolled in an elite (a word they do not take kindly to) school, hearing someone speak in complete sentences is a real novelty.

People who take pains with their language are not just now in danger, through their vast number, of bringing about a population explosion. They are instead a bit difficult to find; you won't, certainly, find them concentrated in any one place. You won't find many of them among the professoriat; in fact, much of the dreariest abstract language we now have was first put into circulation by social scientists, though nowadays historians, philosophers, and literary scholars are hot on the social scientists' gummy heels. It used to be said that the working class provided pungent and solidly concrete additions to the language and the upper-class provided standards of correctness. But today no social class is notable for correct or interesting speech.

Once upon a time, though not so recently as all that, careful English was part of the partrimony of the well-born. Edith Wharton, in her memoir *A Backward Glance*, noted that a strong element in her upbringing was "a reverence for the English language as spoken according to the best usage," and this despite the fact that her parents read little and had scarcely any intellectual interests. "Usage, in my childhood, was as authoritative an element in speaking English as tradition was in social conduct," she writes. The kind of English Edith Wharton was taught to speak was "easy, idiomatic English, neither pedantic nor 'literary'," and while her parents' sensitivity to careful English remained a mystery to her, they always wanted their children's English to be better, "that is, easier, more flexible and idiomatic." English like that ain't spoke here no more.

English is still spoke, of course, but it is rarely bespoke, as one imagines it was in Edith Wharton's New York, or at Henry Adams' Harvard. Language today seems chiefly to come off the rack, no matter what social class is speaking or writing it. Not that there aren't people who make very deliberate efforts to say precisely what they mean; or that there aren't writers—novelists and critics, essayists and poets, historians and philosophers, the occasional scientist—who command styles of true power, real elegance, and general felicity. There are, but their number and social provenance are not—probably cannot be—known. They have determined to take pains. But why do they bother? Why, now that one's use of language has scarcely any effect on one's financial fate or social standing, does anyone any longer bother?

Although the honors list of those who have taken up the cause of good linguistic hygiene has over the centuries included Confucius, Cervantes, Swift, Samuel Johnson, William Hazlitt, and George Orwell, the same cause, it must be allowed, has attracted prigs, pedants, intellectual bullies, and snobs. "She is, I am sorry to have to say," a woman I know reported to me of another woman, "one of those people who is always misusing 'hopefully'." More recently, I met a man who told me that, in the middle of delivering a wedding toast, he was corrected for incorrectly using the word "fulsome." No doubt there were people in fifth-century B.C. Athens who discovered solecisms in Pericles's funeral oration as there were those in twentieth-century London who discovered solecisms in Winston Churchill's World War II broadcasts. Purists have always existed who write and speak with the linguistic equivalent of their little fingers crooked above the cup of language, people—they, I suspect, would prefer the word "persons"—of whom H. W. Fowler once remarked, "There speaks one of those friends from whom the English language may well pray to be saved, one of the modern precisians who have more zeal than discretion." In the lengthy saga that one thinks of as the perpetual decline of the English language—it has been going on for nearly a thousand years—the current villains are well known: the perpetrators of the hopelessly abstract, the devotees of the too precise, the schoolmasters who invent unnecessary rules, the populists who decry the need for any rules whatsoever.

The heroes of this saga are those extraordinary writers who in every age demonstrate that more can be done with the language than might have hitherto been thought. Some among them, viewing the world in ways no one before them has done, forge new styles to give expression to their new views; others work within traditional styles, but through their individuality develop them to a higher power. Whether avant-garde or traditional, such writers, whose unshakeable assumption is that everything in the world can be rendered in words, freshen and regularly refreshen the language, saving it from ossification and from rot.

On occasion such writers have themselves complained of the spoliation of the language. Jonathan Swift, writing to his prime minister, held that "daily improvements [in English] are by no means in proportion to its daily corruptions; that pretenders to polish and refine it have chiefly multiplied abuses and absurdities; and that in many instances it offends against every part of grammar." In his now famous essay "Politics and The English Language," George Orwell, in plain Orwellian fashion, set out the possibilities for deep corruption when politicians go to work on language. Evelyn Waugh, the most elegant and efficient of twentieth-century prose writers, used to fume against the horrendous lapses in English usage he claimed to find all around him—further evidence, of course, of the general degradation of the modern world. Edmund Wilson was not shy about returning certain of his correspondents' letters with his corrections of their grammar, syntax, and semantics indelicately written in the margins.

Apart from demonstrating how language ought to be used through their own writing and sending up occasional wails about its debasement by politicians, social scientists, advertising types, and other linguistical thugs, writers have not generally been much interested in fighting the trench warfare of language. This has been left to such foot soldiers as lexicographers and linguists, many of them academics, but perhaps the most impressive among them not. The English have been particularly strong in this line, a line that begins with James Murray (1837–1915), who personally edited roughly half the great *Oxford English Dictionary*, Henry Watson Fowler (1858–1933), who with his brother Frank edited the *Concise Oxford Dictionary* and alone wrote *A Dictionary of Modern English Usage*, Eric Partridge (1894–1979), whose many lexicographical works include the *Dictionary of Slang and Unconventional English, Usage and Abusage*, and *Origins, A Short Etymological Dictionary of Modern English*, and Sir Ernest Gowers (1880–1966), who revised Fowler's *Dictionary of Modern English Usage* and produced two remarkable brief books of his own entitled *Plain Words* and *ABC of Plain Words*, which, taken together, have appeared in various editions as THE COMPLETE PLAIN WORDS.

Of these extraordinary books, perhaps the most remarkable is the one you now hold in your hands. Written by a non-specialist for non-specialists, it is neither technical nor scholarly nor otherwise daunting. THE COMPLETE PLAIN WORDS has a plain enough purpose: to make the task of writing easier for those who wish to write better than they now do. "Writing," remarks Sir Ernest on the opening page of his Prologue, "is an instrument for conveying ideas from one mind to another; the writer's job is to make the readers apprehend the meaning readily and precisely." All the author's efforts in this useful volume are bent toward helping his readers achieve that end. So subtle is Gowers' tact, so graceful and becalming his manner, that one soon reads along in his book quite forgetting that one is in the hands of a consummate teacher. One of his chief lessons is that the considerate writer must put himself in the mind of the reader he is addressing. THE COMPLETE PLAIN WORDS teaches that careful writing is arrived at by a combination of courtesy and good sense and taking pains with small details. By dealing one by one with the problems of writing through his own courtesy, good sense, and attention to detail, Ernest Gowers eliminates the element of mystification from writing while inspiring in his readers the belief that their own writing can be improved, and vastly so.

James Murray, H. W. Fowler, Eric Partridge and Ernest Gowers were all born while Queen Victoria ruled, all had what one has come to think of as nineteenth-century energy, all had the quite sensible Victorian belief in self-improvement. K. M. Elisabeth Murray, in *Caught in the Web of Words*, has chronicled her grandfather James Murray's prodigious efforts in the composition of the *OED*. Of Eric Partridge, who was born a New Zealander and whose death occurred fewer than ten years ago, nowhere near so much is known, or at any rate has been revealed. Rather more is known of H. W. Fowler, who was in so many ways an extraordinary character, and I shall get to some of it presently. Sir Ernest Gowers is a man about whom very little is known, and this by design, for he was an English civil servant—a "public servant," in the older and better phrase—and as such felt altogether content with anonymity.

Although Henry Fowler was born twenty-two years before Ernest Gowers and Gowers died thirty-three years after Fowler, and although the two men never met, one tends to think of them as a tandem. Gowers, of course, performed a singular service in revising Fowler's *Dictionary of Modern English Usage*, tactfully bringing it up to date without allowing any serious loss in its idiosyncratic character. Gowers, in "H. W. Fowler: The Man and His Teaching," has written the most intelligent essay on Fowler. But above and beyond these services that the younger man performed for the older, Gowers seems to complement Fowler as Fowler felt that the word meticulous should have complemented the word punctilious, "the two covering between them the positive accuracy that omits no detail and the negative accuracy that admits no error."

As befits a man who took it upon himself to shape up the English language, H. W. Fowler kept himself in top physical trim. Until nearly the end of his life, he was a runner and a swimmer; he ran to his swim, swam, and then home he ran. A photograph of Fowler that appears in *The Oxford University Press, An Informal History* shows him outside his cottage in Guernsey, bald, goateed, in shorts that fall just below the knees and in an English football jersey, holding a towel that he will doubtless use after his swim. He is a shortish man, well set-up physically—neither muscle-bound nor thin but without any trace of softness or fat, compact—with a confident smile that seems to come easily to him. Short, solid, humorous, H. W. Fowler may be said to resemble nothing quite so much as one of his own entries in *A Dictionary of Modern English Usage*.

How does one happen to set oneself up as arbiter of the entire English language? In H. W. Fowler's case the answer is that he had first to fail at a number of much smaller tasks. The son of a school-master, Fowler, after winning a scholarship to Balliol College, Oxford, failed to get a first and had to settle for a second-class degree. Upon leaving Oxford, the master of Balliol, Benjamin Jowett ("There's no knowledge, but I know it"), gave him the following characteristically curt recommendation:

I have a very high opinion of Mr. H. W. Fowler. While at Balliol College he has made himself respected. He is quite a gentleman in manner and feeling and has good sense and good taste. He is a very fair scholar and has, I think, a natural aptitude for the profession of Schoolmaster.

A schoolmaster Fowler became, first teaching at a school in Scotland and then settling in at a quite good public school called Sedbergh in the northwest corner of Yorkshire, where he remained for seventeen years. Shy and fastidious as a young man, he had not the gift of easy intimacy, and consequently was a teacher of the kind that his students did not adore but came eventually—sometimes even in later life—to admire. Fowler left Sedberg over a religious dispute with the headmaster, who asked that his housemasters put their students through confirmation, which Fowler, who was up for a housemaster-ship, felt himself unprepared and unwilling to do. When the head-master remained adamant on the point, Fowler wrote to him: "the choice is between acquiescence and resigning my post, and the latter is what I now feel compelled to do. . . . It is better to recognize that we have a perfectly friendly, but irreconcilable difference of opinion, and to regard the matter as settled." Along with keeping himself in physical trim, Fowler, as this incident reveals, liked to keep himself in moral trim.

Fowler was forty-one years old when his teaching career was finished. He next turned to journalism. He moved to London and attempted to write for the British weeklies. He did publish in the *Spectator*, though not frequently enough to be thought a regular contibutor. According to G. G. Coulton, upon whose lengthy memoiristic account of H. W. Fowler I have been drawing,* he put

---

* "H. W. Fowler" by G. G. Coulton can be found in *Society for Pure English Tract Number XLIII*. pp. 99–158; the Clarendon Press, 1934.

together two volumes in typescript of essays he had written, but no publisher was interested in them. He did bring out one of these volumes, which he entitled *More Popular Fallacies*, at his own expense. Of this volume, Coulton remarks: "It fell flat: being neither good enough nor bad enough for popular success." Doubtless the difficulty was in part owing to Fowler's style. Gowers, in his essay on Fowler, notes that "Fowler's style is mathematical rather than literary," adding: "His first concern was precision not elegance, and, as we all know, it is not easy to combine the two."

When Fowler was attempting to make his way as a journalist, the *Spectator* accepted one of his essays, but, having long delayed its publication, informed him that they would no longer be able to run it, though they enclosed a check for full payment. Fowler, with no spite but only his customary moral scrupulousness intended, returned the check. In 1915, with England at war, Fowler, at age fifty-seven, enlisted, claiming to be forty-four. (His brother Frank, at forty-five, also enlisted.) Given his own program of physical fitness, Fowler apparently found military training no hardship. What he did find a hardship was that, when his battalion was sent to France, he and his brother were not permitted to fight but instead were given various dogswork—dishwashing, coalheaving, porterage—which caused him to write a formal letter, owning up to his true age and requesting that he either be permitted to do real soldiering or be discharged. In the event, he and his brother were discharged, but the incident once again illustrates H. W. Fowler's scrupulosity, his moral fastidiousness.

Much earlier, in 1903 in fact, Fowler departed London to live in Guernsey. There he built a cottage fifty yards' distance from his brother Frank's cottage and roughly a mile from the sea, which made possible a daily swim and a two-mile run. It also made possible editorial collaboration with Frank, whose training in classics was quite as good as Henry's and whose intellectual interests were congruent with his older brother's. Their first combined enterprise was a translation, in four volumes, of the Greek writer Lucian (c. 117–180 A.D.), which appeared under the authoritative imprint of the Clarendon Press, of the Oxford University Press. Before the *Lucian* appeared, Henry Fowler inquired of the editor of the Oxford University Press of his interest in his and his brother's next project:

We have just begun to collect materials for a little book which we think
might serve a useful purpose, but which would perhaps not be in your line.
This is a sort of English composition manual, from the negative point of
view, for journalists and amateur writers. There is a vast number of writers
nowadays who have something to say and know how to make it lively or
picturesque, but being uneducated cannot write a page without a blunder or
cacophony or piece of verbiage or false pathos or clumsiness or avoidable
dulness. . . . It might possibly, we think, be mildly entertaining as well as
serviceable.

Charles Cannan, the editor of the Oxford University Press, replied
that "we in the office would welcome an antibarbarus," and went on
to explain that there were two possible publics for such a book: "one
is the schools which desire something in the nature of a Rhetoric (in
the old sense). The other is that which you have in mind: the editor
of the *Spectator* and the people who write in the *Times*." The book
was eventually published, in 1906, under the title *The King's English*
by H. W. Fowler and F. G. Fowler. Peter Sutcliffe, the author of
the informal history of the Oxford University Press, writes, correctly,
that the Fowlers' book "was never really suitable for schools, and it
was taking a narrow view to suppose that it would serve as a guide
for journalists." Nor did the book receive a hardy critical welcome.
Desmond MacCarthy, whom one tends to think a generous critic,
wrote of *The King's English* that "it is clear that such rules must often
involve the consideration of barely perceptible subtleties which waste
the writer's time." The greater significance of *The King's English*,
however, is that it formed the basis on which Henry Fowler, after
his younger brother's death, would write *A Dictionary of Modern
English Usage*.

A Dictionary of Modern English Usage is one of a shelf of fifty or so
great books written in English in this century. It is immensely helpful,
happily memorable, and endlessly re-readable; it stands in a splen-
didly synecdochic relation to the culture that produced it: from the
part that is this book one can infer the entire tradition of correctness,
lucidity, and wit that once seemed emblematic of English intellectual
life at its best. *A Dictionary of Modern English Usage* is also clearly
the book that all Fowler's previous experience led him to write. After
working on *The Concise Oxford Dictionary* and *The Pocket Oxford*

Dictionary, both bearing the names of the two Fowler brothers (Frank died in 1918), Henry Fowler announced that he had grown tired of straightforward lexicography. He thought about turning to a dictionary that would leave out the obvious words and concentrate instead on idioms and other aspects of language that exist in a state of jumbled inexactitude in the minds of even the most highly intelligent people. Fowler thought of it as his "Idiom Dictionary," though at Oxford University Press one of the principal editors referred to it, in a letter to Fowler, as "A Utopian dictionary [that] would sell very well—in Utopia." But Fowler, as Englishmen of his own day might have said, pressed on, finishing the work, which was given the title *A Dictionary of Modern English Usage*, in 1925. It was reprinted four times the year of publication, 1926, along with a special impression for the United States of fifty thousand copies.

Whenever a serious book becomes a best-seller, even a modest best-seller, an explanation is required. The most cogent explanation for the success of *A Dictionary of Modern English Usage* is to be found in the character of its author. Pedagogue, lexicographer, essayist, late Victorian, all the elements in Fowler's character conjoined to make this remarkable book, product of his intellectual maturity, the capstone to his career. Sir Ernest Gowers felt that the appeal of *Modern English Usage* "lies partly in the way the author reveals his idiosyncrasy to the reader," taking his definition of *idiosyncrasy* from Fowler's own entry on the word in *Modern English Usage*:

Its meaning is peculiar mixture, & the point of it is best shown in the words that describe Brutus: *His life was gentle & the elements so mixed in him that Nature might stand up and say to all the world "This was a man."*

No supposed reference work has ever been more suffused by the spirit of a single man than H. W. Fowler's *Dictionary of Modern English Usage*, including Samuel Johnson's *Dictionary*. In this wondrous work, Fowler, freed from the stringent demands of straight and strict lexicogaphy, let fly, never restraining his wit or whimsy or opinionation. Every writer seeks his true form, and Fowler's was evidently the dictionary article, which one scarcely considers a literary form at all, though he was able to turn it into one. Even in Fowler's hands, an odd form it is; it is a form with a beginning, which usually formulates the problem; a middle, which provides illustrations of error occasioned by ignorance of the problem; and generally no end whatsoever, for the article frequently trails off after the final illustration with no summarizing statement from the author. The wit and whimsy, the point and pique, are found at the front, as in this opening for the article "Sturdy Indefensibles," which sounds the characteristic Fowlerian note:

Many idioms are seen, if they are tested by grammar or logic, to express badly, even sometimes to express the reverse of, what they are nevertheless well understood to mean. Good people point out the sin, & bad people, who are more numerous, take little notice & go on committing it; then the good people, if they are foolish, get excited & talk of ignorance and solecisms, & are laughed at as purists; or, if they are wise, say no more about it & wait. The indefensibles, sturdy as they may be, prove one after another to be not immortal.

No one, I more than suspect, would ever think to look up such material in an entry with the title of "Sturdy Indefensibles," or look to "Elegant Variation" to deal with the problem of repetitions, or expect to find abbreviations under "Curtailed Words." To be sure, many items in *Modern English Usage* are precisely where one would expect to find them—"Split infinitive," "Participles," "Subjunctives"—as are entries on specific words that are not always used with sufficient distinctiveness: "barbarian," "barbaric," "barbarous," for example. But who would have thought to look up the vaguely archaic language of certain nineteenth-century novels under "Novelese," or would search out the wish to avoid perfectly useful common words under "Novelty Hunting"? The entry "Superiority" turns out to be about apologizing for using slang in one's prose, and has the following extraordinary beginning:

Surprise a person of the class that is supposed to keep servants cleaning his own boots, & either he will go on with the job while he talks to you, as if it were the most natural thing in the world, or else he will explain that the bootboy or scullery-maid is ill & give you to understand that he is, despite appearance, superior to bootcleaning. If he takes the second course, you conclude that he is not superior to it; if the first, that perhaps he is.

Owing to this often slightly bizarre arrangement, *A Dictionary of Modern English Usage* is a book best approached serendipitously (see the Fowler entry "Love of The Long Word"). It is a particularly fine volume to wander around in. When not going to the book for help with a particular problem—I looked a while back to see if Fowler had anything to say about the word "pique," which I used a few paragraphs before: apart from brief advice on pronunciation, he didn't—I tend to roam around in its pages, usually stopping at an entry on a word I have used myself but never with full confidence. Such a word I recently looked up in Fowler is "palpable," which he says provides a useful illustration "of the need of caution in handling dead metaphors." He then tells exactly what the word does mean, even in a generous definition, and closes with the admonition that "P. is one of the words that are liable to clumsy treatment of this sort because they have never become vernacular English, & yet are occasionally borrowed by those who have no scholarly knowledge of them."

I enjoy Fowler when he is dispensing not merely instruction but advice, particularly of a moralizing kind. I enjoy the Fowler who begins his entry "French Words" by remarking, "Display of superior knowledge is as great a vulgarity as display of superior wealth— greater, indeed, inasmuch as knowledge should tend more definitely than wealth toward discretion & good manners. . . . To use French words that your reader or hearer does not know or does not fully understand, to pronounce them as if you were one of the select few to whom French is second nature when he is not one of those few (& it is ten thousand to one that neither you nor he will be so), is inconsiderate & rude." *Modern English Usage* is a chest filled with such didactic gems. "Men, especially," wrote Fowler in his entry "Didacticism," "are as much possessed by the didactic impulse as women by the maternal instinct." The Victorian schoolmaster in Fowler was never for long in abeyance. If his *Modern English Usage* is in effect a book of instruction in manners—in how to conduct oneself on the page—it is also a book of moral instruction. For the Victorians, as their historian Gertrude Himmelfarb has convincingly argued, the separation between manners and morals did not exist; manners were morals, morals created manners, and with impressively salubrious result.

In a dispute over the grammatical construction that Fowler termed the "fused participle," Otto Jespersen, the Danish philologist, called H. W. Fowler an "instinctive grammatical moraliser." Sir Ernest

Gowers, in his essay on Fowler, tells us that Fowler resented the attack but not the epithet. Gowers nicely deals with the charge of "instinctive grammatical moralising," when he writes: "The prime mover of Fowler's instinctive moralizing was not grammatical grundyism; it was intellectual fastidiousness. He had the soul of a craftsman and could not bear slovenly work." Fowler detested affectation and empty authority. He was ever the critic of the slipshod journalist, the pompous scholar, the precious aesthete. His hatred of humbug could on occasion take a moral turn, but he was inevitably moral on the side of good sense.

It may well be that the moral tone in Fowler, combined with the frequency with which he uses such words as "barbarous" and "vulgar," have lent *A Dictionary of Modern English Usage* the reputation of a crotchety work composed by a heavy-breathing reactionary. Such a reputation, along with being unearned, couldn't be more wrong. Nor will it do to score Fowler off as an amiable pedant with a penchant for moralizing and an agile wit. In a way that Fowler himself would no doubt have found amusing, he has come to stand, in matters having to do with English usage, for the stodgy, the staid, the stuffy. In point of plain fact, H. W. Flower was in his day a radical. "Here," as Sir Ernest Gowers writes, "was an emancipator from the fetters of the grammatical pedants that had bound us for so long."

English is not static—neither in vocabulary nor in grammar, nor yet in that elusive quality called style. The fashion in prose alternates between the ornate and the plain, the periodic and the colloquial. Grammar and punctuation defy all the efforts of grammarians to force them into the mould of a permanent code of rules. Old words drop out or change their meanings; new words are admitted. What was stigmatised by the purists of one generation as a corruption of the language may a few generations later be accepted as an enrichment, and what was then common currency may have become a pompous archaism or acquired a new significance.

It is salutary to remember that two such smart fellows as Joseph Addison and Jonathan Swift objected to the emergence of the useful word "mob" (which derives from "mobile"). No doubt others have looked down upon "gazebo," "gismo," and "go-go." A new word is a fine thing when it is vivid and crisp and amusing and needed. New formations of old words, the most common mechanism of which derives from turning old nouns into new verbs ("finalize," "prioritize"), has to be viewed with the gravest suspicion, but at the same time it is useful to recall as THE COMPLETE PLAIN WORDS reminds us that this is the way the words "diagnose" and "sterilize" entered the language. Mike Tyson, the current heavyweight champion, speaking of his wife's initial distrust of boxers, not long ago remarked that this changed. "I took her off her feet," he said. "I suaved her." As a verb, "suave" is mildly amusing, but even now I see the word's ruination in an advertising campaign: "Suave her with Soave Bolla."

The problem is that it is difficult to object to most new words, or terms, or even trends, on principle. Usually there is no principle involved. One despises a new word because it sounds barbarous; yet once that word barbarous is past one's lips, the game is up—the charge of snobbery has already been entered. I do not mind the charge all that much myself, but I prefer to argue from more solid ground. Too often the ground in these matters slides away from under one. The argument from etymology, for example, is not usually convincing. I am someone who uses the word "presently" in the sense of "soon" or "by and by" and not, as it is nowadays more often used, as a synonym for "currently." I have all along been doing so under the assumption that I had the authority of etymology on my side. Wrong. The Gowers-revised Fowler entry on "presently" has it that the word originally meant "instantly," and so its etymology is really closer to "currently" than to my usage. I shall continue to use the word in the way I have, but henceforth with a slight suspicion that I may merely be suaving myself.

When I say that it is difficult to object to new words, terms, or trends on principle, what I mean, more precisely, is that it is difficult to object to them on general principles. One has, as in traffic and divorce courts, to take each case as it comes, arguing the demerits of every separate entry. I do not like the word "arguably," for example, as it is used in the sentence, "Anthony Powell is arguably one of the great English novelists of the twentieth century." I think that, in this usage, in which the word "arguably" means "a respectable argument for the case could be made," it is a weasel-word, which allows one to get around answering the question of whether Powell is or isn't one of the century's great English novelists. I am not much for the word "intriguing" either, as in the sentence, "I find women of her kind intriguing." I cannot see what advantage "intriguing" in this usage has over "interesting" or "fascinating," except perhaps to make the person who uses it himself sound, you should pardon the expression, "intriguing." Fowler says of the word used in this sense that "it is one of the Gallicisms, & Literary Critics Words, that have no merit whatever except that of unfamiliarity to the English reader, & at the same time the great demerit of being identical with & therefore confusing the sense of a good English word." I would only add that, so often has the word come to be used in the way I have described it, it no longer has the merit of unfamiliarity.

In his day, Sir Ernest did not have to deal with the vexing problem of ethnic sensitivities, where even the nomenclature of groups is regularly changing, so that one cannot know if, say, a word such as "Chicano" is or is not in good form on a given day. He also escaped the earth before the most recent wave of feminists arrived with the demand that language be—get ready for a word that is going to look like a loose piece of barbed-wire—"desexitized." Not only do the more exacting feminists wish to eliminate feminine nouns such as actress and poetess but they are none too pleased with masculine ones such as chairman and mankind. The current editors of THE COMPLETE PLAIN WORDS suggest that one does best to write one's way around the problem. "You will avoid giving offence," they write, "by using *human accomplishments* instead of *man's accomplishments* and *working hours* instead of *man hours*."

That is probably sound enough advice, though I do not myself think that the day of equality will be at hand when everyone uses "Ms.," and heads of academic departments all refer to themselves as "chair," and people who do not know the sex of their unseen audience address them in letters as "Dear Gentlepersons." I do not like "Ms." because you cannot say it without hissing; I do not like "chair" because it is patently ridiculous; and as for "gentlepersons," the aroma of a bloodless vegetarianism clings to it, like horse manure to a football cleat. No, in my view the problem of sex and language cuts much deeper than such superficialities. It is much better engaged at the level where one can no longer think of a man as "enraged," while a woman at the same pitch of anger is declared "hysterical." It is better engaged at the level where one no longer thinks of certain work, or subjects, or points of view as belonging exclusively to one or another sex. Meanwhile, though my experience here may be unusual, I have yet to meet a man who was eager to fall into line with the rules of feminist thought-control whom I thought truly respected the intelligence of women.

Which brings me to another category of words I think fit for outlawing. These are words that once seemed quite all right, but have now to be turned in for overuse and ill-use. "Experience" used as a verb is such a word: "Kent," the cigarette ad runs. "Experience it!" (Death, the surgeon general adds, risk it.) "No problem" is a phrase that has had it, especially "no problem" with the ejaculatory "hey" before it; "no problem" is also coming, in the United States, to replace "You're welcome." "Special" as an adjective is now at the Hallmark greeting card level of language, particularly when it is followed by "person." A "special person" usually turns out to be a "caring person," as one need scarcely add. Well, one could go on, and I doubtless shall, the flecks of foam forming at the corners of my mouth, but not here and not now.

Many have been the events and moments in recent history when one has wished that certain figures from the past had been alive to comment upon them. How fine to have had H. L. Mencken's report on the creationism-evolutionism controversy, or A. J. Liebling on the gloating of the press around the time of Watergate, or Max Beerbohm on the Pop Art movement, or Edmund Wilson on any of the past ten years' meetings of the Modern Language Association. As for H. W. Fowler and Sir Ernest Gowers, they, were they alive today, would find plenty to keep them busy. Fowler, after sampling some of the work of contemporary academics—feminists, structuralists, Marxists—would doubtless wish to begin his *Dictionary of Modern English Usage* over from scratch. Gowers would readily see the need for another *Plain Words*, this one written for literary critics. Funny business, language—like the man said, the pay may not be high, but you're never out of work.

JOSEPH EPSTEIN
Evanston, Illinois
March, 1988

Preface

Her Majesty's Stationery Office, the British Government department that publishes official material, issued this third edition of THE COMPLETE PLAIN WORDS as part of its 1986 bicentennial celebration.

The first edition of the book appeared in 1954. Sir Ernest Gowers, a distinguished civil servant, had previously written two books—*Plain Words* (1948) and *The ABC of Plain Words* (1951)—at the invitation of the British Treasury as a contribution to what they were doing to improve official English. He thus addressed those whose duties included answering letters received by government departments; writing regulations and every sort of government matter such as notices on post office walls; designing official forms; and corresponding with other civil servants. In THE COMPLETE PLAIN WORDS, Gowers combined the two previous books and at the same time took the opportunity to revise what he had written earlier.

THE COMPLETE PLAIN WORDS was an immediate success and has been reprinted many times. It has attracted devoted followers, not only among civil servants in Britian and abroad, but among all those nonprofessional writers whose jobs nevertheless demand that they write: business people, legal aides, technologists, librarians, teachers, and students. Such men and women do not readily accept advice, although they may advise others every day of their working lives; but having once come to the book for guidance, they stay to enjoy its elegance and wit. Gowers' reputation as a sensible and practical authority on usage and style made him the obvious choice to revise that other classic guide to good English, Fowler's *Modern English Usage* (1965).

The English that Gowers advocates is necessarily British English. Although he welcomes the "vigorous word-making habit of the Americans" as an enrichment of our common language—where would we all be without *doodle* and *teenager?*—he comments that "we still have defenders of our tongue who scrutinise [incoming Americanisms] very closely." It is just as common in Britain today as it was in 1954 for the self-appointed guardians of British English to become hysterical over the infiltration by American vocabulary and grammar. As civil servants, Gowers says, we must "try to put ourselves in the position of our correspondent, to imagine his feelings as he writes his letters, and to gauge his reaction as he receives ours." Such a correspondent may well be the kind of language purist who attacks the BBC and the *Times* for using what he conceives to be an Americanism of vocabulary (*transportation* for *transport*), of grammar (*meet up with* for *meet*), or of spelling (*center* for *centre*). If he encounters any novelties of language in official writing it will irritate him, and make him, as Gowers warns, "less likely to be influenced in the way you intend."

Gowers himself displays an urbanely cordial attitude to American innovations, accepting or rejecting each on its own merits. (It is interesting that many of these innovations, such as the new sense of *hopefully*, have been sharply criticised in America too.) It goes without saying that he would never presume to censure the use of normal educated American English *by Americans*; but that is not what the book is about. Nearly all of it concerns the "common core" of good English the world over, so that his rulings can be followed anywhere with almost equal pleasure and profit.

But usage and attitudes change with time. If Gowers' work is to remain a practical guide, it requires periodic revision to take account of developments in the language. Gowers himself introduced some changes each time the book was reprinted.

The second edition of the book was published in 1973. This major revision was successfully undertaken by Sir Bruce Fraser, another distinguished civil servant. Fraser devoted himself to the task with reverence and admiration for Gowers' work; he endeavoured to retain as much as possible of Gowers' original text and to follow in his amendments and additions the vitality and vigour of Gowers' style.

In his preface Fraser explained the principles that guided his revision. Wherever he could, he substituted contemporary examples for those that seemed dated. Occasionally, he omitted passages that he felt were no longer necessary because of changes in the language or the acceptance of usages that were once condemned. He reduced the number of literary allusions, since most of his contemporary readers would not have had the literary education that Gowers assumed. Some passages on style he abbreviated, because the faults they criticised were no longer committed frequently. In a few passages he disagreed with Gowers; sometimes he gave Gowers' view and then his own, but sometimes he simply replaced Gowers with Fraser. Fraser also added several completely new chapters. Fraser was a worthy successor to Gowers. His edition was reprinted frequently and he, too, introduced changes in succeeding impressions. What Fraser said in his preface about the book's deep and lasting influence in the public service remains true for his edition:

The work is recommended reading in most parts of the service, and it is widely read, or at least widely referred to, by both senior and junior staff. Its influence is felt even by those who have never read it, for its precepts, and many of its illustrations, are used in many booklets for staff and in many training and refresher courses.

This edition is a revision of Fraser's edition, and we have generally followed the principles and practices of Fraser (though he is in no way responsible for the changes we have made). We have not hesitated to make changes that reflect developments in the language or in accepted usage. Like Fraser, we have been conscious that we are revising a classic, and we have attempted to retain the flavour of the original Gowers and as much of the Gowers text as possible.

In the previous editions, several chapters contained lists of words with comments on them. For the convenience of readers, we have brought these lists together in a single alphabetical list in chapter 17.

With this third edition, it has become difficult to enumerate the precise contributions of Gowers, Fraser, Greenbaum, and Whitcut. It would be tedious to do so, and of little interest to most users of the book. But it may be worth saying that the core of the book (chapters 3–14) remains essentially Gowers, despite numerous amendments; and similarly, the epilogue (chapter 18) is almost pure Gowers.

Gowers' frequent use of the first person and pronoun "I" presents a difficulty for revisers. Fraser decided to retain the "I," and he tried to preface the parts of the book that were wholly or mainly written by each of the authors. We have reluctantly renounced any attempt to distinguish in this way between the "I" of each of our predecessors and to add to them the "*we*" of Greenbaum and Whitcut, although we have sometimes indicated that our judgments have diverged from those expressed in the previous editions. In this third edition "we" generally represents Greenbaum and Whitcut in agreement with Gowers and Fraser; but it occasionally means that we have aligned ourselves with Gowers or with Fraser or with neither. As in previous editions, most judgments and comments appear without mentioning the first person pronoun of their originators.

We are deeply indebted to the Cabinet Office and other Government Departments for sending us an abundance of material for this edition. We also acknowledge with thanks the help we obtained from the Forms Information Centre at the University of Reading, which supplied us with batches of examples of official and commercial language. Some of our best specimens of bad writing we received from Mr. Ivan Kingston. We have consulted many works of reference; they include guides to contemporary usage, dictionaries, and the recently published *Comprehensive Grammar of the English Language* (of which Sidney Greenbaum is a co-author). We have also examined the publications on writing plain English by the National Consumer Council and the Campaign for Plain English. Both of us are associated with the Survey of English Usage, and we have occasionally consulted the Survey files.

Finally, we are very grateful to Mr. W. J. Sharp CB, Controller and Chief Executive of Her Majesty's Stationery Office, for his many helpful comments on our work.

JANET WHITCUT

Contents

1
Prologue

Do but take care to express yourself in a plain, easy Manner, in well-chosen, significant and decent Terms, and to give a harmonious and pleasing Turn to your Periods; study to explain your Thoughts, and set them in the truest Light, labouring as much as possible, not to leave them dark nor intricate, but clear and intelligible.

Cervantes, Preface to Don Quixote

The final cause of speech is to get an idea as exactly as possible out of one mind into another. Its formal cause therefore is such choice and disposition of words as will achieve this end most economically.

G. M. Young

The main purpose of this book is to help officials in their use of written English as a tool of their trade. It is possible that this project will be received by many of them without any marked enthusiasm or gratitude. 'Even now', they may say, 'it is all we can do to keep our heads above water by turning out at top speed letters in which we say what we mean after our own fashion. Not one in a thousand of the people we write to knows the difference between good English and bad. What is the use of all this highbrow stuff? It will only prevent us from getting on with the job.'

But what is this job that must be got on with? Writing is an instrument for conveying ideas from one mind to another; the writers' job is to make the readers apprehend the meaning readily and precisely. Do these letters always say just what the writers mean? Indeed, do the writers themselves always know just what they mean? Even when they know what they mean, and say it in a way that is clear to them, is it always equally clear to their readers? If not, they have not been getting on with the job. The test of good writing is whether you can convey to your readers exactly what you intend to convey. Let us take one or two examples to illustrate particular faults, and, applying this test to them, ask ourselves whether the reader is likely to grasp at once the meaning of

Prices are basis prices per ton for the representative-basis-pricing specification and size and quantity.

or of

Where particulars of a partnership are disclosed to the Executive Council the remuneration of the individual partner for superannuation purposes will be deemed to be such proportion of the total remuneration of such practitioners as the proportion of his share in partnership profits bears to the total proportion of the shares of such practitioner in those profits.

or of

The treatment of this loan interest from the date of the first payment has been correct—i.e. tax charged at full standard rate on Mr X and treated in your hands as liability fully satisfied before receipt.

All these were written for plain people, not for experts. What will the plain person make of them? The recipient of the last may painfully and dubiously reach the right conclusion—that no more money is wanted from him. But the recipient of the first example will be unable to unlock the secret of the jargon without a key, and what the second will make of the explanation given to him is anyone's guess. Yet the writers may be presumed to have known exactly what they meant; the obscurity was not in their thoughts but in their way of expressing themselves. The fault of writing like this is not that it is unscholarly but that it is inefficient. It wastes time: the time of the readers because they have to puzzle over what should be plain, and the time of the writers because they may have to write again to explain their meaning. A job that needed to be done only once has had to be done twice because it was bungled the first time.

Professional writers realise that they cannot hope to convey to their readers exactly what they intend to convey without care and practice in the proper use of words. The need for the official to take pains is even greater, for if what the professional writer has written is wearisome and obscure, readers can toss the book aside and read no more, but only at their peril can they so treat what officials have tried to tell them. By proper use we do not mean grammatically proper. It is true that there are rules of grammar and syntax, just as in music there are rules of harmony and counterpoint. But one can no more write good English than one can compose good music merely by keeping the rules. On the whole they are aids to writing intelligibly, for they are in the main no more than the distillation of successful experiments made by writers of English through the centuries in how best to handle words so as to make a writer's meaning plain. Some, it is true, are arbitrary. One or two actually increase the difficulty of clear expression, but these too should nevertheless be respected, because lapses from what for the time being is regarded as correct irritate educated readers, and distract their attention, and so make them less likely to be influenced in the way you intend. But we shall not have much to say about text-book rules because they are mostly well known and well observed in official writing.

The golden rule is to pick those words that convey to the reader the meaning of the writer and to use them and them only. This golden rule applies to all prose, whatever its purpose, and indeed to poetry too. Illustrations could be found throughout the gamut of purposes for which the written word is used. At the one end of it we can turn to Shakespeare, and from the innumerable examples that offer themselves choose the lines

> Kissing with golden face the meadows green,
> Gilding pale streams with heavenly alchymy

which, as a description of what the rising sun does to meadows and rivers on a 'glorious morning', must be as effective a use of thirteen words as could be found in all English literature. At the other end we can turn (for the golden rule can be illustrated from official writing in its observance as well as in its breach) to the unknown member of the staff of the General Post Office who by composing the notice that used to be displayed in every post office

Postmasters are neither bound to give change nor authorised to demand it

used twelve words hardly less efficiently to warn customers of what must have been a singularly intractable dilemma. At first sight there seems little in common between the two. Their purposes are different; one is descriptive and emotional, the other instructional and objective. But each serves its purpose perfectly, and it is the same quality in both that makes them do so. Every word is exactly right; no other word would do as well; each is pulling its weight; none could be dispensed with. As was said of Milton's prose in the quotation that heads Chapter 6, 'Fewer would not have served the turn, and more would have been superfluous'.

You need to choose the right words in order that you may make your meaning clear not only to your reader but also to yourself. The first requirement for all writers is to know just what meaning they want to convey, and it is only by clothing their thoughts in words that they can think at all. And the less one makes a habit of thinking, the less one is able to think: the power of thinking atrophies unless it is used. The following was written about politicians, but it is true of all of us:

> A scrupulous writer in every sentence that he writes will ask himself . . . What am I trying to say? What words will express it? . . . And he probably asks himself . . . Could I put it more shortly? But you are not obliged to go to all this trouble. You can shirk it by simply throwing open your mind and letting the ready-made phrases come crowding in. They will construct your sentences for you—even think your thoughts for you to a certain extent—and at need they will perform the important service of partially concealing your meaning even from yourself.*

'Go to all this trouble' is not an overstatement. Few common things are more difficult than to find the right word, and many people are too lazy to try. This form of indolence sometimes betrays itself by a copious use of inverted commas. 'I know this is not quite the right word', the inverted commas seem to say, 'but I can't be bothered to think of a better'; or, 'please note that I am using this word facetiously'; or, 'don't think I don't know that this is a cliché'. If the word is the right one, do not be ashamed of it: if it is the wrong one, do not use it. The same implied apology is often made in conversation by interposing 'you know' or by ending every sentence with phrases such as 'or something' or 'sort of thing'. Officials cannot do that, but in them the same phenomenon is reflected in an unwillingness to venture outside a small vocabulary of shapeless bundles of uncertain content—words and phrases like *position, situation, basis, arise, involve, in connection with, in terms of, with reference to, issue, consideration* and *factor*—a disposition, for instance, to 'admit with regret the position which has arisen in connection with' rather than to make the effort to tell the reader specifically what is admitted with regret. Clear thinking is hard work, but loose thinking is bound to produce loose writing. And clear thinking takes time, but time that has to be given to a job to avoid making a mess of it cannot be time wasted and may in the end be time saved.

It is wise therefore not to begin to write, or to dictate, until you are

---

* George Orwell in *Horizon*, April 1947.

quite certain what you want to say. That sounds elementary, but the elementary things are often the most likely to be neglected. Some, it is true, can never be sure of clarifying their thoughts except by trying to put them on paper. If you are one of these, never be content with your first draft; always revise it; and you will find that practice, though it may not make perfect, will greatly improve your efficiency.

'But', you may object, 'my work is very urgent. There's no time for this pernickety perfectionism.' Well, perhaps. We can make allowances for what is produced under great stress for internal communication. But not all your work is desperately urgent and not all is for departmental reading only. When it comes to writing for the public you should fear more the danger of putting out slipshod work by omitting to revise it than that of delaying public business by excessive polishing. Very few can write what they mean and influence their readers precisely as they intend without revising their first attempt. There *is* a happy mean between being content with the first thing that comes into your head and the craving for perfection that makes a Flaubert spend hours or even days on getting a single sentence to his satisfaction. The article you are paid to produce need not be polished but it must be workmanlike.

Much official writing, such as routine letters to other authorities or to members of the public, explanatory circulars, and so on, needs merely to be clear, workmanlike and inoffensive. It had much better be flat and clear than eloquent and obscure, or even eloquent and clear; for the reader is looking only for plain, honest bread and butter and he does not want it spread with jam, or even caviar, any more than he wants it spread with glue or engine-grease.

2
A preliminary digression

So as to avoid any misunderstanding about the scope of this book, it will be as well to begin with a digression explaining why certain uses of language are outside it.

Legal English

Acts of Parliament, statutory rules and other legal instruments have a special purpose, to which their language has to be specially adapted. The legal draftsmen, whether they are public officials or not, have to ensure to the best of their ability that what they say will be found to mean precisely what they intended, even after it has been subjected to detailed and possibly hostile scrutiny by acute legal minds. For this purpose they have to be constantly aware, not only of the natural meaning which their words convey to the ordinary reader, but also of the special meaning which they have acquired by legal convention and by previous decisions of the Courts.

Legal drafting must therefore be unambiguous, precise, comprehensive and largely conventional. If it is readily intelligible, so much the better; but it is far more important that it should yield its meaning accurately than that it should yield it on first reading, and legal draftsmen cannot afford to give much attention, if any, to euphony or literary elegance. What matters most to them is that no one will succeed in persuading a court of law that their words bear a meaning they did not intend, and, if possible, that no one will think it worth while to try.

All this means that their drafting is not to be judged by normal standards of good writing, and that they are not really included among those for whom this book is primarily intended—'those who use words as tools of their trade, in administration or business'.

By normal standards of good writing legal drafting is usually both cumbrous and uncouth. No doubt it is sometimes unnecessarily so;* it

* For a striking example, see p.145.

would be surprising indeed if it were not. But it often needs a skilled lawyer to say whether a particular passage could have been put more elegantly without losing its accuracy; the non-lawyer should be slow to criticise—or to imitate.

Writing on the law that is addressed to non-lawyers is quite a different matter. It is legitimate to evaluate it by normal standards of good writing, and we return to this in Chapter 3. Explanations about the law often appear in communications to the public by Government Departments: in forms, leaflets, and official letters. They also appear in consumer contracts and in letters of lawyers to their clients. People have a right to understand forms and contracts they are required to sign; they can reasonably expect to interpret written advice without needing to consult a lawyer.

Expert to expert

When experts are writing only for their fellow experts they may achieve their aim of conveying to their readers exactly what they intend to convey by the use of language which the rest of us find obscure or even quite unintelligible. We are not concerned with this kind of writing, which frequently appears in learned journals. It is always possible to cite passages which could have been put more clearly, with fewer technical or unfamiliar words. But non-experts are not really entitled to criticise scientific or technical writing on this score; what is unclear to them may be perfectly clear to the intended readers.

This is not to say that such writing always *is* clear, even to the intended readers. Its obscurities are sometimes due, not to the requirements of the subject matter, but to muddled thinking or mere pretentiousness; and for obscurities of this kind, as for any other misuses of language, the writers are not to be forgiven merely because they are writing for fellow experts.

But writing on scientific or technical subjects is, of course, entirely within the scope of this book if it is addressed to the non-expert reader. You will find more about this in Chapter 15.

Departmental shorthand

This is really a variant of writing by experts to their fellow experts. It occurs not only in Government Departments but in most large organisations where there has to be written communication between different parts of the organisation. Familiar words take on unfamiliar special meanings; procedures and categories acquire pet names; new words and new terms are invented to meet particular needs; acronyms and other forms of abbreviation are devised; the language becomes allusive and, to the uninitiated, hopelessly obscure.

Take the following (imaginary) examples:

These are all time-expired clause 4 optants and delay in referral would distort the quarterly submission-ratio.

If the claimant is ineligible for transitional supplement only because he has no dormant assets, the initiating officer should consider extra-statutory disregard.

All Wilberforce concessions should be separately recorded on QAB 4's and the relevant claims in the non-grant-aidable list should be de-asterisked.

These passages are, in the strict sense of the word, jargon. But they are entirely justifiable, ugly though they are, because they are doing efficiently what they set out to do. Both writer and reader know precisely what a *time-expired clause 4 optant* is, what special meanings attach to *referral*, *submission–ratio*, *dormant* and *disregard*, what is the difference between a Wilberforce concession and (say) a Shaftesbury one, and so on. Purists may blench at *non-grant-aidable list* and *de-asterisked*, and neither is suitable for general use. But purists do not know, as the official does, that in this particular context a lot turns on whether a claim is categorised as asterisked, unasterisked or de-asterisked; they must not even recommend *de-starred* instead, because for all they know *starred*, *unstarred* and *de-starred* are already in use for some quite different and equally precise purpose. And we cannot blame busy officials for using *non-grant-aidable list* as shorthand for *list of claims that do not satisfy the conditions for grant*.

To put these passages in a form intelligible to the uninitiated would probably take at least five times the space and render them, if anything, less clear to the initiated—to whom alone they are addressed. They are therefore a laudable way of conveying ideas as exactly as possible from one mind to another.

The danger for officials, or for anyone else who habitually uses private language of this kind for internal communication, is that they may slip into using it for external communication too. Clearly this is inefficient as well as impolite, for readers will be puzzled as well as annoyed. To call a man *a time-expired clause 4 optant* in a departmental minute may earn official approval: to call him one in reply to his letter may earn an unofficial punch on the nose.

The spoken word

The spoken word (whether conversation or public discussion or oratory) is very different from the written word. What is effective or allowable in the one may not be in the other. Extempore speakers cannot correct themselves by revision as writers can and should. It is therefore not fair to take a report of a speech or of an oral statement and criticise it as if it were a piece of considered writing.

What has been prepared in writing and is then read out (such as a paper to a learned society, or a formal statement or lecture) is, however, fair game. So are speeches, as soon as the author has revised them for publication. Many reported speeches, for instance in Parliament, are partly prepared and partly extempore, and it is not always easy to tell from reading them which parts are which. In a few instances quotations are taken from speeches in *Hansard* and are then identified as such.

3
The elements

If any man were to ask me what I would suppose to be a perfect style of language, I would answer, that in which a man speaking to five hundred people, of all common and various capacities, idiots or lunatics excepted, should be understood by them all, and in the same sense which the speaker intended to be understood.

Defoe

There is one golden rule to bear in mind always: that we should try to put ourselves in the position of our correspondent, to imagine his feelings as he writes his letters, and to gauge his reaction as he receives ours. If we put ourselves in the other man's shoes we shall speedily detect how unconvincing our letters can seem, or how much we may be taking for granted.

Inland Revenue Staff Instruction

Having thus cleared the decks, we can return to the various other purposes for which official writing has to be used. The relative importance of these, in quantity at any rate, has been changed by the immense volume of modern social legislation and the innumerable ways in which public authorities, and the laws which they administer, now impinge on the life of the community. Official writing used to consist mostly of departmental minutes and instructions, inter-departmental correspondence, and despatches to Governors and Ambassadors. These things still have their places. But in volume they have been left far behind by the vast output now necessary for explaining the law to the public and telling them what their rights and obligations are.

Explaining the law can be a difficult and delicate task. An official interpreting the law is often looked on with suspicion. It is for the legislature to make the laws, for the executive to administer them, and for the judiciary to interpret them. The official must avoid all appearance of encroaching on the province of the Courts. For this reason it used to be a rule in the service that when laws were brought to the notice of those affected by them the actual words of the statute must be used; in no other way could the official be sure of escaping all imputation of putting his own interpretation on the law. But this rule, which was perhaps never quite so important as it was made out to be, has long since yielded to the pressure of events.

Immense pains are now taken in preparing forms, standard letters, leaflets, and other written material that help members of the public to know their rights and obligations and to understand the law in such matters as PAYE and National Insurance. The material is reviewed regularly to identify ways of improving style and presentation.

Guiding principles that are generally accepted as good practice are to use plain English and avoid technical terms; to address the reader personally (preferably as *you*); not to try to give all the details of the law relevant to the subject but to be content with stating the essentials; to explain to the reader that the statements are only an approximation when these are made in the writer's words and not in the words of the Act; to tell the reader where to find fuller information and further advice; and to make sure that the reader knows his or her rights of appeal.

But there is another part of this subject: the answering of letters from individual correspondents about their own cases. These answers cannot be written, like the pamphlets and leaflets, by people who are experts both in the subject matter and in English composition. Often, it is true, an existing leaflet provides the answer to the correspondent's query, and the reply can merely say 'You will see from the enclosed leaflet that . . .'. Or the same query may be posed so often that a stock form of reply has been devised. But these easy expedients are often not available. The official then has the task of composing a reply. Writing a letter on behalf of the Government needs in some respects a special technique, but the principles of it are the same as those of all good writing, whatever its purpose. We have here in its most elementary form—though not on that account its least difficult—the problem of writing what one means and influencing one's reader precisely in the way one wishes. If therefore we begin our study of the problems of official English by examining the technique of this part of it, that will serve as a good introduction to the rest of the book, for it will bring out most of the points that we shall have to study more closely later. It is in this field of an official's duties more than in any other that good English can be defined simply as English which is readily understood by the reader. To be clear is to be efficient; to be obscure is to be inefficient. Your style of letter-writing is to be judged not by literary conventions or grammatical niceties but by whether it carries out efficiently the job you are paid to do.

But 'efficiency' must be broadly interpreted. It connotes a proper attitude of mind towards your correspondents. They may not care about being addressed in literary English, but they will care very much about being treated with sympathy and understanding. It is not easy nowadays to remember anything so contrary to all appearances as that officials are the servants of the public; and the official must try not to foster the illusion that it is the other way round. So your style must not only be simple but also friendly, sympathetic and natural, appropriate to one who is a servant, not a master.

Let us now translate these generalities into some practical rules.

(1) Be sure that you know what your correspondent is asking before you begin to answer him. Study his letter carefully. If he is obscure, spare no trouble in trying to get at his meaning. If you conclude that he means something different from what he says (as he well may) address yourself to his meaning not to his words, and do not be clever at his expense. Get into his skin, and adapt the atmosphere of your letter to suit that of his. If he is troubled, be sympathetic. If he is rude, be specially courteous. If he is muddle-headed, be specially lucid. If he is pig-headed, be patient. If he is helpful, be appreciative. If he convicts you of a mistake, acknowledge it freely and even with gratitude. But never let a flavour of the patronising creep in.

(2) Begin by answering his question. Do not start by telling him the relevant law and practice, and gradually lead up to a statement of its application to his case. Give him his answer briefly and clearly at the outset, and only then, if explanation is needed, begin your explanation. Thus he will know the worst, or the best, at once, and can skip the explanation if he likes.

(3) So far as possible, confine yourself to the facts of the case you are writing about and avoid any general statement about the law.

(4) Avoid a formal framework if you can. Formal official letters are sometimes necessary to notify matters of policy or important decisions made by or on behalf of the Minister. Such letters must be written in a precise and dignified manner but must not be pompous. (An official letter to a big firm or a local authority may have to be read aloud at a board or council meeting. Consider how it will sound there.)

But write ordinary letters to the public in as informal and friendly a way as possible. Do not use the impersonal passive, with its formal unsympathetic phrases such as 'it is felt', 'it is regretted', 'it is appreciated'. You should want your readers to feel that they are dealing with human beings rather than robots. How feeble is the sentence 'It is thought you will now have received the form of agreement' compared with 'I expect you will have received the form of agreement by now'.

(5) Be careful to say nothing that might give your correspondents the impression, however mistakenly, that you think it right that they should be put to trouble in order to save you from it. Do not use paper stamped 'Date as postmark'. Do not ask them to repeat information they have already given you unless there is some good reason for doing so, and, if there is, explain the reason.

(6) Use no more words than are necessary to do the job. Superfluous words waste your time and official paper, tire your reader and obscure your meaning. There is no need, for instance, to begin each paragraph with phrases like *I am further to point out, I would also add, You will moreover observe*. Go straight to what you have to say, without precautionary words, and then say it in as few words as are needed to make your meaning clear.

(7) Keep your sentences short. This will help both you to think clearly and your correspondent to take your meaning. If you find you have slipped into long ones, split them up.

(8) Be compact; do not put a strain on your reader's memory by widely separating parts of a sentence that are closely related to one another.

Why, for instance, is this sentence difficult to grasp on first reading?

Section 11(1) of the Act provides that a person who has information which he knows or believes might be of material assistance in preventing an act of terrorism, or in securing the apprehension, prosecution or conviction of any person for an offence involving the commission, preparation or instigation of such an act of terrorism, and who fails without reasonable excuse to disclose that information as soon as reasonably practicable to a constable is guilty of an offence.

The structure of the sentence is too diffuse; readers have to keep in mind the opening words all the way through. Only at the very end do they find out that the person is guilty of an offence. Now consider a revised version:

Section 11(1) of the Act provides that a person is guilty of an offence if he has information which he knows or believes might be of material assistance in preventing an act of terrorism, or in securing the apprehension, prosecution or conviction of any person for an offence involving the commission, preparation or instigation of such an act of terrorism, and if he fails without reasonable excuse to disclose that information as soon as reasonably practicable to a constable.

The original sentence comes from the Report of a Royal Commission and is not addressed to the average reader. Even so, it might well be shortened and made clearer by (say) changing *might be of material assistance in preventing* to *might help to prevent*. But merely the minimal change we have introduced has improved the sentence. Why is the revised version much easier to grasp? The reason is that it employs a device that is very useful when officials have to say (as they frequently have to) that a class of people who have certain attributes or who have acted in certain ways have certain rights or obligations or incur certain penalties. The device is to use *if*-clauses instead of *who*-clauses: in our example to say that a person is guilty if he has failed to act in certain ways rather than to say that a person who has failed to act in certain ways is guilty. The advantage is that it avoids the wide separation of the main verb (and what goes with it) from the main subject; the subject *a person* comes immediately before *is guilty*. The device is particularly useful when otherwise you would need a series of *who*-clauses or perhaps just one long *who*-clause.

Two other simple expedients help to make such a sentence clearer: (i) If you need a long *if*-clause or more than one, put the *if*-clause at the end, as in the revised version; this enables your readers to reach the main point quickly. (ii) If your readers themselves are possibly members of the specified class, use the second person *you* as subject in the *if*-clauses, as in this sentence from a leaflet of Income Tax instructions:

If you have income from abroad, you may be able to claim relief against your United Kingdom income tax for tax paid overseas.

Here is a further example of a sentence that puts a strain on the reader's memory:

A deduction of tax may be claimed in respect of any person whom the individual maintains at his own expense, and who is (i) a relative of his, or of his wife, and incapacitated by old age or infirmity from maintaining himself or herself, or (ii) his or his wife's widowed mother, whether incapacitated or not, or (iii) his daughter who is resident with him and upon whose services he is compelled to depend by reason of old age or infirmity.

The sentence comes from an old leaflet of Income Tax instructions. A recent version is far easier to understand, not only because it splits the sentence up but also because it changes the arrangements of words within each sentence:

> You may claim for
> **either** a relative of yours or your wife's who is unable to work because of old age, or permanent illness or disablement
> **or**   your mother or mother-in-law if she is separated, divorced or a widow.
> The relative must be maintained by you . . .

You may claim if you are maintaining your son/daughter and he/she is living with you and looking after you or your wife because you are old, or permanently ill or disabled.

(9) **Do not say more than is necessary.** The feeling that prompts you to tell your correspondent everything when explaining is commendable, but you will often help him more by resisting it and confining yourself to the facts that will enable him to understand what has happened.

> I regret however that the Survey Officer who is responsible for the preliminary investigation as to the technical possibility of installing a telephone at the address quoted by any applicant has reported that owing to a shortage of a spare pair of wires to the underground cable (a pair of wires leading from the point near your house right back to the local exchange and thus a pair of wires essential for the provision of telephone service for you) is lacking and that therefore it is a technical impossibility to install a telephone for you at . . .

This explanation is obscure partly because the sentence is too long, partly because the long parenthesis has thrown the grammar out of gear, and partly because the writer, with the best intentions, says far more than is necessary even for a thoroughly polite and convincing explanation. It might have run thus:

> I am sorry to have to tell you that we have found that there is no spare pair of wires on the cable that would have to be used to connect your house with the exchange. I regret therefore that it is impossible to install a telephone for you.

(10) Explain technical terms in simple words. You will soon become so familiar with the technical terms of the law you are administering that you will feel that you have known them all your life, and may forget that to others they are unintelligible.

(11) Do not use what have been called the 'dry meaningless formulae' of commercialese. Against some of these a warning is not needed: officials do not write *your esteemed favour to hand* or address their correspondents as *your good self*. But if they are not careful they may find themselves using *same* as a pronoun (on which see pp. 117–8), or *enclosed please find* instead of *I enclose*. *Per* should not be permitted to get too free with the English language. Such convenient abbreviations as *m.p.h.* and *r.p.m.* are no doubt with us for good. But generally it is well to confine *per* to its own language—e.g. *per cent*, *per capita*, *per stirpes*, *per contra*, and not to prefer *per day* to *a day*, or *per passenger train* to *by passenger train*, or *as per my letter* to *as I said in my letter*.

Even for phrases in which *per* is linked to a Latin word there are often English equivalents which serve as well, if not better. A letter can as well be signed *AB for CD* as *CD per pro AB*. £100 *a year* is more natural than £100 *per annum*. *Per se* does not ordinarily mean anything more than *by itself* or *in itself*.

Another Latin word better left alone is *re*. It means *in the matter of*. It is used by lawyers for the title of lawsuits, such as '*In re* John Doe deceased'. It has passed into commercialese as an equivalent of the English preposition *about*. It has no business there, or anywhere else outside a lawyer's office. It is not needed either to introduce a heading ('*re* your application for a grant'), which can stand without its support, or in the body of a letter, where an honest *about* will serve your purpose better. Avoid that ugly and unnecessary symbol *and/or* when writing letters; it is fit only for forms and lists and specifications and things of that sort. It can always be dispensed with. Instead of writing (say) 'soldiers and/or sailors' we can write 'soldiers or sailors or both'. Finally, there is no reason for preferring the Latin abbreviations *inst.*, *ult.* and *prox.* to the name of the month, which is also capable of abbreviation and has the advantage over them of conveying an immediate and certain meaning.

Here is an example of the baleful influence of commercialese:

Payment of the above account, which is now overdue at the date hereof, appears to have been overlooked, and I shall be glad to have your remittance by return of post, and oblige.

Yours faithfully,

The superfluous *at the date hereof* must have been prompted by a feeling that *now* by itself was not formal enough and needed dressing up. The word *oblige* is grammatically in mid-air. It has no subject, and is firmly cut off by a full stop from what might have been supposed to be its object, the writer's signature.

The fault of commercialese is that its mechanical use has a bad effect on both writer and reader—the writer because it deadens his appreciation of the meaning of words, the reader because he feels that the writer's approach to him lacks sincerity.

(12) Use words with precise meanings rather than vague ones. Since, as we have seen, you will not be doing your job properly unless you make your meaning readily understood, this is an elementary duty. Yet it is still too often disregarded. All entrants into the service come equipped with a vocabulary of common words of precise meaning adequate for all ordinary purposes. But when they begin to write as officials they have a queer trick of forgetting them and relying mainly on a smaller vocabulary of less common words with a less precise meaning. It is a curious fact that in the officials' armoury of words the weapons readiest to hand are weapons not of precision but of rough and ready aim; often, indeed, they are of a sort that were constructed as weapons of precision but officials have bored them out into blunderbusses.* They have been put in the front rank of the armoury; the official reaches out for a word and uses one of these without troubling to search in the ranks behind for one that is more likely to hit the target in the middle. For instance, the blunderbuss *integrate* is now kept in front of *join, combine, amalgamate, coordinate* and other words, and the hand stretching out for one of these gets no farther. *Develop* blocks the way to *happen, occur, take place* and *come*. *Alternative* (a converted weapon of precision) stands before many simple words such as *different, other, new, fresh, revised*. *Realistic* is in front of others, such as *sensible, reasonable, practicable, workable* and *feasible*. *Involve* throws a whole section of the armoury into disuse, though not so big a one as that threatened by *overall*; and rack upon

* The *OED* defines this word as 'A short gun with a large bore, firing many balls or slugs, and capable of doing execution within a limited range without exact aim'.

rack of simple prepositions are left untouched because before them are kept the blunderbusses of vague phrases such as *in relation to*, *in regard to*, *in connection with* and *in the case of*.

It may be said that it is generally easy enough to guess what is meant. But you have no business to leave your reader guessing at your meaning, even though the guess may be easy. That is not doing your job properly. If you make a habit of not troubling to choose the right weapon of precision you may be sure that sooner or later you will set your reader a problem that is past guessing.

(13) If two words convey your meaning equally well, choose the common one rather than the less common. Prefer *about* to *regarding*, *respecting* or *concerning*, say *refer* instead of *advert*, and use *say* or *tell* rather than *state*, *inform*, *acquaint* or *advise*. *Furthermore* is a prosy word used too often. It may be difficult to avoid it in cumulative argument (*moreover . . . in addition . . . too . . . also . . . again . . . furthermore*), but prefer one of the simpler words if they have not all been used up. Do not say *hereto*, *herein*, *hereof*, *herewith*, *hereunder*, or similar compounds with *there*, unless like *therefore* they have become part of everyday language. Most of them put a flavour of legalism into any document in which they are used. Use a preposition and pronoun instead. For instance:

> With reference to the second paragraph thereof. (In its second paragraph.)
> I have received your letter and thank you, for the information contained therein. (. . . contained in it.)
> I am to ask you to explain the circumstances in which the gift was made and to forward any correspondence relative thereto. (. . . any correspondence about it.)

To take a few more examples of unnecessary choice of stilted expressions, do not say *predecease* for *die before*, *ablution facilities* for *wash basins*, *it is apprehended that* for *I suppose*, *capable of locomotion* for *able to walk*, *will you be good enough to advise me* for *please tell me*, *I have endeavoured to obtain the required information* for *I have tried to find out what you wanted to know*, *it will be observed from a perusal of* for *you will see by reading*. The reason why it is wrong for you to use these starchy words is not that they are bad English; most of them are perfectly good English in their proper places. The reason is twofold. First, some of the more unusual of them may actually be outside the vocabulary of your correspondents and convey no meaning at all to them. Secondly, their use runs counter to your duty to show that officials are human. These words give the reader the impression that officials are not made of common clay but are, in their own estimation at least, beings superior and aloof. They create the wrong atmosphere; the frost once formed by a phrase or two of this sort is not easily melted. If you turn back to the two versions of the income tax leaflet given under rule (8), you will see how careful the writer of the revised version has been about this. The word *individual* (a technical term of income tax law to distinguish between a personal taxpayer and a corporate one) and the phrase *at his own expense* were unnecessary and have disappeared. *A deduction of tax may be claimed in respect of* is translated into *you may claim for*, *incapacitated* into *unable to work*, *is resident with* into *is living with*, *upon whose services he is compelled to depend* into *is looking after you or your wife*, *by reason of* into *because of* or *because you are*, and *infirmity* into *permanent illness or disablement*.

These rules can be summarised as 'Be short, be simple, be human'. Since they were first formulated, they have been used by all Government Departments in their own way. A handbook issued by the Civil Service Department cautions new civil servants:

> You must learn the importance of using words in their exact meanings, so that they convey, to somebody you have never seen, exactly what you intend to convey, and not something roughly approximating to it. If there is any ambiguity in your phrasing, somebody is sure to misunderstand; so say what you mean, simply and clearly. Keep your sentences short and avoid officialese.

The rules are the foundation of a short booklet, *The word is . . . Plain English*, published by the Cabinet Office and widely distributed in the Civil Service; also of more specialised booklets produced by other Departments for their own particular purposes, in which the lessons are rubbed home by practical examples drawn from the Department's daily work. For example, Customs and Excise advise their staff to write not like this:

> The general position as we see it is that gifts as such are not exempt from Customs charges. There is in existence, however, a limited concession under which C & E Officers are able to waive value (except for gifts of highly dutied goods such as cigarettes or spirits) forwarded to individuals in this country by post.

but rather like this:

> In general, gifts are not exempt from Customs charges. However, there is a limited concession under which duty and value-added tax may be waived on many low value, genuine private gifts received by post from abroad. This does not apply to gifts of highly duted goods such as cigarettes or spirits.

A standard letter from the Office of Fair Trading used to begin as follows:

> Your company has already been told by this office that particulars of the above agreement, to which you are a party, have been placed on the public register of restrictive trading agreements.

The new version begins:

> In my letter of . . ., I told you that the Office has decided that this agreement should be placed on the public register of restrictive trading agreements.

Sometimes, no doubt, the advice in these admirable publications is not followed, but they have certainly done a great deal to raise the standard of letters sent by Government Departments to members of the public, particularly routine correspondence conducted by local offices. They have also done a great deal to improve other kinds of official writing, notably forms and explanatory leaflets. A form issued by the Department of Health and Social Security once contained the following:

> So that your proper entitlement to supplementary benefit can be decided you must produce evidence about your circumstances. You should therefore bring any of the following items you have for yourself, your wife or any dependants:–

The revised version now reads:

> We need to see some papers to sort out your claim. They are listed in the box on your right.

The rules for official writing are well tabulated in the following advice given to its staff by the Ministry of Housing and Local Government (now part of the Department of the Environment), which is directed to the composition of minutes and memoranda as well as letters of all kinds:

You must know	Before you begin to write make sure that you:
Your subject	(*a*) have a clear understanding of the subject;
Your reason for writing	(*b*) know why you are writing—what does your correspondent want to know and why does he want to know it?
Your reader	(*c*) adapt your style and the content of the letter or minute to suit your correspondent's needs and his present knowledge of the subject.

You must be	When writing you should:
Clear	(*a*) make your meaning clear; arrange the subject in logical order; be grammatically correct; not include irrelevant material;
Simple and brief	(*b*) use the most simple and direct language; avoid obscure words and phrases, unnecessary words, long sentences; avoid technical or legal terms and abbreviations unless you are sure that they will be understood by the reader; be as brief as possible; avoid 'padding';
Accurate and complete	(*c*) be as accurate and complete as possible; otherwise further correspondence will follow, resulting in extra work and loss of time;
Polite and human	(*d*) in your letters to the public be sympathetic if your correspondent is troubled; be particularly polite if he is rude; be lucid and helpful if he is muddled; be patient if he is stubborn; be appreciative if he is helpful; and *never* be patronising;
Prompt	(*e*) answer promptly, sending acknowledgements or interim replies if necessary—delays harm the reputation of the Department, and are discourteous.

Check your writing	Look critically at your written work. Can you answer 'yes' to the following questions about it?
Is it (a) clear?	(i) Can the language be easily understood by the recipient? (ii) Is it free from slang? (iii) Are the words the simplest that can carry the thought?

	(iv)	Is the sentence structure clear?
(b) *Simple and brief?*	(i)	Does it give only the essential facts?
	(ii)	Does it include only essential words and phrases?
(c) *Accurate?*	(i)	Is the information correct?
	(ii)	Do the statements conform with rules, policy, etc.?
	(iii)	Is the writing free from errors in grammar, spelling and punctuation?
(d) *Complete?*	(i)	Does it give all the necessary information?
	(ii)	Does it answer all the questions?
(e) *Human?*	(i)	Is the writing free from antagonistic words and phrases?
	(ii)	Is it, where appropriate, tactful, helpful, courteous, sympathetic, frank, forceful?
	(iii)	Will the tone bring the desired response?

The rules discussed in this chapter apply equally to writing by others than civil servants: letters, notices, and leaflets from quasi-government agencies or from local authorities; insurance policies, mortgages, and other consumer contracts; labels and instructional leaflets for consumer products; letters and bills from companies; letters of advice from lawyers to their clients. At least some organisations outside the Civil Service also recognise that the public have a right to understand and have revised their written material. Pressure groups such as the National Consumer Council, the Campaign for Plain English, and Clarity (a movement for the simplification of legal English) campaign to encourage clearer writing. And business companies and other organisations, as well as Government Departments, are put to shame when appalling passages of unintelligible writing are held up to public ridicule in the annual competition arranged by the Plain English Campaign and the National Consumer Council.

This chapter is called 'The Elements' because it suggests certain elementary rules—'be short, be simple, be human'—for officials to follow in writing letters to explain the law to members of the public. They will be elaborated in Chapters 5 to 8, in which much of what has been said in this chapter will be expanded. There is nothing novel in this chapter's precepts. Similar precepts were laid down for the Egyptian Civil Service some thousands of years ago:

Be courteous and tactful as well as honest and diligent.
All your doings are publicly known, and must therefore
Be beyond complaint or criticism. Be absolutely impartial.
Always give a reason for refusing a plea; complainants
Like a kindly hearing even more than a successful
Plea. Preserve dignity but avoid inspiring fear.
Be an artist in words, that you may be strong, for
The tongue is a sword. . . .

If we may judge from the following letter, those brought up in this tradition succeeded in avoiding verbiage. The letter is from a Minister of Finance to a senior civil servant:

Apollonius to Zeno, greeting. You did right to send the chickpeas to Memphis. Farewell.

4
Correctness

My Lord, I do here, in the name of all the learned and polite persons of the nation, complain to Your Lordship as First Minister, that our Language is extremely imperfect; that its daily improvements are by no means in proportion to its daily corruptions; that the pretenders to polish and refine it have chiefly multiplied abuses and absurdities; and that in many instances it offends against every part of grammar.

Swift

If language is not correct, then what is said is not what is meant; if what is said is not what is meant, then what ought to be done remains undone.

Confucius

There is little doubt that most of the new features that are intensely disliked by linguistic conservatives will triumph in the end. But the language will not bleed to death. Nor will it seem in any way distorted once the old observances have been forgotten.

Robert Burchfield

We will now turn to the implications of the remark made on p. 3, 'Lapses from what for the time being is regarded as correct irritate educated readers, and distract their attention, and so make them less likely to be influenced in the way you intend'. We shall have to add a fourth rule to the three with which we finished the last chapter—be correct. It applies to both vocabulary and grammar.

Correctness of vocabulary seems once to have been enforced more sternly on officials than it is now. More than two centuries ago the Secretary to the Commissioners of Excise wrote this letter to the Supervisor of Pontefract.

The Commissioners on perusal of your Diary observe that you make use of many affected phrases and incongruous words, such as 'illegal procedure', 'harmony', etc., all of which you use in a sense that the words do not bear. I am ordered to acquaint you that if you hereafter continue that affected and schoolboy way of writing, and to murder the language in such a manner, you will be discharged for a fool.*

* Quoted in *Humour in the Civil Service*, by John Aye, Universal Publications, 1928.

To us the punishment seems disproportionate to the offence, though the same penalty today might prove gratifying to those who think we have too many officials. But we can have nothing but admiration for the sentiment of the letter or for the vigorous directness of its phrasing. It serves moreover to illustrate a difficulty presented by this precept. What is correctness and who is to be the judge of it? It cannot be the same now as it was then. A Collector of Customs and Excise today might certainly use the expression 'illegal procedure' without being called in question; he might even refer to the harmony of his relations with the Trade without running much risk. On the other hand it would not do for him to say, as the Supervisor of Pontefract might have said, that the Local Bench were an indifferent body, meaning that they performed their duties with impartiality, or that he prevented the arrival of his staff at his office, meaning that he always got there first.

English is not static—neither in vocabulary nor in grammar, nor yet in that elusive quality called style. The fashion in prose alternates between the ornate and the plain, the periodic and the colloquial. Grammar and punctuation defy all the efforts of grammarians to force them into the mould of a permanent code of rules. Old words drop out or change their meanings; new words are admitted. What was stigmatised by the purists of one generation as a corruption of the language may a few generations later be accepted as an enrichment, and what was then common currency may have become a pompous archaism or acquired a new significance.

Eminent men with a care for the language have from time to time proposed that an Authority should be set up to preserve what is good and resist what is bad. 'They will find', said Swift, 'many words that deserve to be utterly thrown out of the language, many more to be corrected, and perhaps not a few long since antiquated, which ought to be restored on account of their energy and sound.'* Swift's plea, which was made in the form of a letter to the Lord Treasurer, came to nothing. This, Lord Chesterfield drily observed, was not surprising, 'precision and perspicuity not being in general the favourite objects of Ministers'. Dr Johnson thought the task hopeless:

Academies have been instituted to guard the avenues of the language, to retain fugitives and to repulse invaders; but their vigilance and activity have

---

* *Proposal for correcting, improving and ascertaining the English Tongue.*

been vain; sounds are too volatile and subtile for legal restraints; to enchain syllables and to lash the wind are equally the undertakings of pride, unwilling to measure its desires by its strength.

Dr Johnson was right, as usual. One has only to look at the words which Swift wanted to expel to realise how difficult, delicate and disappointing it is to resist new words and new meanings. He condemns, for instance, *sham, banter, mob, bully* and *bamboozle*. A generation later Dr Johnson called *clever* a 'low word' and *fun* and *stingy* 'low cant'. Should we not have been poorer if Swift and Johnson had had their way with these? There is no saying how things will go. The fight for admission to the language is quickly won by some assailants and long resistance is maintained against others. The word that excited Swift to greatest fury was *mob*, a contraction of *mobile vulgus*. Its victory was rapid and complete. So was that of *banter* and *bamboozle*, which he found hardly less offensive. And if *rep* for *reputation* proved ephemeral, and *phiz* for *physiognomy* never emerged from slang status, and is now dead, that is not because Swift denounced them, but because public opinion disliked them or got tired of them. *Reliable* was long opposed on the curious ground that it was an impossible construction; an adjective formed from *rely* could only be *reli-on-able*. This objection was a survival of the theory, widely held in pre-Fowler days, and not yet wholly exorcised, that no sentence could be 'good grammar', and no word a respectable word, if its construction violated logic or reason. It is not the habit of the English to refrain from doing anything merely because it is illogical; in any case it was less illogical to accept *reliable* than to strain at it after swallowing *available* and *objectionable*.

Some words gatecrash irresistibly because their sound is so appropriate to the meaning they are trying to convey. *Blurb*, imported from American English, has been described as 'an admirable word, quite indispensable'. The meaning of *livid* has moved from 'black-and-blue' through 'pallid' to 'reddish' perhaps because of its resemblance in sound to *vivid* and *lurid*; it has also acquired the colloquial figurative meaning 'furiously angry'. The quaint playful sound of the acronym *quango* has encouraged its speedy acceptance. Vidkun Quisling won instant admission to the company of the immortals, who, like the Earl of Sandwich, Mr Joseph Aloysius Hansom, General Shrapnel and Captain Boycott, have given their names to enrich the language. There has been stout resistance against certain words that attacked the barrier in the nineteenth century with powerful encouragement from Dickens—*mutual, individual, phenomenal* and *aggravate*. *Mutual* in the sense of *common*, shared by two or more, as in *Our Mutual Friend*, goes back to the sixteenth century, according to the *OED*, but is 'now regarded as incorrect'. Perhaps the reason why it is so difficult to restrain the word to its 'correct' meaning is the ambiguity of *common*. 'Our common friend' might be taken as a reflection on the friend's manners or birth. On the other hand it would be a great pity if *mutual* became so popular in its 'incorrect' sense that we could no longer rely on it when we need it for its correct one. The use of *individual* that is unquestionably correct is to distinguish a single person from a collective body, as it is used in the Income Tax Acts to distinguish between a personal taxpayer and a corporate one. But its use as a facetious term of disparagement (like the French *individu*) used to be common and still lingers. That was how Mr Jorrocks understood it when Mr Martin Moonface described him as an 'unfortunate individual', and provoked the retort 'You are another indiwidual'. *Phenomenal* to the purists means nothing more than 'perceptible to the senses', and a *phenomenon* is an occurrence so perceptible. But the purists have lost at least half this battle. It is still unusual to use *phenomenon* by itself to denote something striking or rare; it still tends to need a descriptive adjective or adjectival clause (such as 'striking' or 'rare'). But *phenomenal* in the sense of *extraordinary* is now common. Over *aggravate* there was a long-drawn-out struggle between those who, like Dickens, use it in the sense of *annoy* and those who would confine it to its original sense of *make worse*. The Dickens team have won, in the writing of good authors as well as in speech; but here too their victory must not be allowed to disqualify the word for its original purpose.

Today the newcomers are mostly from the inventive and colourful minds of the Americans. We have changed our outlook since Dean Alford declared nearly a hundred years ago that the way the Americans corrupted our language was all of a piece with the character of that nation 'with its blunted sense of moral obligation and duty to men'. But we have not yet accepted H. L. Mencken's suggestion that, since Americans far outnumber Britons, American English should be regarded as the norm. We therefore still have defenders of our tongue who scrutinise these immigrants very closely. That is as it should be, for some of them are certainly undesirables. But we ought not to forget how greatly our language has been enriched by the vigorous word-making habit of the Americans. Among the very many words we have acquired in the last few decades have been *gatecrasher*, *debunk*, *cold war*, *baby-sitter*, *stockpile*, *bulldoze*, *teenager* and *commuter*. For more about the influence of America see Chapter 15.

It is around new verbs that the battle now rages most hotly. New verbs are ordinarily formed in one of three ways, all of which have in the past been employed to create useful additions to our vocabulary. The first is the simple method of treating a noun as a verb; it is one of the beauties of our language that nouns can be so readily converted into adjectives or verbs. This was the origin, for instance, of the verb *question*; and there are many other such verbs, such as *function*, *condition*, *experience* and *mention*. The second is what is called 'back-formation', that is to say, forming from a noun the sort of verb from which the noun might have been formed if the verb had come first. In this way the verb *diagnose* was formed from *diagnosis* and the verb *televise* from *television*. The third is to add *ise*★ to an adjective, as *sterilise* has been formed from *sterile*.

All these methods are being used today with great zest. New verbs for something that is itself new (like *pressurise*) cannot be gainsaid. *Service* is a natural and useful newcomer in an age when almost everyone keeps a machine of some sort that needs periodical attention. But it provides an interesting example of the way these new verbs take an ell, once you give them an inch. *Service* is already trying to oust *serve*, as in:

A large number of depots of one sort or another will be required to service the town.

To enable a Local Authority to take advantage of this provision it is essential that sites should be available, ready serviced with roads and sewers.

A Welsh secretariat should be established in Brussels to service the needs of Welsh organisations.

The verb *contact*, which has been described as 'loathsome' and 'an abomination', has now made its way into the language, perhaps because it combines concisely the notions of 'write to', 'speak to' (in person or by telephone), and 'send a message to through someone else'. Earlier editions of this book recorded some people as still

★ On the question whether this should be *ise* or *ize* see p. 239.

strongly objecting to the use as verbs of *feature*, *glimpse*, *position*, *sense* and *signature*, though all had long since found their way into the dictionaries. All have now won their way, except perhaps *signature* (which indeed does not deserve to). The verbs *loan*, *gift* and *author* were verbs centuries ago and are now trying to come back again after a long holiday, spent by *loan* in America, by *gift* in Scotland and by *author* in oblivion. These have not yet succeeded, presumably because they compete with the established alternatives *lend*, *give* and *write*; on the other hand, the verb *co-author* has been admitted as shorter than 'be co-author of'. We shall not be disposed to welcome such a word as *re-accessioned*, used by a librarian of a book once more available to subscribers. Nor shall we welcome the verb *demagogue*, used by a spokesman to explain why the Republican president could not make a particular proposal ('The Democrats would pick it up and demagogue it').

But these words are merely skirmishers. The main body of the invasion consists of verbs ending in *ise* (and their accompanying nouns ending in *isation*). Earlier editions of this book noted that 'among those now nosing their way into the language' were *casualise* (employ casual labour), *civilianise* (replace military staff by civilian), *diarise* (enter in a diary), *editorialise* (make editorial comments on), *finalise* (finally settle), *hospitalise* (send to hospital), *publicise* (give publicity to), *servicise* (replace civilian staff by military), *cubiclise* (equip with cubicles), *randomise* (shuffle). Of these no one today raises an eyebrow at *editorialise*, *finalise*, *hospitalise*, *publicise*, or *randomise* (in the statistical sense); and the other noses have retreated. Advances in technology have produced, reasonably enough, *miniaturise*, *containerise*, *computerise*, *denuclearisation* and many others. The usual reason for inventing such words is that they enable us to say in one word what would otherwise need several. Whether that will prove a valid passport, time alone can show. In complaining of a glut of words ending in *-ise* and *-isation*, earlier editions singled out as among the least palatable the words *trialise*, *itinerise*, *reliableise* and *extemporisation*. Of these *extemporisation* (as well as the verb *extemporise*) has been swallowed with good grace, but *trialise*, *itinerise* and *reliableise* have not been admitted to the table. New words ending in *-ise* and *-isation* continue to multiply. Among recent additions are *privatise* and *privatisation*; they have slipped easily into the language without opposition. If these words were all, they might eventually be swallowed, though with some wry faces. But they are by no means all; a glut of this diet is being offered to us (*coordinatise, discretise, routinise, prioritise, cosmeticise, comprehensivisation, precinctisation*), and we are showing signs of nausea.

Another popular way of making new words is to put *de, dis* or *non* at the beginning of a word in order to create one with an opposite meaning. *De* and *dis* are termed by the *OED* 'living prefixes with privative force' (that is to say, they denote the removal of something). 'Living' is the right word; they have been living riotously of late. Anyone, it seems, can make a new verb by prefixing *de* to an existing one. Earlier editions of this book cited among 'some remarkable creations of this sort' the verbs *debureaucratise, decontaminate, dedirt, dehumidify, deinsectise, deratizate, derestrict, dewater, dezincify*.

Some of these, happily, have proved to be freaks of an occasion and are seen no more. But there is a class which will always have a strong claim to survival, whether we like it or not. It includes *decontaminate, derestrict* and *deschedule*. Their origin is the same: they all denote the undoing of something the doing of which called for—or at any rate was given—a special term. If to affect with gas is to *contaminate*, to enforce a speed limit is to *restrict*, to commandeer a house is to *requisition*, and to mark an area of the country as qualifying for special development grants is to *schedule*, then the cancellation of those things will inevitably be *decontaminate, derestrict, derequisition* and *deschedule*; and it is no use saying that they ought to be *cleanse, exempt, release* and *disqualify*, or any other words that are not directly linked with their opposites. Some people may still wince on reading that the authorities have decided to detrunk a road, as though it were an elephant, and on hearing that witnesses in a postponed trial have been dewarned. But they must learn to be brave. Many established *de*-words are unlikely to trouble anyone; among them are *deactivate, declassify, decode, defrost, dehydrate* and *desegregate*. An interesting word on the fringes of this class is *debrief*. One might think it meant telling the recipient of a brief that his brief is withdrawn, but in fact it means asking him how he got on in carrying it out; and it is as well established in this meaning for space pilots in the 1980s as it was for aircraft pilots in the 1940s. It is in use for others too, for example diplomats and spies.

Most of the new *dis*-words in the last fifty years have been invented by economists (several by *The Economist* itself). *Disincentive* and *disinflation*, received at first with surprised disapproval, have quite settled down. It is recognised that the old-fashioned opposites of *incentive* and *inflation—deterrent* and *deflation*—will not do; we need special words for that particular form of deterrent that discourages men from working hard, and for that process of checking inflation which is something less than deflation. And we now have *reflation* for the policy of deliberate controlled inflation. Among other *dis*-words that we may similarly excuse are *diseconomy* and *dissaving*.

It would yield economies that would far outweigh the diseconomies that are the inevitable price of public ownership and giant size.
Some 13.4 million of the 22 million income earners . . . kept their spending in such exact step with their incomes that they saved or dissaved less than £25 in that year.

These have also been accepted on the ground that in the first no positive word—neither *extravagance* nor *waste* nor *wastefulness*—would express the writer's meaning so well as *diseconomies*, and that in the second *dissaved* is the only way of expressing the opposite of *saved* without a clumsy periphrasis that would destroy the nice balance of the sentence. Other such fairly new *dis*-words are *disengagement*, *disinformation* and *disinvestment*. These words can certainly claim to have sprung from deliberate and provocative choice and not from mental indolence. What is deplorable is that so many of those who go in for the invention of opposites by means of 'living prefixes with privative force' do not know when to stop. It becomes a disease. *Disincentive* replaces *deterrent*; then *undisincentive* ousts *incentive*, and then *disincentive* itself has to yield to *non-undisincentive*. This tendency is well parodied by George Orwell; in the 'newspeak' which he pictured as the language imposed by a despotic government in 1984 *very bad* has become *doubleplusungood*.

The same warning is needed about the prefix *non*. To put *non* in front of a word is a well-established way of creating a word with the opposite meaning. *Non-appearance*, *non-combatant*, *nonconformist* and *non-existent* are common examples. But the lazy habit of using *non* to turn any word upside-down, so as not to have the trouble of thinking of its opposite, is becoming sadly common. 'Institutions for the care of the *non-sick*' presumably means something different from 'institutions for the care of the healthy', but the difference is not apparent. *Non-total* appears where *partial* is meant and *non-professional* is sometimes unnecessarily preferred to *unprofessional*, *lay*, or *amateur*.

This is not to say that new words with *non* are always to be condemned. They are sometimes needed because words with the negative prefixes *un* and *in* cannot always replace them. Words with *non* express simple negation, but words with *un* and *in* tend to express active opposition or failure. Thus, *noninformative* may be used of a type of communication that does not purport to be informative, but *uninformative* is used when it is expected to be informative; *nonproductive* may apply to managers, inspectors, or clerical staff who are not directly concerned with production, but *unproductive* refers to those who fail to produce. Words with *non* are also sometimes needed because of a certain ambiguity in the prefix *un*. Thus, your coat may be described as 'unbuttoned' either when you have undone the buttons or when you have never done them up. Similarly with *uncovered, undone, undressed, unfastened* and many others. For this reason certain countries may prefer to be described as 'non-aligned' rather than 'unaligned' so as to avoid any possible implication that they were once aligned. Our social security system makes a valid distinction between *unemployed* and *non-employed*. Even when the adjective has *un* the noun is often happier with *non*. If you wish to remain uninvolved, uncooperative or undiscriminating you will adopt a policy of non-involvement, non-cooperation or non-discrimination. It is relevant to mention here the adjective *inflammable*. It is connected with *inflame*, but because it looks negative you will do well to replace it with *flammable* when you want to mean 'capable of catching fire easily and of burning very quickly'. *Noninflammable* and *nonflammable* are synonymous and safely negative.

Yet another favourite device for making new words is the suffix *ee*. This is an erratic suffix, not conforming wholly to any rule. But in its main type it serves to denote the object of a verb, either the indirect object, as in *assignee, referee* and *trustee*, or the direct object, as in *examinee, trainee* and *employee*. Nevertheless, the suffix is occasionally used to form a word that refers to the subject of the verb, as in *absentee, escapee* and *refugee. Amputee* is illogical, since the word refers to the person and yet it is the limb and not the person that has been amputated. We may legitimately object to a new *ee* word if a perfectly good word is already on the job: *prosecutee* is not needed when we have *defendant*. But it would be idle to object to new *ee* words on principle or because they do not conform to the main rule for the suffix. Their purpose seems to be the same as that of many of our new verbs: to enable us to use one word instead of several. But since many *ee* words are ugly, we should not invent new ones unless they are really necessary.

While the age-long practice of creating new words has quickened its tempo, so has the no less ancient habit of extending the meaning of established words. Here again we ought to examine the novelties on merit, without bias. The main test for both is whether the new word, or the new meaning, fills a need in the vocabulary. If it is trying to take a seat already occupied—as the enlarged meanings of *anticipate* and *claim* are squatting in the places of *expect* and *assert*—they are clearly harming the language by 'blurring hard-won distinctions'. Still more are words like *overall* and *involve* open to that charge: they are claiming the seats of half a dozen or more honest words. But those that claim seats hitherto empty may deserve admittance. *Stagger*, for example, has enlarged its meaning both logically and usefully in such a phrase as *staggered holidays*. *Deadline* (originally a line around a military prison beyond which a prisoner might be shot) has done the same in taking over the task of signifying a limit of any sort beyond which it is not permissible to go. Nor do I see why purists should condemn the use of *nostalgia* not only for a feeling of homesickness but also for the emotion aroused by thinking of days that are no more. An appeal to etymology is not conclusive.

Sophisticated was once an uncomplimentary word implying sophistry and even artfulness (*unsophisticated* being its opposite). But it is now commonly used either as the opposite of *naive* with no uncomplimentary implication, or in the sense of *complicated*, particularly in technological contexts. A computer is a more sophisticated tool than an abacus, a ballistic missile a more sophisticated weapon than a musket; and the old connection with sophistry has quite disappeared. There is neither hope nor good sense in resisting this enlargement of meaning. If we want to accuse a man of sophistry, *sophistical* is still available. *Prestigious* is another example. At one time it was related to *prestidigitation*, or sleight of hand, but it has come to be used as an adjective from *prestige* (which has the same etymological origin). A prestigious person is now a VIP, not a conjuror, and a prestigious project is one undertaken to enhance the promoter's prestige, though not necessarily his bank balance. There is no other word which does this job. *Prestigious* passes. Metaphorical extension has given us new meanings for *hawk*, a militant person, and *dove*, a conciliatory person. These are useful additions, and do not prevent these words from continuing to function in their older meanings. The noun *wet* (somewhat similar in its political sense to *dove*) has not yet made its way into literary use, though it has established itself in journalistic practice.

When a word starts straying from its derivative meaning it may often be proper, and sometimes even useful, to try to restrain it; there are many now who would like to restrain the wanderlust of *alibi* and *shambles*. The ignorant misuse of technical terms excites violent reactions in those who know their true meanings. The popular use of *to the nth degree* in the sense of *to the utmost* exasperates the mathematician, who knows that strictly the notion of largeness is not inherent in *to the nth* at all. The use of *by and large* in the sense of *broadly speaking* exasperates the sailor, who knows that the true meaning of the phrase—alternately close to the wind and with the wind abeam or aft—has not the faintest relation to the meaning given to it by current usage. But there is a point where it becomes idle pedantry to try to put back into their etymological cages words and phrases that escaped from them many years ago and have settled down firmly elsewhere. To do that is to start on a path on which there is no logical stopping-point short of such absurdities as insisting that the word *anecdote* can only be applied to a story never told before, whereas we all know that it is more likely to mean one told too often.

Sometimes words appear to have changed their meanings when the real change is in the popular estimate of the value of the ideas they stand for. Only recently have the dictionaries recognised that *appeasement* can be anything but praiseworthy. *Imperialism*, which Lord Rosebery defined as 'a greater pride in Empire, a larger patriotism', has fallen from its pedestal. *Academic* has suffered a similar debasement owing to the waning of love of learning for its own sake and the growth of mistrust of intellectual activities that have no immediate utilitarian results. It is frequently used to mean *irrelevant*, *theoretical*, or *impractical*. *Elite* and *paternal* are going the same way; *élitist* is a term of abuse in many modern mouths and *paternalism* implies bossiness or interference rather than kindliness or protectiveness. On the other hand, *aggressive* and *innovative* have risen in value; *aggressive* is used to compliment an energetic and enterprising business executive and *innovative* is for many a term of praise that looks on novelty as an intrinsic value.

Public opinion decides all these questions in the long run; there is little that individuals can do about them. Our national vocabulary is a democratic institution, and what is generally accepted will ultimately be correct. I have no doubt that if anyone should read this book in fifty years' time he would find current objections to the use of certain words in certain senses as curious as we now find Swift's denunciation of *mob*.

The duty of officials is, however, clear: neither to perpetuate what is obsolescent nor to give currency to what is novel, but, like good servants, to follow what is generally regarded by their masters as the best practice for the time being. Among their readers will be vigilant guardians of the purity of English prose, and they must not be offended. So the vocabulary of officials must contain only words that by general consent have passed the barrier and they must not give a helping hand to any that are still trying to get through, even though they may think them deserving.

> For last year's words belong to last year's language
> And next year's words await another voice.

The sentence that is right, adds Eliot, is one

> . . . where every word is at home,
> Taking its place to support the others
> The word neither diffident nor ostentatious,
> An easy commerce of the old and the new,
> The common word exact without vulgarity,
> The formal word precise but not pedantic,
> The complete consort dancing together.*

Chapter 17 contains an alphabetic list of words and phrases that are used in senses often regarded as incorrect or that are apt to be used unsuitably. It is not easy to decide which words should be assigned to the 'incorrect' category and which to the 'unsuitable', and it seems more convenient to readers to put all the words into one list.

We must now consider what correctness means not in the choice of words but in handling them when chosen. That takes us into the realm of grammar, syntax and idiom—three words that overlap and are often used loosely, with grammar as a generic term covering them all.

* T. S. Eliot, *Little Gidding*, Faber & Faber, 1943.

Grammar has fallen from the high esteem that it used to enjoy. Over a hundred and fifty years ago William Cobbett said that 'grammar perfectly understood enables us not only to express our meaning fully and clearly but so to express it as to defy the ingenuity of man to give our words any other meaning than that which we intended to express'. The very name of grammar school serves to remind us that grammar was long regarded as the only path to culture and learning. But that was Latin grammar. When our mother-tongue encroached on the paramountcy of the dead languages, questions began to be asked. Even at the time when Cobbett was writing his grammar, Sydney Smith was fulminating about the unfortunate boy who was 'suffocated by the nonsense of grammarians, overwhelmed with every species of difficulty disproportionate to his age, and driven by despair to pegtop and marbles'. Very slowly over the past hundred years the idea seems to have gained ground that the grammar of a living language, which is changing all the time, cannot be fitted into the rigid framework of a dead one; nor can the grammar of a language such as Latin, which changes the forms of its words to express different grammatical relations, be profitably applied to a language such as English, which has got rid of most of its inflections, and expresses grammatical relations by devices like prepositions and auxiliary verbs and by the order of its words. Most grammarians today follow the practice of describing how people actually use the language, and they are aware of variations in the use of language: there are differences, for example, between how people write and how they speak or between their formal writing and their casual writing.

The old-fashioned grammarian certainly has much to answer for. He created a false sense of values that still lingers. Too much importance is still attached to grammarians' fetishes and too little to choosing the right words. But we cannot have grammar jettisoned altogether; that would mean chaos. Among educated writers, there are certain grammatical conventions that are, so to speak, a code of good manners. They change, but those current at the time must be observed by writers who wish to express themselves clearly and without offence to their readers.

Strictly, idiom is different from grammar: the two are often in conflict. Idiom is defined by the *OED* as 'a peculiarity of phraseology approved by usage and often having a meaning other than its logical or grammatical one'. When anything in this book is called 'good English idiom' or 'idiomatic', what is meant is that usage has established it as correct. Idiom does not conflict with grammar or logic as a matter of course; it is usually grammatically and logically neutral. Idiom requires us to say *capable of doing*, not *capable to do*, and *able to do*, not *able of doing*. Logic and grammar do not object to this, but they would be equally content with *capable to do* and *able of doing*. At the same time idiom is 'a tyrannical, capricious, utterly incalculable thing', and if logic and grammar get in its way, so much the worse for logic and grammar. It is idiomatic—at least in speech—to say 'I won't be longer than I can help' and 'it's me'. Yet during the reign of pedantry attempts were constantly made to force idiom into the mould of logic. We were not to speak of a *criminal being executed*, for 'a sentence can be executed but not a person'; we were not to say *vexed question* for 'though many a question vexes none is vexed'; nor *most thoughtless* for 'if a person is without thought there cannot be degrees of his lack of that quality'; nor *light the fire*, for 'nothing has less need of lighting'; nor *round the fireside*, for 'that would mean that some of us were behind the chimney'. Some trace still lingers of the idea that what is illogical or ungrammatical 'must' be wrong, such as condemnation of *under the circumstances* and of the use of a plural verb with *none*. The truth is, as Logan Pearsall Smith says:

Plainly a language which was all idiom and unreason would be impossible as an instrument of thought; but all languages permit the existence of a certain number of illogical expressions; and the fact that, in spite of their vulgar origin and illiterate appearance, they have succeeded in elbowing their way into our prose and poetry, and even learned lexicons and grammars, is proof that they perform a necessary function in the domestic economy of speech.*

In Chapters 9–13, we offer advice about common troubles in the handling of words. The troubles will be classified under those in arrangement (Chapter 9), conjunctions and prepositions (Chapter 10), pronouns (Chapter 11), and verbs (Chapter 12). Finally, Chapter 13 deals with a miscellany of potential problems, including principally those involving negatives.

---

* *Words and Idioms*, Constable & Co., 5th ed., 1943.

5
The choice of words: introductory

The craftsman is proud and careful of his tools: the surgeon does not operate with an old razor-blade: the sportsman fusses happily and long over the choice of rod, gun, club or racquet. But the man who is working in words, unless he is a professional writer (and not always then), is singularly neglectful of his instruments.

Ivor Brown

What appears to be a sloppy or meaningless use of words may well be a completely correct use of words to express sloppy or meaningless ideas.

Anonymous diplomat

Here we come to the most important part of our subject. Correctness is not enough. The words used may all be words approved by the dictionary and used in their right senses; the grammar may be faultless and the idiom above reproach. Yet what is written may still fail to convey a ready and precise meaning to the reader. That it does so fail is the charge brought against much of what is written nowadays, including much of what is written by officials. Matthew Arnold once said that the secret of style was to have something to say and to say it as clearly as you can. This is over-simple, but it will do well enough as a first principle for the kind of writing in which emotional appeal plays no part. The most prevalent disease in present-day writing is a tendency to say what one has to say in as complicated a way as possible. Instead of being simple, terse and direct, it is stilted, long-winded and circumlocutory; instead of choosing the simple word it prefers the unusual; instead of the plain phrase the cliché.

The forms most commonly taken by the disease will be examined in the following three chapters. In this one we are concerned (to borrow a bit of jargon from the doctors) with its aetiology and with prescribing some general regimen for writers that will help them to avoid catching it. It is largely a matter of acquiring good habits and eschewing bad ones; for very few people are incurably bad writers by nature, just as very few are congenitally diseased or deformed.

Why do so many writers prefer complexity to simplicity? Officials are far from being the only offenders. It seems to be a morbid condition contracted in early adulthood. Children show no signs of it. Here, for example, is the response of a child of ten to an invitation to write an essay on a bird and a beast:

The bird that I am going to write about is the owl. The owl cannot see at all by day and at night is as blind as a bat.

I do not know much about the owl, so I will go on to the beast which I am going to choose. It is the cow. The cow is a mammal. It has six sides—right, left, an upper and below. At the back it has a tail on which hangs a brush. With this it sends the flies away so that they do not fall into the milk. The head is for the purpose of growing horns and so that the mouth can be somewhere. The horns are to butt with, and the mouth is to moo with. Under the cow hangs the milk. It is arranged for milking. When people milk, the milk comes and there is never an end to the supply. How the cow does it I have not yet realised, but it makes more and more. The cow has a fine sense of smell; one can smell it far away. This is the reason for the fresh air in the country.

The man cow is called an ox. It is not a mammal. The cow does not eat much, but what it eats it eats twice, so that it gets enough. When it is hungry it moos, and when it says nothing it is because its inside is all full up with grass.

The writer had something to say and said it as clearly as he could, and so has unconsciously achieved style. But why do we write, when we are ten, 'so that the mouth can be somewhere' and perhaps when we are thirty 'in order to ensure that the mouth may be appropriately positioned environmentally'? Let us hazard a few possible reasons.

The first affects only the official. It is a temptation to cling too long to outworn words and phrases. The British Constitution, as everyone knows, has been shaped by retaining old forms and putting them to new uses. Among the old forms that we are reluctant to abandon are those that have long been traditional in State documents and the accepted language of administration, Parliamentary government and diplomacy. In their proper place these words and phrases do no harm because no one ever reads them attentively; they are no longer intended to convey thought from one brain to another. But officials, living in this atmosphere, properly proud of the ancient traditions of the public service, sometimes allow their style of letter-writing to be affected by it—*adverting* and *acquainting* and *causing to be informed*. There may even be produced in their minds a feeling that all common words lack the dignity that they are bound to maintain. As suggested on p. 177, the tendency to preserve governmental dignity is not to be wholly derided; but there is no doubt that it is too often overdone.

Another possible reason is that many people retain in maturity the adolescent's love of the long word. Most of us can remember how delighted we were at discovering the meaning of lovely long words like *irrelevant*, *disenchantment*, *confrontation*, *intractable*, *discriminatory*, *opportunistic* and so on, how proud we were of these additions to our schoolboy or schoolgirl vocabulary, and how eagerly we sought opportunities of showing off our new toys. All young people of sensibility feel the lure of rippling and reverberating polysyllables. So it is perhaps because the writer has not quite grown up that he or she finds a satisfaction in 'transferred to an alternative location' which cannot be got from 'moved to another site'; that 'ablution facilities' strikes a chord which does not vibrate to 'wash-basins'. Far-fetched words are by definition 'recherché' words, and are thought to give distinction; thus such words as *allergic*, *ambivalent*, *catalyst* and *viable* acquire their vogue. A newly-discovered metaphor shines like a jewel in a drab vocabulary; thus *blueprint*, *escalation*, *ceiling* and *target* are eagerly seized, and the dust settles on their discarded predecessors—*plan*, *growth*, *limit* and *objective*. But it will not do. The very subject matter of official writing rules out ornament; it asks only to be put across.

There is another reason that affects mainly the official. It is sometimes dangerous to be precise. 'Mistiness is the mother of safety', said Newman. 'Your safe man in the Church of England is he who steers his course between the Scylla of "Aye" and the Charybdis of "No" along the channel of "No meaning".' Ecclesiastics are not in this respect unique. Politicians have long known the dangers of precision of statement, especially at election time.

'And now for our cry', said Mr Taper.

'It is not a Cabinet for a good cry', said Tadpole; 'but then, on the other hand, it is a Cabinet that will sow dissension in the opposite ranks, and prevent them having a good cry.'

'Ancient institutions and modern improvements, I suppose, Mr Tadpole.'

'Ameliorations is the better word; ameliorations. Nobody knows exactly what it means.'

That was written by Disraeli, but no student of modern politics will say that it is out of date. Policies of 'dynamic realism,' 'imaginative pragmatism' or 'purposive abrasiveness' would have appealed to Mr Tadpole in exactly the same way.

When officials do not know their Ministers' minds, or Ministers do not know their own minds, or Ministers think it wise not to speak their minds, officials must sometimes cover the utterance with a mist of vagueness. Civil Service methods are often contrasted unfavourably with those of business. But to do this is to forget that no Board of Directors of a business concern have to meet a committee of their shareholders every afternoon, to submit themselves daily to an hour's questioning on their conduct of the business, to get the consent of that committee by a laborious process to every important step they take, or to conduct their affairs with the constant knowledge that there is a shadow board eager for the shareholders' authority to take their place. The systems are quite different and are bound to produce different methods. Ministers are under daily attack, and their reputations are largely in the hands of their staff. Only with full and explicit authority from their Ministers can civil servants show in an important matter that promptness and boldness which are said to be the attributes of the business world.

The words which he writes will go on record, possibly for all time, certainly for a great many years. They may have to be published, and may have a wide circulation. They may even mean something in international relationships. So, even though mathematical accuracy may in the nature of things be unattainable, identifiable inaccuracy must at least be avoided. The hackneyed official phrase, the wide circumlocution, the vague promise, the implied qualification are comfortingly to hand. Only those who have been exposed to the temptation to use them know how hard it is to resist. But with all the sympathy that such understanding may mean, it is still possible to hold that something might be done to purge official style and caution, necessary and desirable in themselves, of their worst extravagances.

This is a quotation from a leading article in *The Times*. It arose out of a correspondent's ridicule of this extract from a letter written by a Government Department to its Advisory Council:

In transmitting this matter to the Council the Minister feels that it may be of assistance to them to learn that, as at present advised, he is inclined to think that, in existing circumstances, there is, *prima facie*, a case for . . .

It is as easy to slip into this sort of thing without noticing it as to see the absurdity of it when pointed out. One may surmise that the writer felt himself to be in a dilemma: he wanted the Advisory Council to advise the Minister in a certain way, but did not want them to think that the Minister had made up his mind before getting their advice. But he might have done this without piling qualification on qualification and reservation on reservation; all that he needed to say was that the Minister thought so-and-so but wanted to know what the Advisory Committee thought before taking a decision.

This quotation illustrates another trap into which official writing is led when it has to leave itself a bolt-hole, as it so often has. Cautionary clichés are used automatically without thought of what they mean. There are two of them here: *inclined to think* and *as at present advised*. Being *inclined to think*, in the sense of inclining to an opinion not yet crystallised, is a reasonable enough expression, just as one may say colloquially *my mind is moving that way*. But excessive use of the phrase may provoke the captious critic to say that if being inclined to think is really something different from thinking, then the less said about it the better until it has ripened into something that can be properly called thought. We can hardly suppose that the writer of the following sentence really needed time to ponder whether his opinion might not be mistaken:

> We are inclined to think that people are more irritated by noise that they feel to be unnecessary than by noise that they cause themselves.

As at present advised should be used only where an opinion has been formed on expert (e.g. legal) advice, never, as it is too often, as the equivalent of saying: 'This is what the Minister thinks in the present state of his mind but, as he is human, the state of his mind may change'. That may be taken for granted.

There is often a need for caution, and it is a temptation to hedging and obscurity. But it is no excuse for them. A frank admission that an answer cannot be given is better than an answer that looks as if it meant something but really means nothing. Such a reply exasperates the reader and brings the Service into discredit.

Politeness plays its part too: what is vague is less likely to give offence. Politeness often shows itself in euphemism, a term defined by the dictionary as 'the substitution of a mild or vague expression for a harsh or blunt one'. It is prompted by the same impulse as led the Greeks to call the Black Sea the Euxine (the hospitable one) in the hope of averting its notorious inhospitableness, and the Furies the Eumenides (the good-humoured ladies) in the hope that they might be flattered into being less furious. For the Greeks it was the gods and the forces of nature that had to be propitiated; for those who govern us today it is the electorate. Hence the prevalence of what the grammarians call *meiosis* (understatement) and the use of qualifying adverbs such as *somewhat* and *rather* and the popularity of the *not un-* device. This last is useful in its place. There are occasions when a writer's meaning may be conveyed more exactly by (say) *not unkindly*, *not unnaturally* or *not unjustifiably* than by *kindly*, *naturally* or *justifiably*. But the 'not un-' habit is liable to take charge, with disastrous effects, making the victim forget all straightforward adjectives and adverbs. When an Inspector of Taxes writes 'This is a by no means uncomplicated case', we may be pretty sure that he is employing meiosis. And 'I think the officer's attitude was not unduly unreasonable' seems a chicken-hearted defence of a subordinate. George Orwell recommended that we should all inoculate ourselves against the disease by memorising this sentence: 'A not unblack dog was chasing a not unsmall rabbit across a not ungreen field'.

Similarly, 'less than truthful' is a euphemism for 'lying' and 'no little' a meiosis for 'great'. But the writer of the following pays so much more attention to avoiding the stark than to conveying his meaning that he ends by conveying exactly the opposite.

> In communicating these data to your organisation after fullest consultation with all my colleagues also concerned, I would certainly be less than truthful if I were to say that this has occasioned the Ministry (and this Section in particular) no little difficulty but that the delay is nevertheless regretted.

He might more easily have said 'I am sorry we could not send you this information sooner, but we have found this a very difficult case': what he has succeeded in saying is that the case was easy and that he does not regret the delay.

Or a vague word may be preferred to a precise one because the vague is less alarming; or the natural word may be rejected because it has acquired unpleasant associations. The poor have become the lower income brackets, backward countries are developing countries, unsuccessful teachers (and others) are described as coming from the lower end of the achievement range. Even a prison is now sometimes a correctional facility. There are no stupid, backward or troublesome children; they are intellectually unendowed or maladjusted or disturbed—and as like as not underprivileged and socially disadvantaged as well.

The old are senior citizens, secondhand cars are pre-owned, a price rise is an upward adjustment, and a loss is a negative contribution to profits. Employees are let go rather than sacked, and they then become involuntarily leisured. The word *race* has become almost unusable because of its overtones of racial discrimination and colour prejudice; we have to use *ethnic origin* instead. Salesmen and station masters have become salespeople and station managers, to avoid the sexist implication that only a man need apply for the job.

This sort of substitution is natural and often benevolent in intention, but it has its limitations. If the unpleasantness, or the supposed unpleasantness, attaches to the thing itself it will taint the new name; in course of time yet another will have to be found, and so *ad infinitum*. Homosexuals and lesbians are working their way through our vocabulary at an alarming rate: for some time now we have been unable to describe our more eccentric friends as *queer*, or our more lively ones as *gay*, without risk of misunderstanding. We do not seem to have done ourselves much good when we assigned the blameless but unsuitable word *lavatory* to a place where there is nowhere to wash; we merely blunted the language; and now *toilet* and *powder-room* are blunted in their turn.*

Another reason is the love of showing off. There are several different manifestations of this, all of which are dealt with more fully elsewhere in this book. Writers want to parade their knowledge of long or unfamiliar or foreign words; or they want to show that they are familiar with the latest fashion (that they are 'with it'); or they want to impress by their use of language lest they should fail to do so by what they are saying—in other words they are afraid of being damned as

---

* For a neat commentary on the tendency to use language which is at once polysyllabic, euphemistic and fashionable—three of the types mentioned in this chapter—consider the drawing of a small girl pointing to her young brother and shouting 'Mummy! Johnny's polluted his environment again'. But sooner or later this drawing may not even raise a smile: the caption may be what everyone says in these circumstances.

superficial or amateur. All these may combine to produce such flatulent writing as appears in the examples just below.

There remains one more reason—laziness. Clear thinking is hard work. A great many people go through life without doing it to any noticeable extent. And as George Orwell pointed out, sloppy and ready-made phrases 'will construct your sentences for you and even think your thoughts for you to a certain extent'. It is as though the builder of a house did not take the trouble to select with care the materials that he thought most suitable for his purpose, but collected chunks of masonry from ruined houses built by others and stuck them together anyhow. That is not a promising way to produce anything significant in meaning, attractive in form, or of any practical use.

So much for what we have termed the 'aetiology' of the disease. Before turning to treatment it may be useful to illustrate the symptoms. The examples come from various sources, both in the United States and in our own country. The first four are accompanied by translations; the fifth seems to defy translation.

Example

(Quoted *The Economist*, from which the translation also is taken.) NATO has expressed its fundamental change of policy as "evolving in place of the overriding medium-term defence hypothesis to which all economic planning was functionally subordinate, an antithesis of balancing *desiderata*, such as the politico-strategical necessity against the economico-social possibility and further these two components against the need for a maximum of flexibility".

Translation

What this really means is that, whereas a national defence programme has been taken hitherto as something imposed from above which could not be altered, now the military requirements of NATO will be made to match the economic achievements of the individual countries.

The attitude of each, that he was not required to inform himself of, and his lack of interest in, the measures taken by the other to carry out the responsibility assigned to such other under the provision of plans then in effect, demonstrated on the part of each lack of appreciation of the responsibilities vested in them, and inherent in their positions.

Neither took any interest in the other's plans, or even found out what they were. This shows that they did not appreciate the responsibilities of their positions.

Example

(Quoted in *The Lancet*, from which the translation also is taken.) Experiments are described which demonstrate that in normal individuals the lowest concentration in which sucrose can be detected by means of gustation differs from the lowest concentration in which sucrose (in the amount employed) has to be ingested in order to produce a demonstrable decrease in olfactory acuity and a noteworthy conversion of sensations interpreted as a desire for food into sensations interpreted as a satiety associated with ingestion of food.

It is suggested that although there is not necessarily any need for any form of welfare referral—that would depend on all the circumstances—officers can, through greater understanding of these universal phenomena, firstly behave more sensitively at a time when the claimant is especially vulnerable and, secondly, avoid making precipitate judgments on the basis of temporary reactions—judgments which could lead to inappropriate referral on the one hand, or irritated reactions to unco-operative behaviour on the other.*

To reduce the risk of war and establish conditions of lasting peace requires the closer co-ordination in the employment of their joint resources to underpin these countries' economies in such a manner as to permit the full maintenance of their social and material standards as well as to adequate development of the necessary measures.

Translation

Experiments are described which demonstrate that a normal person can taste sugar in water in quantities not strong enough to interfere with his sense of smell or take away his appetite.

Although welfare help may not be wanted staff should, by a better understanding of human behaviour, be aware that the claimant is going through a particularly difficult time; they should avoid jumping to conclusions which might lead either to an unwanted referral or to a charge of uncooperative behaviour.

* Unlike the other examples, this one never saw the light of day. It is taken from the first draft of a training instruction in a Government Department; the translation shows how it was redrafted before being issued. The technical sense of *referral*, which appears in both versions, is legitimate 'departmental shorthand' (see pp. 8–9).

We can now turn to the question whether some general advice can be given to fortify the writer against infection. Several distinguished men have tried their hands at this. This is what Fowler said:

Anyone who wishes to become a good writer should endeavour, before he allows himself to be tempted by more showy qualities, to be direct, simple, brief, vigorous and lucid.

This general principle may be translated into general rules in the domain of vocabulary as follows:

Prefer the familiar word to the far-fetched.
Prefer the concrete word to the abstract.
Prefer the single word to the circumlocution.
Prefer the short word to the long.
Prefer the Saxon word to the Romance.

'These rules', he added, 'are given in order of merit; the last is also the least.'

He also pointed out that

all five rules will often be found to give the same answer about the same word or set of words. Scores of illustrations might be produced; let one suffice: *In the contemplated eventuality* (a phrase no worse than anyone can pick for himself out of his paper's leading article for the day) is at once the far-fetched, the abstract, the periphrastic, the long and the Romance, for *if so*. It does not very greatly matter by which of the five roads the natural is reached instead of the monstrosity, so long as it *is* reached. The five are indicated because (1) they differ in directness, and (2) in any given case only one of them may be possible.

Later authorities have not allowed Fowler to have the last word; and indeed his rules would have absurd results if applied too rigidly. The best that could be said for prose containing nothing but familiar, concrete, single, short, Saxon words is that it would be less intolerable than prose which always opted the other way. His fourth and fifth rules have attracted most disagreement, and rightly so; for we cannot fully exploit the richness of the English language if we are frightened of all words that are Latin in origin or more than two or three syllables in length. The advice to prefer the Saxon word to the Romance also raises the practical difficulty that it is not given to many of us always to be sure which is which. Any virtue there may be in these two rules is really already implicit in the rule to prefer the familiar word to the far-fetched; and most people are likely to think that what Bradley had written, before Fowler formulated his rules, is all that need be said on the subject:

> The cry for 'Saxon English' sometimes means nothing more than a demand for plain and unaffected diction, and a condemnation of the idle taste for 'words of learned length and thundering sound' which has prevailed at some periods of our literature. So far it is worthy of all respect; but the pedantry that would bid us reject the word fittest for our purpose because it is not of native origin ought to be strenuously resisted.

What we are concerned with is not a quest for literary style as an end in itself, but to study how best to convey our meaning without ambiguity and without giving unnecessary trouble to our readers. This being our aim, the essence of the matter may be expressed in the following three rules, and what remains to be said in the domain of vocabulary will be little more than an elaboration of them.

Use no more words than are necessary to express your meaning, for if you use more you are likely to obscure it and to tire your reader. In particular do not use superfluous adjectives and adverbs and do not use roundabout phrases where single words would serve.

Use familiar words rather than the far-fetched, if they express your meaning equally well; for the familiar are more likely to be readily understood.

Use words with a precise meaning rather than those that are vague, for they will obviously serve better to make your meaning clear; and in particular prefer concrete words to abstract, for they are more likely to have a precise meaning.

As Fowler pointed out, rules like these cannot be kept in separate compartments; they overlap. But in the next three chapters we will follow roughly the order in which the rules are set out and examine them under the headings 'Avoiding the superfluous word', 'Choosing the familiar word' and 'Choosing the precise word'.

6

The choice of words: avoiding the superfluous word

A reader of Milton must be always upon duty; he is surrounded with sense, it arises in every line, every word is to the purpose; there are no lazy intervals, all has been considered, and demands and merits observation. Even in the best writers you sometimes find words and sentences which hang on so loosely you may blow 'em off; Milton's are all substance and weight; fewer would not have serv'd the turn, and more would have been superfluous.

Jonathan Richardson, quoted by F. E. Hutchinson
in *Milton and the English Mind*, p. 137

The fault of verbiage (which the *OED* defines as 'abundance of words without necessity or without much meaning') is too multiform for analysis. But certain classifiable forms of it are specially common, and in this chapter we will examine some of these, ending with an indeterminate class which we will call 'padding', to pick up what has been left outside the others.

Verbosity in adjectives and adverbs

Palmerston* wrote of one of Her Majesty's Ministers abroad who had neglected an admonition to go through all his despatches and strike out all words not necessary for fully conveying his meaning: 'If Mr Hamilton would let his substantives and adjectives go single instead of always sending them forth by twos and threes, his despatches would be clearer and easier to read'.

It has been wisely said that the adjective is the enemy of the noun. If we make a habit of saying 'The true facts are these', we shall come under suspicion when we profess to tell merely 'the facts'. If a *crisis* is always *acute* and an *emergency* always *grave*, what is left for those

---

* Quoted by C. K. Webster in *Politica*, August 1934.

words to do by themselves? If *active* constantly accompanies *consideration*, we shall think we are being fobbed off when we are promised bare consideration. If a decision is always qualified by *definite*, a decision by itself becomes a poor filleted thing. If conditions are customarily described as *prerequisite* or *essential*, we shall doubt whether a *condition* without an adjective is really a condition at all. An *unfilled vacancy* may leave us wondering whether a mere vacancy is really vacant. If a part is always an *integral part* or a *component part* there is nothing left for a mere part except to be a spare part.

Cultivate the habit of reserving adjectives and adverbs to make your meaning more precise, and suspect those that you find yourself using to make it more emphatic. Use adjectives to denote kind rather than degree. By all means say an *economic crisis* or a *military disaster*, but think well before saying an *acute crisis* or a *terrible disaster*. Say if you like 'The proposal met with noisy opposition and is in obvious danger of defeat'. But do not say 'The proposal met with considerable opposition and is in real danger of defeat'. If that is all you want to say it is better to leave out the adjectives and say 'The proposal met with opposition and is in danger of defeat'.

Official writers seem to have a curious shrinking from certain adjectives unless they are adorned by adverbs. It is as though they were naked and must hastily have an adverbial dressing-gown thrown around them. The most indecent adjectives are, it seems, those of quantity or measure such as *short* and *long*, *many* and *few*, *heavy* and *light*. The adverbial dressing-gowns most favoured are *unduly*, *relatively* and *comparatively*. These adverbs can only properly be used when something has been mentioned or implied which gives a standard of comparison. But we have all seen them used on innumerable occasions when there is no standard of comparison. They are then meaningless. Their use is merely a shrinking from the nakedness of an unqualified statement. If the report of an accident says that 'about a hundred people were taken to hospital but comparatively few were detained', that is a proper use of the adverb. But when a circular says that 'our diminishing stocks will be expanded in a relatively short period', without mentioning any other period with which to compare it, the word signifies nothing.

Sometimes the use of a dressing-gown adverb actually makes the writer say the opposite of what he or she intended. The writer of the circular which said, 'It is not necessary to be unduly meticulous in

. . .' meant to say 'you need not be meticulous', but actually said 'you may be meticulous but need not be unduly so', leaving the reader to guess when the limit of dueness in meticulousness has been reached.

Undue and *unduly* seem to be words that have the property of taking the reason prisoner. 'There is no cause for undue alarm' is a phrase that may be used in all sorts of circumstances by all sorts of people, from a Government spokesman about a water shortage to a headmistress on the occurrence of a case of AIDS. It is, I suppose, legitimate to say 'Don't be unduly alarmed', though your reader may not find much reassurance in it. But 'there is no cause for undue alarm' differs little, if at all, from 'there is no cause for alarm for which there is no cause', and that hardly seems worth saying. *Undue hardship* is another phrase which makes its appearance far more often than it makes sense.

The following is an example, not of *undue* superfluous, but of *undue* nonsensical:

It does not require undue prescience to anticipate that the enlarged EEC will soon be an effective member of the 'big league'.

Nothing that is undue can ever be required. Reason demands some such word as *unusual*. (See also p. 205 for this use of *anticipate*.)

Undue and *unduly* have of course their own proper job to do, as in 'The speech was not unduly long for so important an occasion'.

As some adjectives seem to attract unnecessary adverbs, so do some nouns unnecessary adjectives. We have mentioned *consideration's* fondness for the company of *active*, but it often walks out with other charmers too, such as *careful, sympathetic* and *thorough*, whose tendency to cling does it little good; it has recently become dissatisfied with *careful* and taken up with *in depth* instead. *In depth* is also in great demand as a companion for *study, review, research* and others, and seems quite capable of ruining all of them. *Danger* is another word that is often given support it does not need, generally *real* and *serious*.

The special needs of children under 5 require as much consideration as those of children aged 5–7, and there is a serious danger that they will be overlooked in these large schools. . . . There is a real danger . . . that the development of the children would be unduly forced. . . .

Here we have *serious, real* and *unduly* all used superfluously. *Serious* is prompted by a feeling that *danger* always needs adjectival support, and *real* is presumably what grammarians call 'elegant variation'* to avoid repeating the same word. *Unduly* is superfluous because the word *forced* itself contains the idea of undue. *Real* danger should be reserved for contrast with imaginary danger, as, for instance, 'Some people fear so-and-so but the real danger is so-and-so'. These things may seem trivial, but nothing is negligible that is a symptom of loose thinking.

Vague adjectives of intensification like *considerable, appreciable* and *substantial* are too popular. None of these three should be used without three questions being asked. Do I need an adjective at all? If so, would not a more specific adjective suit better? Or, failing that, which of these three (with their different shades of meaning) is most apt? If those who write 'This is a matter of considerable urgency' were to ask themselves these questions, they would realise that 'This is urgent' serves them better; and those who write 'A programme of this magnitude will necessarily take a considerable period' will find it more effective to say 'a long time'. Strong words like *urgent, danger, crisis, disaster, fatal, grave, overriding, prime, paramount* and *essential* lose their force if used too often. Reserve them for strong occasions, and then let them stand on their own legs, without adjectival or adverbial support. Otherwise you may find yourself writing like this extract from a ministerial speech:

> Although it is overriding obviously that the prime responsibility of the ballistic missile early warning system must remain paramount at all times . . .

It would be a fairly safe bet that *respective* (or *respectively*) is used unnecessarily or wrongly in legal and official writings more often than any other word in the language. It has one simple straightforward use, and that is to link up subjects and objects where more than one is used with a single verb. Thus, if we say 'Men and women wear trousers and skirts' you are left in doubt which wears which—which indeed is no more than the truth nowadays. But if we add the word *respectively* we allot the trousers to the men and the skirts to the women. It can also be used harmlessly in a distributive sense, as in the sentence 'Local Authorities should survey the needs of their respective areas'. But it contributes nothing to the sense; there is no risk of Local Authorities thinking that they are being told to survey one another's areas.

* see p. 113

Anyway it is neater to write 'Each Local Authority should survey the needs of its area'. *Respective* and *respectively* are used wrongly or unnecessarily far more often than they are used rightly, and it is better to leave them alone. You can nearly always get on without them. Even in the above example you can say 'Men wear trousers and women skirts', which has the advantage of being crisper and therefore better English. One of the many traps set by this capricious word is that of trying to make it distribute two things among three, which leaves the reader guessing. If one says 'Men and women wear trousers and knickers and skirts respectively', the question arises 'Who has the knickers?'

Here is an example, taken from a departmental circular, of the magnetism of this word:

> Owing to the special difficulty of an apportionment of expenditure between (1) dinners and (2) other meals and refreshments respectively . . .

Having taken elaborate care so to arrange the sentence as to make *respectively* unnecessary, the writer found the lure of it irresistible after all.

Definite and *definitely* must be a good second to *respective* and *respectively* in any competition for the lead in adjectives and adverbs used unnecessarily. It can hardly be supposed that the adverb in the injunction—'Local Authorities should be definitely discouraged from committing themselves'—would make any difference to the official who has to carry it out; the distinction between discouraging a Local Authority definitely and merely discouraging it is too fine for most of us. Other examples are:

> This is definitely harmful to the workers' health.
> The recent action of the committee is approving the definite appointment of four home visitors.
> This has caused two definite spring breakages to loaded vehicles.

It is wise to be sparing of *very*. If it is used too freely it ceases to have any meaning; it must be used with discrimination to be effective. An academic authority, commenting on the standard of writing among university candidates, wrote:

> . . . it is very evident from much of the current work being produced that standards have undoubtedly slipped.

This, we must assume, was dictated by someone too busy to revise it by striking out *very*, *being produced* and *undoubtedly*.

Other adverbs of intensification, like *necessarily* and *inevitably*, are also apt to do more harm than good unless you want to lay stress on the element of necessity or inevitability. An automatic *inevitably*, contributing nothing to the sense, is common:

> The Committees will inevitably have a part to play in the development of the service.
> The ultimate power of control which flows inevitably from the agency relationship.

And there can never be any excuse for *must inevitably* or *must necessarily*. The adverbs throw an unwarrantable aspersion on *must's* ability to do its job.

Other intrusive words are *incidentally*, *specific* and *particular*. In conversation, *incidentally* (like *actually* and *definitely*) is often a noise without meaning; in writing it is an apology for irrelevance, sometimes expedient but often unnecessary or even ambiguous:

> The Concert will include horn concertos by Haydn and Mozart, both incidentally written to order.

Incidentally to the announcer's announcement or to the composer's career?

Particular intrudes (though perhaps more in a certain type of oratory than in writing) as an unnecessary reinforcement of a demonstrative pronoun:

> No arrangements have yet been made regarding moneys due to this particular country.
> We would point out that availabilities of this particular material are extremely limited.
> On the same day on which you advised the Custodian of the existence of this particular debt . . .

Verbosity in prepositions

In all utility writing today, official and commercial, the simple prepositions we have in such abundance tend to be forgotten and replaced by groups of words more imposing perhaps, but often less precise. Here are some compound prepositions, with some suggested simpler equivalents:

> as a consequence of (because of)
> by means of (by, with, using)
> by virtue of (by, under)
> for the purpose of (to)
> for the reason that (because)
> in accordance with (by, under)
> in addition to (besides)
> inasmuch as (since)
> in association with (with)
> in case of (if)
> in excess of (more than, over)
> in favour of (for)
> in order to (to)
> in the absence of (without)
> in the course of (during)
> in the event of (if)
> in the nature of (like)
> in the neighbourhood of (about)
> in the vicinity of (near)
> in view of (because of)
> on the grounds of (because of)
> on the part of (by, among)
> prior to (before)
> subsequent to (after)
> with a view to (to)
> with the exception of (except)

It is easy to paraphrase the above groups in the interest of conciseness; but those in the following list may have no obvious paraphrase:

> as regards
> as to
> in connection with
> in regard to
> in relation to
> in respect of
> in terms of
> in the case of

in the context of
on the basis of
with respect to
relative to
with reference to
with regard to

These are useful in their proper places, but they are generally made to serve merely as clumsy devices to save a writer the labour of selecting the right preposition. In the collection that follows the right preposition is added in brackets:

A firm timetable *in relation to* the works to be undertaken should be drawn up (for).

It has been necessary to cause many dwellings to be disinfested of vermin, particularly *in respect of* the common bed-bug (of).

The Authority are fully conscious of their responsibilities *in regard to* the preservation of amenities (for).

It will be necessary to decide the priority which should be given to nursery provision *in relation to* other forms of education provision (over).

The rates vary *in relation to* the age of the child (with).

The Concorde is not needed *in the context of* the ordinary man's holiday-making (for).

We must be realistic *in terms of* recruitment possibilities in determining the overall manpower figure for the civil service (about). (But see also p. 257 for *realistic* and pp. 250–1 for *overall*).

Denuclearisation *in respect of* war-like purposes (of?).

This may impose severe restrictions *as to* Britain's food imports from the old Commonwealth (on).

The extra expenditure made little difference *in terms of* the extra employment created (to).

There may be difficulties *with regard to* the provision of suitable staff (in).

Similar considerations apply *with regard to* application for a certificate (to).

The best possible estimate will be made at the conference *as to* the total number of houses which can be completed in each district during the year (of).

The Lord Chancellor should give a clear indication *as to* his intentions (of).

Sometimes more drastic treatment is needed than the substitution of a single preposition:

A series of changes in the structure of inclusive tour control prices, which have already borne fruit *in terms of* increased traffic (have already produced more traffic).

As to deserves special mention because it leads writers astray in other ways besides making them forget the right preposition. It may tempt them into a more elaborate circumlocution:

The operation is a severe one as to the after-effects. (The after-effects of the operation are severe.)

It is no concern of the Ministry as to the source of the information. (The source of the information is no concern of the Ministry.)

As to also has a way of intruding itself where it is not wanted, especially before such words as *whether, who, what, how*. All the following examples are better without *as to*:

Doubt has been expressed as to whether these rewards are sufficient.

I have just received an enquiry as to whether you have applied for a supplement to your pension.

I am to ask for some explanation as to why so small a sum was realised on sale.

The Company must decide as to what would be a suitable remuneration.

As to serves a useful purpose at the beginning of a sentence by way of introducing a fresh subject:

As to your liability for previous years, I will go into this and write further to you.

Verbosity in adverbial and other phrases

Certain words beget verbosity. Among them are the following.

Case and *instance*. The sins of *case* are well known; it has been said that there is perhaps no single word so freely resorted to as a trouble-saver and consequently responsible for so much flabby writing.

Here are some examples to show how what might be a simple and straightforward statement becomes enmeshed in the coils of phrases formed with *case*:

The cost of maintenance of the building would be higher than was the case with a building of traditional construction. (The building would be more expensive to maintain than a building of traditional construction.)

That country is not now so short of sterling as was formerly the case. (. . . as it used to be.)

Since the officiating president in the case of each major institute takes up his office on widely differing dates. (Since the officiating presidents of the major institutes take up office on widely differing dates.)

The National Coal Board is an unwieldy organisation, in many cases quite out of touch with the coalfields. (Often)

This trick use of *case* is even worse when the reader might be misled, if only momentarily, into thinking that a material case was meant:

Cases have thus arisen in which goods have been exported without the knowledge of this Commission.

Water for domestic use is carried by hand in many cases from road standpipes.

There are, of course, many legitimate uses of the word, and writers should not be frightened away from it altogether. There are, for instance (to borrow from Fowler):

A case of measles.
You have no case.
In case of need, or fire, or other emergency.
A case of burglary or other crime.
A law case of any sort.
Circumstances alter cases.

But do not say 'That is not the case' when you mean 'That is not so', or 'It is not the case that I wrote that letter', when you mean 'It is not true that I wrote that letter', or merely 'I did not write that letter'.

Instance beguiles writers in the same way as *case* into roundabout ways of saying simple things:

In the majority of instances the houses are three-bedroom. (Most of the houses are three-bedroom.)

Most of the factories are modern, but in a few instances the plant is obsolete. (In a few of them)

In the first instance can generally be replaced by *first*, and *in this instance* by *here*, and *in some instances* by *sometimes*.

Another such word is *concerned* in the phrase *as* (or *so*) *far as . . . is concerned*. It is perhaps putting the case too high to say that this phrase could always be replaced by a single preposition. We do not think that the phrase can be dispensed with by those who wish to emphasise that they have blinkers on, and are concerned only with one aspect of a question. 'So far as I am concerned, you may go home' implies that someone else has a say too. Or again:

> So far as the provisions of the Act are concerned, the sum so released may
> . . . be utilised to reimburse you for expenses . . .

There is no other equally convenient way of making clear that the writer is removing only the impediment created by the Act and is not concerned with any other impediment there may be. (But this does not excuse him for writing *utilised* instead of *used*, see p. 266)

Possibly, though less certainly, this sentence might claim the same indulgence:

> The effect of the suggested system, so far as the pharmaceutical industry is concerned, would be to ensure rewards for research and development work until the new preparations were absorbed into the BP.

It might be argued that we should not get quite the same meaning from 'on the pharmaceutical industry'; this destroys the suggestion that there may be other effects, but the writer is not dealing with them.

But these are exceptions. There is no doubt that the phrase is generally a symptom of muddled thinking:

> Some were opposed to hanging as a means of execution where women were concerned (. . . as a means of executing women.)
> The administration of the improvement grant scheme as far as works to privately owned dwellings are concerned. (The administration of improvement grants to private dwellings.)
> Wood pulp manufacture on a commercial scale is a very recent development so far as time is concerned. (Omit the last six words.)
> The punishments at their disposal may not be of very serious effect so far as the persons punished are concerned. (. . . on the persons punished.)
> That is a matter which should be borne in mind because it does rule out a certain amount of consideration so far as the future is concerned.

We cannot translate this with any confidence. Perhaps it means 'That is a matter which should be borne in mind because it circumscribes our recommendations for the future'.

The fact that is an expression sometimes necessary and proper, but sometimes a clumsy way of saying what might be said more simply; when it is preceded by *in view of* or *because of* or *notwithstanding* or *owing to* or *in spite of* it may be merely an intricate way of saying *because* or *although*.

Owing to the fact that the exchange is working to full capacity. (Because the exchange . . .)

The delay in replying has been due to the fact that it was hoped to arrange for a representative to call upon you. (I delayed replying because I hoped to arrange for a representative to call on you.)

So too *until such time as* is usually merely a verbose way of saying *until*. It may be useful to convey a suggestion that the event contemplated is improbable or remote or has no direct connection with what is to last until it occurs. But it cannot do so in

You will be able to enjoy these facilities until such time that he terminates his agreement.

If the phrase is used, it should be *such time as*, not, as here, *such time that*.

There can surely be no justification for preferring the similar phrase *during such time as* to *while* or *so long as*.

As has other sins of superfluity imputed to it, besides the help it gives in building up verbose prepositions and conjunctions. (See pp. 55–7, 100–1.)

There is reason in saying, of a past date, 'these allowances will be payable as from the 1st January last', but there is none in saying, of a future date, 'these allowances will cease to be payable as from the 1st July next'. 'On the 1st July' is all that is needed. The phrase 'as and from', not unknown, is gibberish.

As such is sometimes used in a way that seems to have no meaning:

The statistics, as such, add little to our information.

If they do not do so as statistics, in what capacity do they? The writer probably meant 'by themselves'.

There is no objection to the sale of houses as such.

Here the context shows the writer to have meant that there was no objection of principle to the sale of houses.

In, like *as*, gives rise to verbosity. Such combinations as *few in number, large in size, pink in colour* and *square in shape* are better reduced to *few, large, pink* and *square*.

Certain pairs of words have a way of keeping company without being able to do any more together than either could have done separately. *Save and except* seems to have had its day, but we still have with us *as and when, if and when* and *unless and until*. *As and when* can perhaps be defended when used of something that will happen piecemeal ('Interim reports will be published as and when they are received'). Nothing can be said for the use of the pair in such a sentence as:

As and when the Bill becomes an Act, guidance will be given on the financial provisions of it as they affect hospital maintenance.

Bills cannot become Acts piecemeal.

If and when might plead that both are needed in such a sentence as 'Further cases will be studied if and when the material is available', arguing that *if* alone will not do because the writer wants to emphasise that material becoming available will be studied immediately, and *when* alone will not do because it is uncertain whether the material ever will be available. But this is all rather subtle, and the wise course will almost always be to decide which conjunction suits you better, and to use it alone. We have not been able to find (or to imagine) the use of *unless and until* in any context in which one of the two would not have sufficed alone. The same is true of those combinations such as *good and sufficient, full and complete, perform and discharge, undertake and agree*, to which lawyers are particularly addicted.

Point of view, viewpoint, standpoint and *angle*, useful and legitimate in their proper places, are sometimes no more than a refuge from the trouble of precise thought, and provide clumsy ways of saying something that could be said more simply and effectively. They are used, for instance, as a circumlocution for a simple adverb, such as 'from a temporary point of view' for 'temporarily'. Here are a few examples:

He may lack the most essential qualities from the viewpoint of the Teaching Hospitals. (He may lack the most essential qualities for work in a Teaching Hospital.)

I can therefore see no reason why we need to see these applications, apart from an information point of view (. . . except for information.)

This may be a source of embarrassment to the Regional Board from the viewpoint of overall planning and administration. (This is a particularly bad one. The plain way of putting it is: 'This may embarrass the Regional Board in planning and administration'.)

Bare boards are unsatisfactory from every angle. (. . . in every respect.)

From a cleaning point of view there are advantages in tables being of a uniform height. (For cleaning . . .)

Each of these issues is examined from the standpoint of its background. (Perhaps this means 'with its history in mind': or perhaps not.)

This development is attractive from the point of view of the public convenience. (This, I am told, provoked a marginal comment: 'What is it like looking in the opposite direction?')

Aspect is the complement of *point of view*. As one changes one's point of view one sees a different aspect of what one is looking at. It is therefore natural that *aspect* should lead writers into the same traps as do *point of view*, *viewpoint* and *standpoint*. It induces writers, through its vagueness, to prefer it to more precise words, and it lends itself to woolly circumlocution. It is hard to believe that there was any clear conception in the head of the official who wrote 'They must accept responsibility for the more fundamental aspects of the case'. *Aspect* is one of the words that should not be used without deliberation, and it should be rejected if its only function is to make a clumsy paraphrase of an adverb.

Verbosity in auxiliary verbs

Various methods are in vogue for softening the curtness of *will not* or *cannot*. The commonest are *is not prepared to*, *is not in a position to*, *does not see his way to* and *cannot consider*. Such phrases as these are no doubt dictated by politeness, and therefore deserve respect. But they must be used with discretion. The recipient of a letter may feel better—though it seems unlikely—if you say that the Minister 'is not prepared to approve' than he or she would have done if the letter had said 'the Minister does not approve'. But there is not even this slender justification for the phrase if what you say is that the Minister *is* prepared to approve.

In view of this further information the Board are prepared to admit your claim in respect of. . . . A payable order for £535 is enclosed accordingly.

Are prepared to admit should be *have admitted*. Since the money is enclosed the preparatory stage is clearly over.

But there is a legitimate use of *prepared to*, as in the following:

In order to meet the present need, the Secretary of State is prepared to approve the temporary appointment of persons without formal qualifications.

Here the Secretary of State is awaiting candidates, prepared to approve them if they turn out all right. But the phrase should never be used in actually giving approval; it is silly, and if the habit takes hold it will lead to such absurdities as:

I have to acknowledge your letter of the 16th June and in reply I am prepared to inform you that I am in communication with the solicitors concerned in this matter.

There are other dangers in these phrases. They may breed by analogy verbiage that is mere verbiage and cannot call on politeness to justify its existence. You may find yourself writing that the Minister *will take steps to* when all you mean is he *will*, or that he will *cause investigation to be made with a view to ascertaining*, when what you mean is that he will *find out*. *Take steps to* is not always to be condemned. It is a reasonable way of expressing the beginning of a gradual process, as in:

Steps are now being taken to acquire this land.

But it is inapposite, because of its literal incongruity, in such a sentence as:

All necessary steps should be taken to maintain the present position.

Similarly, there can seldom be any justification for writing *I am of the opinion that* rather than *I think*, or *we have no option but to* for *we must*.

There is a danger that some of these phrases may suggest undesirable ideas to the flippant. To be told that the Minister is 'not in a position to approve' may excite a desire to retort that he might try putting his feet on the mantelpiece and see if that does any good. The retort will not, of course, be made, but you should not put ideas of that sort about your Minister into people's heads. Pompous old phrases must be allowed to die if they collapse under the prick of ridicule. Traditional expressions such as 'I am to request you to move your Minister to do so-and-so' and 'The Minister cannot conceal from himself' owed their death partly to the risible pictures they conjured up—the one of physical pressure applied to a bulky and inert object and the other of an honest man's prolonged and painful struggle in unsuccessful self-deception.

Verbosity in phrasal verbs

The English language likes to tack an adverbial particle to a simple verb and so to create a verb with a different meaning. Verbs thus formed are called 'phrasal verbs'. This habit of inventing phrasal verbs has been the source of great enrichment of the language. Logan Pearsall Smith said:

> From them we derive thousands of vivid colloquialisms and idiomatic phrases by means of which we describe the greatest variety of human actions and relations. We can take *to* people, take them *up*, take them *down*, take them *off* or take them *in*; keep *in* with them, keep them *down* or *off* or *on* or *under*; get *at* them or *round* them or *on with* them; do *for* them, do *with* them or *without* them, and do them *in*, make *up to* them; set them *up* or *down* or hit them *off*—indeed there is hardly any action or attitude of one human being to another which cannot be expressed by means of these phrasal verbs.

But there is today a tendency to form phrasal verbs to express a meaning no different from that of the verb without the particle. To do this is to debase the language, not to enrich it. *Drown out, sound out, lose out, rest up, miss out on*, are examples of phrasal verbs used, under American influence, in senses no different from that of the unadorned verb. We rightly welcomed the newcomer *measure up to* in the sense of to be adequate to an occasion: it conforms to the usual practice of adding particles to give a verb a different meaning. But *pay off, try out* and *start up* are often used in contexts where the particles do not seem to contribute anything to the sense. See also pp. 106, 184.

Pompo-verbosity

A very common cause of verbosity is the desire to be grand. The dividing line between dignity and pomposity is not always well marked. Something depends on the subject-matter, for language that is aptly used to describe affairs of grave national concern will be merely pompous if applied to the trivial or the humdrum. But there is no doubt that pompo-verbosity is a persistent and insidious danger, both to official writers and to others. We have already (p. 46) quoted the phrase *making precipitate judgments on the basis of temporary reactions*, which is pompo-verbosity for *jumping to conclusions*. Here are a few more examples:

They will have to work with unusually distant time-horizons. (They will have to look unusually far ahead.)

This would make a major contribution to increased efficiency in its own right. (This would in itself do much to increase efficiency.)

The decorating as well as the making processes [in the pottery industry] have been subjected to intensive simplification. (Have been greatly simplified.)

To the extent that [this] is held not to be practicable an obstacle is of course created in the path of successful completion of [the] scheme. (If this is not practicable it will be difficult to complete the scheme.)

The existing Immigration Regulations occasionally—only a very limited number of cases have come to my attention—produce undue hardship as a result of the very strict interpretation. (The strict interpretation of the existing Immigration Regulations occasionally causes hardship, though I know of only very few cases.)

Long passages have visual unattractiveness. (Long passages look ugly *or* are not beautiful.)

The Council has decided to inform your Department that no adverse observations are offered on planning grounds to the proposed redevelopment. (The Council sees no objection on planning grounds to the proposed redevelopment.)

Padding

All forms of verbosity might be described as padding, and the topic overlaps others we shall come to in the chapters on choosing the familiar word and choosing the precise word. We use *padding* here as a label for the type of verbosity Churchill referred to in a memorandum entitled 'Brevity' that he issued as Prime Minister on the 9th August 1940. He wrote:

> Let us have an end of such phrases as these:
> 'It is also of importance to bear in mind the following considerations . . .' or 'consideration should be given to the possibility of carrying into effect . . .'. Most of these woolly phrases are mere padding, which can be left out altogether, or replaced by a single word. Let us not shrink from using the short expressive phrase even if it is conversational.

'Padding' then in the sense in which Churchill used the word consists of clumsy and obtrusive stitches on what ought to be a smooth fabric of consecutive thought. No doubt it comes partly from a feeling that wordiness is an ingredient of politeness, and blunt statement is crude, if not rude. There is an element of truth in this: an over-staccato style is as irritating as an over-sostenuto one. But it is a matter of degree; and official prose is of the sort that calls for plainness rather than elegance. Moreover the habit of 'padding' springs partly from less meritorious notions—that the dignity of an official's calling demands a certain verbosity, and that naked truth is indecent and should be clothed in wrappings of woolly words.

Padding can easily creep into official letters if each paragraph is thought to need introductory words—'I am to add'; 'I am further to observe'; 'I am moreover to remark'; 'Finally I am to point out'; and so forth. This form of padding is not as prevalent in official letters as it used to be, but it is quite common elsewhere.

In addition it is perhaps relevant to mention that . . .

is not, as you might think, from a civil servant's letter in the 1940s. It comes from a formal memorandum submitted by a local authority to a House of Commons Select Committee in 1970.

Here is the same phenomenon in a circular sending a form for a statistical return:

(i) *It should be noted that* the particulars of expenditure . . . relate to gross costs.
(ii) *It is appreciated that* owing to staffing difficulties Local Authorities may not find it possible on this occasion to complete Tables . . .
(iii) *It will be noted that* in Tables . . . the only overhead expenditure . . . which the Authorities are asked to isolate is . . .
(iv) Table 4 . . . is intended to provide a broad picture.

The words italicised in the first three paragraphs are padding. They are no more needed there than in paragraph (iv), where the writer has wisely done without them, perhaps feeling that he or she had run out of stock.

Other examples:

I am prepared to accept the discharge of this account by payment in instalments, but *it should be pointed out that* no further service can be allowed until the account is again in credit.

The opportunity is taken to mention that it is understood . . .

I regret that the wrong form was forwarded. *In the circumstances* I am forwarding a superseding one.

It should be noted that there is a possibility of a further sale.
It is important to add that neither transaction has yet been completed.
It is of significance that several participants failed to complete the course.
It may be recalled that a previous application was rejected in 1982.
It is interesting that no solution has yet been found.

This form of padding deserves special mention both because the temptation affects officials more than most people and because it is comparatively easy to resist. It shows itself more plainly than other more subtle temptations to pad. For the rest, padding can be defined as the use of words, phrases and even sentences that contribute nothing to the reader's perception of the writer's meaning. Among those that seem to be specially tempting are *in this connection* and *for your information*. These have their proper uses, but are more often found as padding clichés. In none of the following examples do they serve any other purpose.

I am directed to refer to the travelling and subsistence allowances applicable to your Department, and in this connection I am to say . . .

Mr X is an applicant for appointment as a clerk in this Department and in this connection I shall be glad if you will complete the attached form.

The Minister's views in general in this connection and the nature and scope of the information which he felt would assist him in this connection was indicated at a meeting . . .

For your information is appropriately used to provide necessary background, or to reassure your reader that no action is necessary:

For your information, I have already notified the Department.

It can add nothing to an instruction to act:

For your information I would inform you that it will be necessary for you to approach the local Agricultural Executive Committee.

Of course is another adverbial phrase that needs watching lest it should creep in as padding. In journalism, especially of the gossip kind, *of course* is used to impress readers by showing the writer's familiarity with an out-of-the-way piece of information or with the families of great personages. Officials who overwork the phrase are more likely to do so from genuine humility. They put it in so as not to seem didactic: 'Don't think that I suppose you to be so stupid that you don't already know or infer what I am telling you, but I think I ought to mention it'. Sometimes *of course* is wisely used for this purpose—if, for instance, the writer has good reason to say something so obvious as to make a touchy reader feel insulted. It is better in such circumstances to say 'of course' than its pompous variant 'as you are doubtless aware'. *Of course* can mean 'It must be reluctantly admitted that'. It might with advantage have been used here:

It may be stated with some confidence that though it is possible for an infected animal to escape the quarantine regulations, the probability of such an occurrence is small.

In this example *It may be stated with some confidence that* is not only padding but also an absurdity. One might say with some confidence that this will not happen, or with complete confidence that it is improbable. But to feel only some confidence about its improbability is carrying intellectual timidity almost to imbecility.

The following introductory sentence to a circular seems to be wholly padding, but we cannot be sure, for we can find no meaning in it.

The proposals made in response to this request show differences of approach to the problem which relate to the differing recommendations of the Committee's Report, and include some modifications of those recommendations.

There are many types of padding other than the one we have been dealing with, and many padders other than Governmental Departments. Consider for instance these three passages:

The completed Research Report *now being prepared and* covering three years of intensive activity over the greater part of Scotland *with its factual matter, conclusions and recommendations* will be *an* invaluable *document* to the new statutory Tourist Board in planning *the provision of future* tourist facilities.

The Commission has been encouraged to look forward *in the future* to *a two-way process of* consultation with the Government before major policy decisions affecting its work are taken.

It is in any case important that senior management should at least involve itself in ensuring the existence of satisfactory policies and procedures for dealing with recruitment, induction, training and industrial relations.

In the first, all the italicised words are unnecessary, and we get quite a good sentence without them. In the second, we can start by omitting the italicised words, but more pruning is still needed. We shall probably finish with something like:

The Government have promised to consult the Commission before taking any important decisions affecting its work.

The third also carries a lot of surplus weight. The first 19 words are obviously heavily padded and should be replaced by something like *Senior management should insist on*. But the phrase *satisfactory policies and procedures for dealing with* also lacks litheness. We might try:

Senior management should always satisfy itself that the staff are being properly recruited and trained and industrial relations well handled.

But padding is too multifarious for analysis. It can only be illustrated, and the only rule for avoiding it is to be self-critical.

7

The choice of words: choosing the familiar word

Literary men, and the young still more than the old of this class, have commonly a good deal to rescind in their style in order to adapt it to business. But the young, if they be men of sound abilities, will soon learn what is not apt and discard it; which the old will not. The leading rule is to be content to be commonplace—a rule which might be observed with advantage in other writings, but is distinctively applicable to these.

Henry Taylor, *The Statesman*, 1836

Boswell tells of Johnson: 'He seemed to take pleasure in speaking in his own style; for when he had carelessly missed it, he would repeat the thought translated into it. Talking of the comedy of "The Rehearsal", he said, "It has not wit enough to keep it sweet". This was easy—he therefore caught himself and pronounced a more round sentence; "It has not vitality enough to preserve it from putrefaction".' The mind of another famous lover of the rotund phrase worked the opposite way. '"Under the impression", said Mr Micawber, "that your peregrinations in this metropolis have not as yet been extensive, and that you might have some difficulty in penetrating the arcana of the Modern Babylon . . . in short", said Mr Micawber in a burst of confidence, "that you might lose your way . . .".' We should not hesitate which of these remarkable men to take as our model. We should cultivate Mr Micawber's praiseworthy habit of instinctively translating the out-of-the-way into the everyday.

Too many writers, official and other, incline rather towards the Johnsonian habit (which might be described as 'verbo-pomposity', a close relation to the 'pompo-verbosity' mentioned in the last chapter). They thus handicap themselves in achieving what we have seen must be their primary object, to influence the reader precisely in the way they intend. The simple reader is puzzled; the sophisticated one is annoyed.

The precept to choose the familiar word (which is also probably the short word) must of course be followed with discretion. Many wise men throughout the centuries, from Aristotle to Churchill, have emphasised the importance of using short and simple words. But no one knew better than these two authorities that sacrifice either of precision or of dignity is too high a price to pay for the familiar word. If the choice is between two words that convey a writer's meaning equally well, one short and familiar and the other long and unusual, of course the short and familiar should be preferred. But one that is long and unusual should not be rejected merely on that account if it is more apt in meaning. Churchill did not hesitate to prefer the uncommon word if there was something to be gained by it. If we were asked whether there was any difference in meaning between *woolly* and *flocculent* we should probably say no; one was commonplace and the other unusual, and that was all there was to it. But Churchill in the first volume of his *Second World War*, uses *flocculent* instead of *woolly* to describe the mental processes of certain people, and so conveys to his readers just that extra ounce of contempt that we feel *flocculent* to contain, perhaps because the combination of *f* and *l* so often expresses an invertebrate state, as in *flop*, *flap*, *flaccid*, *flimsy*, *flabby* and *filleted*. Moreover there is an ugliness of shortness as well as an ugliness of length, and an ostentatious avoidance of long words can be just as irritating to the reader as an ostentatious resort to them. A literary artist like Ernest Hemingway can achieve wonderful force and poignancy by limiting himself almost entirely to words of one or two syllables, but if the rest of us try to write like that we give the impression of grunting.

But there are no great signs at present of any urgent need of a warning not to overdo the use of simple diction. The commonest ways in which failure to choose the simple word can offend the ordinary reader are the use of jargon and legal language and an addiction to showy words, including foreign words and phrases.

Jargon and legal language

When officials are accused of writing jargon, what is generally meant is that they affect a pompous and flabby verbosity. That is not what we mean. We use *jargon* here for technical terms—especially conventional phrases invented by a Government Department—which are understood inside the Department but are unintelligible to outsiders. 'Departmental shorthand' (see Chapter 2) has escaped from its compound. A circular from the headquarters of a Department to its regional officers begins:

> The physical progressing of building cases should be confined to . . .

Nobody but another official could say what meaning this was intended to convey. It is not English, except in the sense that the words are English words. They are a group of symbols used in conventional senses known only to the parties to the convention. It may be said that no harm is done, because the instruction is not meant to be read by anyone unfamiliar with the departmental jargon. But using jargon is a dangerous habit; it is easy to forget that the public do not understand it, and to slip into the use of it in explaining things to them. If that is done, those seeking enlightenment will find themselves plunged in even deeper obscurity. A member of the Department has kindly provided this interpretation of the words quoted above, qualified by the words 'as far as I can discover':

'The physical progressing of building cases' means going at intervals to the sites of factories, etc. whose building is sponsored by the Department and otherwise approved to see how many bricks have been laid since the last visit. 'Physical' apparently here refers both to the flesh-and-blood presence of the inspector and to the material development of the edifice, neither of which is, however, mentioned. 'Progressing', it seems, should have the accent on the first syllable and should be distinguished from pro*gress*ing. It means recording or helping forward the progress rather than going forward. 'Cases' is the common term for units of work which consist of applying a given set of rules to a number of individual problems; 'should be confined to' means that only in the types of cases specified may an officer leave his or her desk to visit the site.

Legal diction, as we have seen, is almost necessarily obscure. As Lord Denning said when presenting the 1982 Plain English awards, 'Lawyers try to cover every contingency, but in so doing they get lost in obscurity.' Explanations of the provisions of legal documents must be translated into familiar words simply arranged.

> With reference to your letter of the 12th August, I have to state in answer to question 1 thereof that where particulars of a partnership are disclosed to the Executive Council the remuneration of the individual partner for superannuation purposes will be deemed to be such proportion of the total remuneration

of such practitioners as the proportion of his share in the partnership profits bears to the total proportion of the shares of such practitioner in those profits.

This is a good example of how not to explain. It seems to mean merely 'Your income will be taken to be the same proportion of the firm's remuneration as you used to get of its profits'. Even if that is an oversimplification, it is hard to believe that language is unequal to any clearer explanation than the unfortunate correspondent received. Liberal punctuation would help.

Here is another example of failure to shake off the shackles of legal language:

Separate departments in the same premises are treated as separate premises for this purpose where separate branches of work which are commonly carried on as separate businesses in separate premises are carried on in separate departments in the same premises.

This sentence is constructed with that mathematical arrangement of words which lawyers adopt to make their meaning unambiguous. Worked out as one would work out an equation, the sentence serves its purpose; as literature, it is balderdash. The explanation could easily have been given in some such way as this:

If branches of work commonly carried on as separate businesses are carried on in separate departments of the same premises, those departments will be treated as separate premises.

This shows how easily an unruly sentence like this can be reduced to order by turning part of it into an 'if' clause.

Even those who write about the proper use of English sometimes fail to practise what they preach. The Report of a Committee on People and Planning (1969) used these brave words:

Whatever medium is used for the communication of ideas it is essential that the language or representation used should be readily understood. . . . The use of jargon between experts is understandable; between experts and the public it is unforgivable. The recipient of the message must be able to understand it. Whatever is said must be said simply and clearly.

But elsewhere in the same report we find:

The continuity of debate which is implicit in the participation process can itself be educative for both planner and public.

The community forum can be the spring-board for involvement of the non-participators.

The measure of the community development officer's success would largely be the extent to which he identifies and activates these points of contact.

What right, we may well ask, has this committee to lecture us about saying things 'simply and clearly'?

An academic writer starts an article about techniques of communication like this:

The efflorescence of a host of specialists in commerce and industry and the ever widening inroad that the Government is forging into our business lives are carcinogens of effective communication; for the jargon of, on the one hand, such people as computer programmers, systems analysts, cyberneticians, psychologists and, on the other hand, the complex prose of Whitehall constitute an invidious growth which is challenging our ability to express ourselves in clear simple terms.

How does one forge an inroad? How can an efflorescence of specialists and a forged inroad be carcinogens? The mixture of metaphors, and the muddled and illogical construction of the sentence after the semicolon, are so blatant that one begins to wonder whether the writer is doing it on purpose, with facetious intent. But the rest of the article expunges this charitable thought.

Foreign words and phrases

The safest rule about foreign words and phrases, and about legal tags or legal technical terms (whether in foreign or English words), is to avoid them if you can. This is partly because you may easily use them wrongly (Chapter 17 mentions the frequent misuse of the Latin phrase *a priori* and of the legal term *leading question*), and partly because even if your understanding and use of them are faultless your reader may be less learned than you and must not be made to feel inferior. Constant use even of familiar foreign expressions like *inter alia* gives the impression that the writer is trying to show off—which indeed is often just what he or she is doing.

We say 'if you can'; and you can very often. You can usually avoid *inter alia*, *per annum*, *prima facie*, *ad hoc*, *pro rata*, *ceteris paribus*, *mutatis mutandis*, *con amore* and *carte blanche* by writing *among others, a year, at first sight, for the purpose, in proportion, other things being equal, with the necessary changes, enthusiastically* and *blank cheque* (or *free hand*). But it would be pedantic to insist on a complete prohibition. Sometimes the foreigner, though still felt as foreign and still often printed in italics, is well on the way to naturalisation and is already accepted and understood by nearly everyone. Perhaps *sub judice, recherché, fait accompli* and *ad infinitum* are now at the stage that *et cetera, agenda, garage* and *hotel* passed some time ago. Some foreigners have no wholly satisfactory English equivalents, and the near-equivalents, though good enough for many purposes, lack a nuance or a precision which can be conveyed only by the foreign word and may be important to the context. The foreign word, in short, may be the *mot juste*. Thus, there are near-equivalents to *dénouement, blasé, imbroglio, frisson, dolce vita* and *détente*, but sometimes none of them will quite do. If you are really certain that you need a particular foreign word to convey your meaning, and that your readers will take the meaning that you intend, you need not be frightened of that word. The important thing, particularly in official writing, is to put the reader's convenience before the writer's self-gratification.

When all this has been said (and there is much more that could be) the basic rule 'avoid them if you can' remains the safest guide.

Overworked metaphors

Those who like showy words are given to overworking metaphors. There is no doubt about the usefulness and attractiveness of metaphors. They enable a writer to convey briefly and vividly ideas that might otherwise need tedious exposition. What should we do, in our economic difficulties, without *target, ceiling, launch* and *break-through*? But the very seductiveness of metaphors makes them dangerous, especially as we may be rather proud to have learned a new one and want to show off. Thus metaphors, especially new ones, tend to be used indiscriminately and soon get stale, but not before they have elbowed out words perhaps more commonplace but with meanings more precise. Sometimes metaphors are so absurdly overtaxed that they become a laughing-stock and die of ridicule. That has been the fate of 'exploring every avenue' and of 'leaving no stone unturned'.

Another danger in the use of metaphors is of falling into incongruity. So long at least as they are 'live'* metaphors, they must not be given a context that would be absurd if the words used metaphorically were being used literally. Nothing is easier to do; almost all writers fall occasionally into this trap. But it is worth while to take great pains to avoid doing so, because a reader who notices it will deride you. So we should not speak of increasing or waiving a ceiling, or say that it is beginning to bite. Possibilities more unpleasant than the writer can have intended are suggested by the warning to Civil Defence Workers that many persons who have experienced a nuclear explosion will have diarrhoea and vomiting and should not be allowed to swamp the medical services. The statesman who said that sections of the population were being squeezed flat by inflation was not then in his happiest vein, nor was the writer who claimed for American sociology the distinction of having always immersed itself in concrete situations, nor the enthusiastic scientist who announced the discovery of a virgin field pregnant with possibilities. The warning issued during a fuel shortage that gas rings might only be used by officers earmarked for the purpose suggests a curious method of identification, and the BBC did not choose their words felicitously when they said that every facet of Negro music would be heard that night; facets, like children, should be seen not heard.

'The sacred cows have come home to roost with a vengeance' is a stock example of the mixed metaphor. Here is a short selection of mixed or inappropriate metaphors:

This pool [i.e. of staff] can also be used as a cushion.

Flexibility is one of the corner-stones of programme budgeting.

We now have 137½ pairs of surgical boots on our hands.

Instead of supersonic aircraft standing on their own feet by charging slightly increased fares, subsonic aircraft are required to cross-subsidise . . .

The road from X to Y has not yet got off the ground.

Thanks to a windfall of heavy tankers . . .

---

* A live metaphor is one that evokes in a reader a mental picture of the imagery of its origin; a dead one does not. If we write 'the situation is in hand' and 'he has taken the bit between his teeth', we are in both going to horsemanship for our metaphor. But to most readers the first would be a dead metaphor, and the sentence would have no different impact from 'the situation is under control'; the second would be a live one, calling up, however faintly and momentarily, the picture of a runaway horse.

The recovery of the house-building programme will require action in a number of fields.

It has no real head of steam to which it can harness itself.

We are at the cross-roads and anyone making concrete forecasts is liable to come unstuck.

. . . a port apparatus that is cited as an example for qualified and fast turnover of ships.

Men and women want to know the future shape of their environment and expect candid guidelines to help them mould it.

No suitable framework for career streams was thrown up by the survey.

Architects have to undertake drastic cheeseparing to bring a project within sight of the yardstick.

8

The choice of words: choosing the precise word

The search for the *mot juste* is not a pedantic fad but a vital necessity. Words are our precision tools. Imprecision engenders ambiguity and hours are wasted in removing verbal misunderstandings before the argument of substance can begin.

Anonymous civil servant

How popular and how influential is the practice [of personifying abstract words] may be shown by such a list of words as the following: Virtue, Liberty, Democracy, Peace, Germany, Religion, Glory—all invaluable words, indispensable even, but able to confuse the clearest issues unless controlled.

Ogden and Richards

The lure of the abstract word

The reason for preferring the concrete to the abstract is clear. Your purpose must be to make your meaning plain. Many concrete words have a penumbra of uncertainty round them, and an incomparably larger one surrounds all abstract words. If you use an abstract word when you might use a concrete one you are handicapping yourself in your task, difficult enough in any case, of making yourself understood.

Unfortunately the very vagueness of abstract words is one of the reasons for their popularity. To express one's thoughts accurately is hard work, and to be precise is sometimes dangerous. We are tempted to prefer the safer obscurity of the abstract. It is the greatest vice of present-day writing. Writers seem to find it more natural to say 'Was this the realisation of an anticipated liability?' than 'Did you expect to have to do this?'; to say 'Communities where anonymity in personal relationships prevails' than 'Communities where people do not know one another'. To resist this temptation, and to resolve to make your meaning plain to your reader even at the cost of some trouble to yourself, is more important than any other single thing if you would convert a flabby style into a crisp one. As G. M. Young said, an excessive reliance on the noun at the expense of the verb will, in the end, detach the mind of the writer from the realities of here and now, from when and how and in what mood the thing was done, and insensibly induce a habit of abstraction, generalisation and vagueness. We are to prefer, in fact, *conclude* rather than 'reach a conclusion', *investigate* rather than 'make an investigation into', *consider* rather than 'take into consideration', and *lie* rather than 'give untruthful evidence'. To what lengths the use of nouns can go may be illustrated by these three examples:

> The desirability of attaining unanimity so far as the general construction of the body is concerned is of considerable importance from the production aspect.
>
> The actualisation of the motivation of the forces must to a great extent be a matter of personal angularity.
>
> Its practicability depends essentially on there being a mutuality of capability and interest.

The first, which relates to the building of vehicles, presumably means that in order to produce the vehicles quickly it is important to agree on a standard body. The meaning of the second is past conjecture. The perpetrator of it is an economist, not an official. The third has something to do with defence and its meaning is perhaps befogged in the interests of national security (see also p. 89).

Here are some less extreme examples of the habit of using abstract words to say in a complicated way something that might be said simply and directly:

> There has been persistent instability in numbers of staff. (Staff has continually varied in numbers.)
>
> A high degree of carelessness, pre-operative and post-operative, on the part of some of the hospital staff, took place. (Some of the hospital staff were very careless both before and after the operation.)
>
> The cessation of the present restrictions cannot be made. (The present restrictions cannot be ended.)
>
> Intervention is contra-indicated. (We should not intervene.)

Sometimes abstract words are actually invented, so powerful is the lure of saying things this way.

> [We are unwilling] to tolerate any multilateralisation of the dialogue.

This way of expressing oneself seems to be tainting official speech as well as writing. 'We want you to deny indirect reception', said the goods clerk of a local railway station, telephoning about a missing case. 'What does that mean?' he was asked. 'Why,' he said, 'we want to make sure that the case has not reached you through some other station.'

Exponents of the newer sciences are fond of expressing themselves in abstractions. Perhaps this is unavoidable, but they do sometimes seem to make things unnecessarily difficult for their readers. Several examples are given elsewhere in this book (see in particular p. 181). Here is one from psychology:

Reserves that are occupied in continuous uni-directional adjustment of a disorder are no longer available for use in the ever-varying interplay of organism and environment in the spontaneity of mutual synthesis.

In official writing the words *availability*, *lack* and *dearth* contribute much to the same practice, though they do not produce the same obscurity.

We would point out that availabilities of this particular material are extremely limited. (. . . that this material is extremely scarce.)

The actual date of the completion of the purchase should coincide with the availability of the new facilities. (The purchase should not be completed until the new facilities are available.)

The lack of attraction in the three services is so deep that it has been found quite impossible to man them on a voluntary basis. (The three services are so unattractive . . .)

Lack is a useful word to denote a deficiency of something, and occasionally, though less commonly, the complete absence of something. But this word is being pressed too much into service. For instance, 'there is a complete lack of spare underground wire' is not the natural way of saying 'we have no spare underground wire' or 'There exists a considerable lack of knowledge about . . .' for 'We do not know much about . . .', or 'A dearth of information exists' for 'We have very little information'.

Here is a remarkable sentence in which *availability* is used to mean *lack*:

The availability of figures may indeed prove to be one of the obstacles in the efficiency of the whole of the proposed statistical content of the exercise.

This means 'Lack of figures may make it difficult to produce accurate statistics.' It is not unnatural that people who write *obstacles in* instead of *obstacles to* and who ask us to consider the efficiency of a content should now and again say exactly the opposite of what they mean.

The headline phrase

More serious is the harm that is being done to the language by excessive use of nouns as adjectives. In the past, the language has been greatly enriched by this free-and-easy habit. We are surrounded by innumerable examples—Customs Officer, Highway Code, Nursery School, Community Centre, Trades Union Congress and so on. But something has gone wrong recently with this useful practice; its abuse is corrupting English prose. It has become natural to say 'World population is increasing faster than world food production' instead of 'The population of the world is increasing faster than the food it produces'. 'The housing position will then be relieved' instead of 'More houses will then be available', 'The balance of payments position exceeds all expectation' instead of 'The balance of payments is more favourable than was expected.' It is old-fashioned to speak of the 'state of the world'; it must be the 'world situation'. The fact is, as Lord Dunsany once remarked, that 'too many *of*s have dropped out of the language, and the dark of the floor is littered with this useful word'. We meet daily, he adds, with things like 'England side captain selection' instead of 'Selection of captain of English eleven'; or even 'England side captain selection difficulty'. Nor would they stop nowadays at 'England side captain selection difficulty rumour'.

This sort of language is no doubt pardonable in headlines, where as many stimulating words as possible must be crowded into spaces so small that *treaties* have had to become *pacts*, *ambassadors envoys*, *investigations probes* and all forms of human enterprise *bids*. Headlines have become a language of their own, knowing no law and often quite incomprehensible until one has read the article that they profess to summarise. 'INSANITY RULES CRITIC' and 'W. H. SMITH OFFER SUCCESS' have quite different meanings from their apparent ones. Who could guess that the headline 'UNOFFICIAL STRIKES CLAIM' introduces a report of a speech by a Member of Parliament who said that there was abundant evidence that unofficial strikes were organised and inspired by Communists as part of a general plan originating from abroad? We do not see how those three words by themselves can have any meaning at all; they convey a vague suggestion of the discovery of oil or gold by someone who ought not to have been looking for it. And if the announcement BULL GRANTS INCREASE is construed grammatically, it does not seem to deserve a headline at all: one would say that that was no more than was to be expected from any conscientious bull.

But what may be pardonable in headlines will not do in the text. *Nursery School* is a legitimate use of the noun-adjective, but *nursery school provision* is not to be preferred as a proper way of saying *the provision of nursery schools. Electricity crisis restrictions* and *world supply situation* may be all right as newspaper headlines but not in English prose. For instance:

> An extra million tons of steel would buy our whole sugar import requirements (. . . all the sugar we need to import.)
> Food consumption has been dominated by the world supply situation. (People have had to eat what they could get.)
> Delays must continue to occur because of the man-power situation. (. . . because there are not enough workers.)

An exceptionally choice example is:

> The programme must be on the basis of the present head of labour ceiling allocation overall.

Here *head of labour* means *number of building operatives. Ceiling* means *maximum. Overall*, as usual, means nothing (see pp. 250–1). The whole sentence means 'The programme must be on the assumption that we get the maximum number of building operatives at present allotted to us'.

> Everything is being done to expedite plant installation within the limiting factors of steel availability and the preparation of sites.

The only thing that can be said for the writer of this is that his conscience pulled him up before the end, and he did not write 'sites preparation'. The sentence should have run 'So far as steel is available and sites can be prepared, everything is being done to expedite the installation of plant'.

The use of a noun as an adjective should be avoided where the same word is already an adjective with a different meaning. Do not, for instance, say 'material allocation' when you mean 'allocation of material', but reserve that expression against the time when you may want to make clear that the allocation you are considering is not a spiritual one. For the same reason this phrase is not felicitous:

In view of the restrictions recently imposed on our capital economic situation . . .

It is possible, of course, to go too far in condemning headline phrases. *Headline phrase* might itself be described as a headline phrase: and if so it is clearly a harmless one. But the constant use of such phrases is usually a sign either of unclear thinking or of unwillingness to say things as briskly and simply as possible. A headline phrase consisting of more than two words should be treated with suspicion, and things tend to get even more awkward if the phrase includes an adjective as well as a number of nouns; it is not always obvious on first reading which noun the adjective qualifies, and tiresome problems of hyphenation sometimes arise (see pp. 167–9). *British history teachers* may turn out to be either teachers of British history or British teachers of history. Few will think that the first sentence of this paragraph would have been better if it had read 'Excessive headline phrase condemnation is, of course, a possibility'; but few can deny that some people do write like this. Officials are by no means the only offenders. The following were produced by officials:

The formulation of personnel management information requirements.
Flexible resource allocation procedures.
The conception of a major weapon system development.
Water-cooled reactor design staff.
Unnecessary file access difficulties.

But the following were not:

The programming of transport facility development.

It seems a pity that this three-word phrase did not take the opportunity of entering the four-word class as *Transport facility development programming*. But even if it had it would have won no prizes.

A non-population oriented maternity service project

scores five, and

> Surplus Government chemical warfare vapour detection kits

wins easily with seven.

Here are some other non-official headline phrase predilection examples:

> I notice that planning permission condition trees never do get planted.

This means that when the planting of trees is a condition of the grant of planning permission they are not in the event planted. The next comes from a circular issued by a commercial firm.

> This compulsion is much regretted, but a large vehicle fleet operator restriction in mileage has now been made imperative in meeting the demand for petrol economy.

This translated into English presumably means:

> We much regret having to do this, but we have been obliged to restrict greatly the operation of our large fleet of vehicles [or to restrict the operation of our fleet of large vehicles?] to meet the demand for economy in petrol.

This is from an article by a politician:

> Avoiding technicalities . . . it might mean either mandatory (though flexible) minimum liquidity ratios, or a once-for-all sterilising of excess ban liquidity . . .

This seems impossible to translate.

Abstract adjective and adverb phrases

By this we mean using a phrase containing an abstract noun (e.g. *character, nature, basis, description, level, manner, degree*) with an adjective, where a simple adjective or adverb would do as well. This too offends against the rule that you should say what you have to say as simply and directly as possible in order that you may be readily understood.

> These claims are of a very far-reaching character. (These claims are very far-reaching.)
> A high degree of carelessness. (Great carelessness.)

New work of high priority which is of an inter-sectoral nature. (Urgent new work which is inter-sectoral. We leave to others the interpretation of *inter-sectoral*.)

In close proximity. (Near.)

In a cautious manner. (Cautiously.)

On a temporary basis. (Temporarily.)

In all probability. (Probably.)

The wages will be low owing to the unremunerative nature of the work.

The translation of the last example will present no difficulty to a student of Mr Micawber, who once said of the occupation of selling corn on commission: 'It is not an avocation of a remunerative description—in other words, it does *not* pay'. (Other examples of this type of abstract adjectival phrase will be found on p. 189.)

Proposition is another abstract word used in the same way.

Decentralisation on a regional basis is now a generally practical proposition. (. . . is now generally feasible.)

Accommodation in a separate building is not usually a practical proposition. (. . . is not usually feasible.)

The high cost of land in clearance areas makes it a completely uneconomic proposition to build cottages in those areas. (. . . makes it completely uneconomic to build cottages there.)

Proposition is becoming a blunderbuss word (see p. 17), constantly used for purposes for which *plan* or *project* would be better.

Basis is specially likely to lead writers to express themselves in roundabout ways. When you find you have written 'on a . . . basis' always examine it critically before letting it stand. You may well allow it to stand if you have written of staff paid on a weekly basis, but do not despise *by the week* or *weekly* as somewhat less pompous alternatives. The following examples would not escape so easily:

[Certain services are] cross-subsidised on a continuing basis by other more profitable services. (Permanently *or* year after year.)

Mr X's services will be available on a consulting basis. (Mr X will be available as a consultant *or* for consultation.)

The objective evidence that exists suggests that the building of large new hospitals on the basis of avoidance of duplicated facilities alone would represent suboptimisation. (. . . for the sole purpose of avoiding . . . But the sentence needs more extensive surgery than this.)

Such officer shall remain on his existing salary on a mark-time basis. (. . . shall mark time on his existing salary.)

The organisation of such services might be warranted in particular localities and on a strictly limited basis. (Scale.)

The machines would need to be available both day and night on a 24-hour basis. (. . . at any time of the day or night.)

Please state whether this is to be a permanent installation or on a temporary line basis. (. . . or a temporary line.)

A legitimate use of *basis* is:

The manufacturers are distributing their products as fairly as possible on the basis of past trading.

Clichés

In the course of this book we have called numerous expressions clichés. A cliché may be defined as a phrase whose aptness in a particular context when it was first invented has won it such popularity that it has become hackneyed, and is used without thought in contexts where it is no longer apt. Clichés are notorious enemies of the precise word. To quote from the introduction to Eric Partridge's *Dictionary of Clichés*:

They range from fly-blown phrases (explore every avenue) through sobriquets that have lost all point and freshness (the Iron Duke) to quotations that have become debased currency (cups that cheer but not inebriate), metaphors that are now pointless, and formulas that have become mere counters (far be it from me to . . .).

A cliché then is by definition a bad thing, not to be employed by self-respecting writers. Judged by this test, some expressions are unquestionably and in all circumstances clichés. This is true in particular of verbose and facetious ways of saying simple things (*conspicuous by its absence, tender mercies, grind to a halt, durance vile*) and of phrases so threadbare that they cannot escape the suspicion of being used automatically (*leave no stone unturned, acid test, psychological moment, operative word, at this point in time, when it comes to the crunch, at the end of the day, leave severely alone*). But a vast number of other expressions may or may not be clichés. It depends on whether they are used unthinkingly as reach-me-downs or deliberately chosen as the best means of saying what the writer wants to say. Eric Partridge's *Dictionary* contains some thousands of entries. But, as he says in his preface, what is a cliché is partly a matter of opinion. It is also a matter of occasion. Many of those in his dictionary may or may not be clichés; it depends on how they are used. Writers would be needlessly handicapped if they were never permitted such phrases as *swing of the pendulum*, *thin end of the wedge* and *white elephant*. These may be the fittest way of expressing a writer's meaning. If you choose one of them for that reason, you need not be afraid of being called a cliché-monger. The trouble is that writers often use a cliché because they think it fine, or because it is the first thing that comes into their heads. It is always a danger-signal when one word suggests another and Siamese twins are born—*part and parcel, intents and purposes, this day and age,* and the like. There is no good reason why *inconvenience* should always be said to be *experienced* by the person who suffers it, and *occasioned* by the person who causes it. Single words too become clichés; they are used so often that their edges are blunted while more exact words are neglected. Many of the words and phrases listed in Chapter 17 must be so classified. It is not the allure of novelty that gives them their popularity; some indeed seem to attract by their very drabness.

Vogue words

The written language is as subject to the whims of fashion as is speech or dress or art. Some words and turns of phrase become fashionable, are rapidly done to death and pass out of fashion in a few years. This is particularly true of the favourite words of politicians. It is quite possible, for instance, that *pragmatic, gritty, purposive* and *abrasive*, which led fairly quiet existences before the mid-1960s, have already had their day as vogue words and are now ready to resume their previous, less glamorous, duties. Some vogue words gain a permanent foothold and are often enrichments to the language. *Flamboyant, stalemate, analysis, dilemma*, which started as technical terms, were doubtless vogue words in their day; they have now lost their meretricious air and are doing an honest non-technical job (as, perhaps, is *meretricious*). Others linger on for many years without ever quite gaining either the respect of good writers or the guerdon of popular usage and eventually die unmourned. There is no saying how things will go. *Bottleneck* was all the rage in the 1940s; and it might well have won an honoured place, for its metaphorical use can be easily understood and is frequently apt. But it was so badly overused and mishandled when it was a new toy that few people now think it worth taking out of the cupboard. *Target, ceiling* and *blueprint*, near-contemporaries of *bottleneck* as vogue words, have also been roughly handled in the toy-room but seem to have lasted better. The use of *image*, in such a sentence as 'This will improve my image', was unknown when Gowers first wrote, but it is now so prevalent that *image* can hardly be classed any longer as a vogue word at all. *Escalate*, no younger than *image*, is not yet nearly as respectable and its ultimate fate seems at present doubtful.

So anything written about particular vogue words is likely to be soon out of date. But there are perhaps some general points which will always remain valid. First, these words are often vivid and enlightening in their proper meaning, but where they are overworked their edge gets blunted and their force broken. Thus *traumatic* is now in danger of meaning little more than *unpleasant*, *breakthrough* of meaning merely some change for the better, *population explosion* of meaning a gradual rise in population. (By extension from this use of *explosion* the word *explode* now sometimes means merely *increase*, as in a statement to the press by a bank manager that 'the amount of cash handled has exploded by more than 100 per cent in the past decade'; he should have remembered the useful word 'doubled'.) In this way the currency is debased and the language impoverished. The process may be inevitable—there is no ultimate appeal from the verdict of popular usage—but it should not be accelerated by those who care about saying what they mean. The careful writer should therefore not use vogue words, merely because they are in vogue, for purposes which blunt their proper meaning.

But it would be foolish to say that he or she should not use vogue words at all. For some of them it is difficult to see any sensible use, but for many of them—perhaps most—there is a respectable job to do. Their services should be neither refused nor solicited merely because they are in fashion. It is the misuse and the overuse of vogue words that the good writer must guard against. Some examples of misuse are given in Chapter 17. Overuse is not so easily illustrated, but it is easily recognised when seen; and unless it is being done just for fun it is a sign of a bad writer. For what makes a writer reach repeatedly for a vogue word? A desire to show off? A reluctance to think? Neither of these is conducive to good writing. It is extraordinary how often you will find vogue words accompanied in the same sentence by pretentiousness or sloppiness or other signs of sickness. No motorist is to be blamed for sounding his horn. But if he sounds it repeatedly we are not only offended by the noise; we suspect him of being a bad driver in other respects too.

The Canadian Defence Department is credited with the invention of the following 'buzz-phrase generator'.

Column 1	Column 2	Column 3
0. integrated	0. management	0. options
1. overall	1. organizational	1. flexibility
2. systematized	2. monitored	2. capability
3. parallel	3. reciprocal	3. mobility
4. functional	4. digital	4. programming
5. responsive	5. logistical	5. concept
6. optimal	6. transitional	6. time-phase
7. synchronized	7. incremental	7. projection
8. compatible	8. third-generation	8. hardware
9. balanced	9. policy	9. contingency

The procedure is simple. You think of a three-digit number at random and take the corresponding word from each column. Thus, 601 gives you the buzz-phrase 'optimal management flexibility', 095 gives 'integrated policy concept', 352 gives 'parallel logistical capability', and so on. The authors claim that the buzz-phrase generator gives its users 'instant expertise on matters pertaining to defence', enabling them to invest anything they write, not with any particular meaning, but with 'that proper ring of decisive, progressive, knowledgeable authority'.

There exists a British development of this invention which has three columns of no fewer than sixty lines each and includes not only most of the vogue words mentioned elsewhere in this book but many others too. This may be over-elaborate for practical use, but its compilation speaks well for British civil servants. It is wonderful how slight the difference is between some of the serious writing produced nowadays on defence matters and some of the parodies produced with the aid of the Canadian or British buzz-phrase generator.

No one can achieve a fresh and lively style by sticking to uses that were current twenty or thirty years ago; and to condemn modernity in the use of English is to insult the spirit of the language. But there is a sort of writing that forces its modernity on the reader by posture and display, like an incompetent model flaunting a new dress rather than a sensible woman wearing one. In 'modish writing' writers go out of their way to parade their knowledge of the latest vogue word or their ability to twist to new uses the vocabulary or the modes of expression that have lately become current in other contexts—the result is affected or pretentious rather than fresh or lively.

This sort of writing is usually the consequence not of an occasional lapse but rather of a wrong approach to the job of writing. It is therefore better illustrated by long passages than by short. But here are some short examples of what we may call 'modish writing'. In the first, for instance, it is hard to believe that the writer would have struck this ungainly posture if he or she had not wanted to appear familiar with the vocabulary of computers.

The study has been designed to provide the essential link between land use planning and the programming of transport facility development, using as input a land use plan expressive of the nature and extent of desirable future development, and providing as output a definition of the transport system which will best serve the future needs of the area and permit its desirable development.

Without an educational system wherein inter-personal relationships are built up in the classroom the methodology of such objects as sex education for boys and girls is foredoomed to failure. The teacher in these reactions is ideally a catalyst in the furtherance of the ability of a child to express himself. In this day and age the child who fails in this respect whatever his endowment will be impoverished emotionally and will be deprived of the fullest health.

It must be noted that this analysis of benefits has concentrated on one formulation of economies of scale. There are of course different forms of the function which still reflect the nature of the postulated relationship between the variables; these alternative forms however would alter the numerical values of the indicators relating to each centre while probably still preserving the order.

These two aspects of programming and control in isolation from the context of monetary economy are only of marginal value. Cash is the incentive to action, and is the critical criterion when assessing options.

The complexity of value decisions that have to be made by personnel in contact with clients may be added (to technology and the nature of the primary tasks) as a potentially important variable in relation to the structure and style of management of social services.

9
The handling of words: troubles in arrangement

Proper words in proper places make the true definition of style.

Swift

Despite the quotation that heads this chapter, something more than 'style' depends on putting words in their proper places. In a language like ours, which, except in some of its pronouns, has got rid of its different forms for the subjective and objective cases, your very meaning may depend on your arrangement of words. In Latin, the subject of the verb and the object have different forms; you may arrange them as you like, and the meaning will remain the same. 'Amor vincit omnia' means exactly the same as 'Omnia vincit amor' (Love conquers all things). But English is different. In the two sentences 'Cain killed Abel' and 'Abel killed Cain' the words are the same, but when they are reversed the meaning is reversed too.

If all you want to say is a simple thing like that, there is no difficulty. But you rarely do. You probably want to write a more complicated sentence telling not only the central event but also its how, why and where. The Americans have a useful word, *modifier*, by which they mean 'words or groups of words that restrict, limit or make more exact the meaning of other words'. The 'modifiers' bring the trouble.

The rule is easy enough to state: words or other units that are most closely related should be placed as near to each other as possible, so as to make clear their relationship. But it is not so easy to keep. We do not always remember that what is clear to us may be far from clear to our readers. Sometimes it is not clear even to us which parts are most closely related, and if there are many 'modifiers' we may be confronted with the sort of difficulties posed by jigsaw puzzles.

The simplest type of faulty arrangement, and the easiest to fall into, is illustrated by the following examples. Their offence is that they obscure the writers' meaning, if only momentarily, and usually make them appear to be guilty of an absurdity.

There was a discussion yesterday on the worrying of sheep by dogs in the Minister's room.

It is doubtful whether this small gas company would wish to accept responsibility for supplying this large area with all its difficulties.

I have discussed the question of stocking the proposed poultry plant with my colleagues.

Bulletin No. 160 on Housing of Pigs from Her Majesty's Stationery Office.

He has given a number of lectures on methods of controlling the flow of gases and liquids to audiences of engineers.

Prices of different models vary and you should take the advice of an expert on the make.

She said that a private contractor could run motorways in Greater Manchester when the Greater Manchester council disappears in April at an annual saving of £50,000.

Faulty arrangement of this sort is not unknown even in model regulations issued by Government Departments to show local authorities how things ought to be done:

No child shall be employed on any weekday when the school is not open for a longer period than four hours.

'For a longer period than four hours' qualifies *employed*, not *open*, and should come immediately after *employed*.

We shall have something more to say on this subject (pp. 159–60) in pointing out the danger of supposing that disorderly sentences can be set right by vagrant commas. But one cause of the separation of 'words or other units most nearly related' is so common that, although we have already touched on it (p. 13), an examination of some more examples may be useful. That is the separation of the subject from the verb by intervening clauses, usually defining the subject.

Officers appointed to permanent commissions who do not possess the qualifications for voluntary insurance explained in the preceding paragraphs and officers appointed to emergency commissions direct from civil life who were not already insured at the date of appointment (and who, as explained in para. 3, are therefore not required to be insured during service) may be eligible.

In this example the reader is kept waiting an unconscionable time for the verb. The simplest way of correcting this will generally be to change the order of the words or to convert relative clauses into *if*-clauses or *though*-clauses, or to do both. For instance:

Officers appointed to permanent commissions may be eligible though they do not possess the qualifications for voluntary insurance explained in the preceding paragraphs. So may officers appointed to emergency commissions direct from civil life who . . .

Here is a similar example:

These proposals, which it is intended should be effected without requiring police authorities to increase manpower or expenditure although there may be some modest increase in expenditure by the Police Complaints Board, are described at Annex A to this paper.

Again a long relative clause intervenes between the main subject and the verb. In this case we can simply split the sentence into two:

These proposals are described at Annex A to this paper. It is intended that they should be effected without . . .

We can fault the next example not only because of the distance between the main subject and the verb but also because the subject is much longer than the rest of the sentence:

. . . the need for delegation of authority and the simplest administration consistent with public accountability is fully recognised.

The sentence is dominated by the subject and collapses in an anti-climax. We might rewrite the sentence by beginning like this: 'We fully recognise the need for delegation of authority'.

Sometimes we may be able to split the subject in two when we want to avoid such faults:

. . . the requirement for dentists to obtain the approval of the Dental Estimates Board before providing bonded crowns on first molar teeth has been removed.

We might put most of the subject after the verb, leaving the main subject in front:

. . . the requirement has been removed for dentists to obtain the approval of . . .

It would be even better to turn the abstract noun into a verb and recast the sentence:

Dentists are no longer required to obtain the approval of . . .

Here is another example of an unbalanced sentence:

The possibility that the students would have to buy books or do without was recognised.

To improve this sentence we might move the relative clause to the end:

The possibility was recognised that the students would have to buy books or do without.

Sometimes the object allows itself to be driven a confusing distance from the verb. In the following example the writer has lumbered ponderously along without looking where he was going and arrived at the object (*officers*) of the verb *are employing* with a disconcerting bump:

One or two of the largest Local Authorities are at present employing on their staff as certifying officers and as advisers to the Mental Deficiency Act Committees officers having special qualification or experience in mental deficiency.

He would have given himself little more trouble, and would have saved his reader some, if he had turned the sentence round and written:

Officers having special qualification or experience in mental deficiency are at present being employed on the staff of one or two of the largest Local Authorities as certifying officers and as advisers to the Mental Deficiency Act Committees.

Other common errors of arrangement likely to give the reader unnecessary trouble, if they do not actually bewilder him, are letting the relative get a long way from its antecedent and the auxiliary a long way from the main verb. Examples:

(Of relative separated from antecedent.)

Enquiries are received from time to time in connection with requests for the grant of leave of absence to school children during term time for various reasons, which give rise to questions as to the power to grant such leave.

What is the antecedent of *which? Enquiries, requests* or *reasons?* Probably *enquiries,* but it is a long way off. In this sentence it matters little, but in other sentences similarly constructed it might be important for the antecedent to be unmistakable. The surest way of avoiding ambiguity, when you have started a sentence like this, is to put a full stop after *reasons*, and begin the next sentence *These enquiries*, or *These requests* or *These reasons*, whichever is meant.

(Of verb separated from auxiliary.)

The Executive Council should, in the case of approved institutions employing one doctor, get into touch with the committee.

The Council should accordingly, after considering whether they wish to suggest any modifications in the model scheme, consult with the committee

. . . provided that she has at the beginning of the eleventh week before the expected week of confinement given continuous service (including any unpaid leave) for at least 2 years and fulfils certain other conditions . . .

You can generally place the intervening part immediately before the subject:

. . . provided that at the beginning of the eleventh week before the expected week of confinement she has given continuous service . . .

It is a bad habit to put all sorts of things between the auxiliary and the verb in this way; it leads to unwieldy sentences and irritated readers.

Adverbs sometimes get awkwardly separated from the words they qualify. They should be placed where it will be perfectly clear which word or words they are intended to qualify. If they qualify an adjective or past participle or another verb their place is immediately in front of it (*accurately placed*, *perfectly clear*). If they qualify another part of a verb, or a phrase, they may be in front or behind. It is usually a matter of emphasis: *he came soon* emphasises his promptitude; *he soon came* emphasises his coming.

The commonest causes of adverbs going wrong are the fear, real or imaginary, of splitting an infinitive (see pp. 143–5) and the waywardness of the adverbs *only* and *even*. *Only* is a capricious word. It is much given to deserting its post and taking its place next to the verb, regardless of what it qualifies. It is more natural to say 'he only spoke for ten minutes' than 'he spoke for only ten minutes'. The sport of pillorying misplaced *only*s has a great fascination for some people, and *only*-snooping seems to have become as popular a sport with some purists as split-infinitive-snooping was a generation ago. A recent book, devoted to the exposing of errors of diction in contemporary writers, contained several examples such as:

He had only been in England for six weeks since the beginning of the war. This only makes a war lawful: that it is a struggle for law against force. We can only analyse the facts we all have before us.

These incur the author's censure. By the same reasoning he would condemn Churchill for writing in *The Gathering Storm*:

Statesmen are not called upon only to settle easy questions.

Fowler took a different view. Of a critic who protested against 'he only died a week ago' instead of 'he died only a week ago' Fowler wrote:

There speaks one of those friends from whom the English language may well pray to be saved, one of the modern precisians who have more zeal than discretion.

But it cannot be denied that the irresponsible behaviour of *only* does sometimes create ambiguity. Take such a sentence as:

His disease can only be alleviated by a surgical operation.

We cannot tell what this means, and must rewrite it either:

Only a surgical operation can alleviate his disease (it cannot be alleviated in any other way),

or:

A surgical operation can only alleviate his disease (it cannot cure it).

Again:

In your second paragraph you point out that carpet-yarn only can be obtained from India, and this is quite correct.

The writer must have meant 'can be obtained only from India', and ought to have so written, or, at the least, 'can only be obtained from India'. What he did write, if not actually ambiguous (for it can hardly be supposed that carpet-yarn is India's only product), is unnatural, and sets the reader puzzling for a moment.

So do not take the *only*-snoopers too seriously. But be on the alert. It will generally be safe to put *only* in what the plain man feels to be its natural place. Sometimes that will be its logical position, sometimes not. When the qualification is more important than the positive statement, to bring in the *only* as soon as possible is an aid to being understood; it prevents the reader from being put on a wrong scent. In the sentence 'The temperature will rise above three degrees only in the south-west of England', *only* is carefully put in its right logical place. But the listener would have grasped more quickly the picture of an almost universally cold England if the announcer had said, 'the temperature will only rise above three degrees in the south-west of England'. What is often still better in such cases is to avoid *only* by making the main statement a negative: 'the temperature will not rise above three degrees, except in the south-west of England'.

Even has a similar habit of getting into the wrong place. The importance of putting it in the right one is aptly illustrated in the *ABC of English Usage* thus:

Sentence: 'I am not disturbed by your threats'.
(i) Even I am not disturbed by your threats (let alone anybody else).
(ii) I am not even disturbed by your threats (let alone hurt, annoyed, injured, alarmed).
(iii) I am not disturbed even by your threats (*even* modifies the phrase, the emphasis being on the threats).

It is also possible, though perhaps rather awkward, to put *even* immediately before *your*, and so give *your* the emphasis (your threats, let alone anybody else's).

Other adverbs and some prepositional phrases enjoy a similar versatility. They include *merely*, *just*, *also*, *mainly*, *in particular*, *at least*. Within the context they usually do not create ambiguity. But you will need to be on the alert with these too.

10

The handling of words: troubles with conjunctions and prepositions

There is sufficient overlap between conjunctions and prepositions to justify including them in the same chapter. Some words, such as *both*, have been included because in certain of their uses they accompany conjunctions.

Conjunctions

(i) *And*.

There used to be an idea that it was inelegant to begin a sentence with *and*. The idea is now dead. And to use *and* in this position may be a useful way of indicating that what you are about to say will reinforce what you have just said. But do not do this so often that it becomes a mannerism. One occasionally sees *And* used to begin a paragraph; this has a slightly affected air. *But*, on the other hand, may be freely used to begin either a sentence or a paragraph.

(ii) *And which*.

There is a grammarians' rule that it is wrong to write *and which* (and similar expressions such as *and who*, *and where*, *but which*, *or which*, etc.) except by way of introducing a second relative clause with the same antecedent as one that has just preceded it. The rule is unknown in French and may be destroyed eventually by usage, but for the present its observance is expected from those who would write correctly. According to this rule, Nelson was wrong grammatically, as well as in other more important ways, when he wrote to Lady Nelson after his first introduction to Lady Hamilton:

> She is a young woman of amiable manners and who does honour to the station to which he has raised her.

To justify the *and who* grammatically a relative is needed in the first part of the sentence, for example:

She is a young woman whose manners are amiable and who . . .

Conversely, the writer of the following sentence has got into trouble by being shy of *and which*:

Things which we ourselves could not produce and yet are essential to our recovery . . .

Here, says the grammarian, *which* cannot double the parts of object of *produce* and subject of *are*. To set the grammar right the relative has to be repeated just as it would have to be if it were an inflective one (e.g. 'Men whom we forget but who should be remembered').

Things which we ourselves could not produce and which are . . .

The wisest course is to avoid the inevitable clumsiness of *and which*, even when used in a way that does not offend the purists. Thus these two sentences might be written:

She is a young woman of amiable manners who does honour to the station to which he has raised her.

Things essential to our recovery which we ourselves could not produce . . .

The next example of *or which* is particularly clumsy because of the preceding *where*:

It is unlikely that he would seek this discharge [from his duty to refer the agreement to the Restrictive Practices Court] *where* there are restrictions on the level of prices or charges *or which* impose unreasonable conditions for supplying goods.

It would be clearer to write the sentence:

It is unlikely that he would seek this discharge *where* there are restrictions on the level of prices or charges *or where* there are restrictions which impose unreasonable conditions for supplying goods.

or, more succinctly:

It is unlikely that he would seek this discharge where there are restrictions *which* control the level of prices or charges *or which* impose unreasonable conditions for supplying goods.

You may here write *or* alone instead of *or which*.

If you use *which*, *who*, or *whom* for one clause, be consistent; do not switch to *and that* in the second relative clause ('restrictions *which* control the level of prices or charges *or that* . . .'). The same requirement for consistency applies to the converse ('restrictions *that* . . . or *which* . . .').

And and *or* join units of the same type. Two unequal phrases are yoked together in this example:

> A woman who is absent from work because of pregnancy or confinement has the right to work in the same grade *and* working the same hours at any time before . . .

We must rewrite the part that follows *and* to harmonise with either 'to work in the same grade':

> . . . has the right to work in the same grade and to work the same hours . . .

or with 'in the same grade':

> . . . has the right to work in the same grade and for the same hours . . .

The next sentence demands an excessive effort to find out what is linked with what. Most readers will give up the struggle:

> On receipt of a complaint against a member of his force the chief officer would cause it to be recorded *and* to have made such preliminary inquiries as were necessary to decide whether the matter should be handled initially by informal resolution or by formal investigation . . .

The infinitive *to have made* goes back to *would cause*, but difficulties arise because the order is peculiar – the expected order would be 'to have such preliminary inquiries made' – and because this peculiar order upsets the parallelism with the previous part. It would be better to write:

> On receipt of a complaint against a member of his force the chief officer would arrange to have it recorded *and* to have such preliminary inquiries made . . .

(iii) *As.*

Earlier editions firmly held to the view that *as* must not be used as a preposition. Readers were told that they must not say 'no one knows the truth as fully as me'; it must be 'as fully as I', since the first *as* is an adverb and the second a conjunction. *As* is now commonly used as a preposition in speech and in much writing, but in formal writing 'as fully as I' remains preferable to 'as fully as me'. However, if 'as fully as I' sounds to you pedantic or too formal, you may prefer to include the verb; nobody can object to 'as fully as I am'. It is always safer to include the verb where the comparison may otherwise be ambiguous. 'I see the Minister as often as the Permanent Secretary' may mean either 'I see the Minister as often as I see the Permanent Secretary' or 'I see the Minister as often as the Permanent Secretary does'.

We say 'as good *as* ever' and 'better *than* ever'. But should we use *as* or *than*, or both, if we say 'as good or better'? The natural thing to say is 'as good or better than ever', ignoring the *as* that *as good* logically needs, and you commit no great crime if that is what you do. But if you want both to run no risk of offending the purists and to avoid the prosy 'as good as or better than', you can write 'as good as ever or better'. Thus you could change:

Pamphlets have circulated as widely, and been no less influential, than those published in this volume.

into:

Pamphlets have circulated as widely as those published in this volume, and have been no less influential.

The use of *as* in the temporal sense of *while* or in the reason sense of *since* may give rise to ambiguity:

As they were working in the next office, they could overhear the argument.

Does this mean 'since they were working in the next office' or 'while they were working in the next office'? If there is any possibility of confusion, change *as* to a conjunction that will convey clearly the sense you intend.

(For the superfluous *as* see p.60.)

(iv) *Both.*

When using *both* . . . *and*, be careful that these words are in their right positions and carry equal weight. Nothing that comes between the *both* and the *and* can be regarded as carried on after the *and*. If words are to be carried on after the *and*, they must precede the *both*; if they do not precede the *both*, they must be repeated after the *and*. For instance:

He was both deaf to argument and entreaty.

Since *deaf to* comes after *both*, it cannot be 'understood' again after *and*. We must adjust the balance in one of the following ways:

He was both deaf to argument and unmoved by entreaty.
He was deaf both to argument and to entreaty.
He was deaf to both argument and entreaty.

Here is a sentence where the unbalanced *both* puts the reader off the scent:

Staff may seek rewards and satisfaction from both their superiors and from their clients.

This seems to say that there are two superiors, from both of whom, as well as from their clients, the staff may seek rewards. But that is not what the writer meant: he should have written 'both from their superiors . . .'

An extreme example of the unbalanced *both* is:

The proposed sale must be both sanctioned by the Minister and the price must be approved by the District Valuer.

The need for proper balancing of *both . . . and* applies also to such pairs as *either . . . or, neither . . . nor, not only . . . but also, not so much . . . as, between . . . and*.

Do not use *both* where it is not necessary because the meaning of the sentence is no less plain if you leave it out:

Both of them are equally to blame. (They are equally to blame.)
Please ensure that both documents are fastened together. (. . . that the documents are fastened together.)

(v) *But*.

But, in the sense of *except*, is sometimes treated as a preposition ('no one knows the full truth but me') and sometimes as a conjunction ('no one knows the full truth but I'). Earlier editions suggested that it was more commonly treated as a conjunction but that seems no longer so. Mrs Hemans was not guilty of 'bad grammar' when she wrote 'whence all but he had fled' and would not be now, but *him* would be the present usual practice. That is the worst of personal pronouns: by retaining the case-inflections that nouns have so sensibly rid themselves of, they pose these tiresome and trivial questions. (See also *I* and *me* pp.115–6 and *who* and *whom* pp. 124–5.) If the sentence could have been 'whence all but the boy had fled' no one could have known whether *but* was being used as a conjunction or a preposition, and no one need have cared.

In using *but* as a conjunction an easy slip is to put it where there should be an *and*, forgetting that the conjunction that you want is one that does not go contrary to the clause immediately preceding but continues in the same sense.

It is agreed that the primary condition of the scheme is satisfied, but it is also necessary to establish that your war service interrupted an organised course of study for a professional qualification comparable to that for which application is made, *but*, as explained in previous letters, you are unable to fulfil this condition.

The italicised *but* should be *and*. The line of thought has already been turned by the first *but*; it is now going straight on.

A similar slip is made in:

The Forestry Commission will probably only be able to offer you a post as a forest labourer, or possibly in leading a gang of forest workers, but there are at the moment no vacancies for Forest Officers.

Either *only* must be omitted or the *but* must be changed to *since.*

(vi) *If.*

The use of *if* for *though* or *but* may give rise to ambiguity or absurdity. It is ambiguous in such a sentence as:

This case, if not proved, is arguable.

Care is also needed in the use of *if* in the sense of *whether*, for this too may cause ambiguity.

Please inform me if there is any change in your circumstances.

Does this mean 'Please inform me now whether there is any change' or 'If any change should occur please inform me then'? The reader cannot tell. If *whether* and *if* become interchangeable, unintentional offence may be given by the lover who sings:

> What do I care,
> If you are there?

(vii) *Inasmuch as.*

This is sometimes used in the sense of *so far as*, but more commonly in the reason sense of *since*. It is occasionally ambiguous: 'We encourage him inasmuch as we can' may mean either 'so far as we can' or 'since we can'. For both uses, *inasmuch as* is clumsy and somewhat old-fashioned, and might well be dispensed with altogether. For the same reasons replace *insomuch as* with either *since* or *so far as* according to the sense you intend. You might also prefer *so far as* to the clumsy and old-fashioned *insofar as*.

(viii) *Like*.

Colloquial English admits *like* as a conjunction, and would not be shocked at such a sentence as 'Nothing succeeds like success does'. In America they go even further, and say 'It looks like he was going to succeed'. But in English prose neither of these will do. *Like* must not be treated as a conjunction. So we may say 'nothing succeeds like success'; but it must be 'nothing succeeds *as* success does' and 'it looks *as if* he were going to succeed'.

But the convention forbidding *like he does*, where *like* is a conjunction, should not frighten writers away from *like him*, where it is a preposition, and make them lean over backwards with such a sentence as 'The new Secretary of State, as his predecessor, is an Etonian'.

(ix) *Provided* (*that*).

This form of introduction of a stipulation is better than *providing*. The phrase should be reserved in the sense of *if and only if* for a true stipulation, as in:

> He said he would go to the meeting provided that I went with him.

and not used loosely for *if* as in:

> I expect he will come tomorrow, provided that he comes at all.

Sometimes this misuse of *provided that* creates difficulties for a reader:

> Such emoluments can only count as qualifying for pension provided that they cannot be converted into cash.

The use of *provided that* obscures the meaning of a sentence that would have been clear with *if*.

(x) *Than*.

Than tempts writers to use it as a preposition, like *as* (see pp. 60, 100–1), in such a sentence as 'he is older than me'. Examples can be found in good writers, including a craftsman as scrupulous as Somerset Maugham. But some grammarians will not have it.

According to them we must say 'he is older than I' (i.e. than I am). We may say 'I know more about her than him' if what we mean is that my knowledge of her is greater than my knowledge of him, but if we mean that my knowledge of her is greater than his knowledge of her, we must say 'I know more about her than he (does)'. Fowler, more tolerant, merely says that, since the prepositional *than* may cause ambiguity, it is to that extent undesirable. But it is so common a colloquialism that those who observe the stricter ruling risk the appearance of pedantry unless they add the verb.

But even the stricter grammarians recognise one exception—*whom*. We must say 'than whom', and not 'than who', even though the only way of making grammatical sense of it is to regard *than* as a preposition. But that is rather a stilted way of writing, and can best be left to poetry:

> Beelzebub . . . than whom, Satan except, none higher sat.

Be careful not to slip into using *than* with words that take a different construction. *Other*, *otherwise*, *else* and *elsewhere* are the only words besides comparatives that take *than*. *Than* is sometimes mistakenly used in place of *as*:

> Nearly twice as many people die under 20 in France than in Great Britain, chiefly of tuberculosis.

(xi) *That.*
For *that* (conjunction) see p. 123.

(xii) *When.*
It is sometimes confusing to use *when* as the equivalent of *and then*.

> Let me have full particulars when I will be able to advise you. (Please let me have full particulars. I shall then be able to advise you.)
> Alternatively the Minister may make the order himself when it has the same effect as if it has been made by the Local Authority. (. . . the Minister may make the order himself, and it then has the same effect . . .)

(xiii) *While.*
It is safest to use this conjunction only in its temporal sense ('Your letter came while I was away on leave'). That does not mean that it is wrong to use it also as a conjunction without any temporal sense, equivalent to *although* ('While I do not agree with you, I accept your ruling'). But in this sense it can sometimes be ambiguous, as in:

While he is short of experience, he will do the job quite adequately.

And it should certainly not be used in both senses in the same sentence, as in:

While appreciating your difficulties while your mother is seriously ill . . .

Moreover, once we leave the shelter of the temporal sense, we are on the road to treating *while* as a synonym for *and*:

Nothing will be available for some time for the desired improvement, while the general supply of linoleum to new offices may have to cease when existing stocks have run out.

There is no point in saying *while* when you mean *and*, and it is much better not to use it for *although* either.* If you are too free with *while* you are sure sooner or later to land yourself in the absurdity of seeming to say that two events occurred simultaneously which could not possibly have done so.

The first part of the concert was conducted by Sir August Manns . . . while Sir Arthur Sullivan conducted his then recently composed *Absent Minded Beggar*.

Careful screening by appraisal interviews would help to . . . while later interviews would provide a means . . .

Prepositions

(i) Ending sentences with prepositions.

Do not hesitate to end a sentence with a preposition if your ear tells you that that is where the preposition goes best. There used to be a rather half-hearted grammarians' rule against doing this, but no good writer ever heeded it, except Dryden, who seems to have invented it. The translators of the Authorised Version did not know it ('but I have a baptism to be baptised with'). The very rule itself, if phrased 'do not use a preposition to end a sentence with', has a smoother flow and a more idiomatic ring than 'do not use a preposition with which to end a sentence'. Sometimes, when the final word is really a verbal particle,

---

* Some people make a distinction between *while* and *whilst*, using *while* only in its temporal sense and *whilst* for *and* or *although*. We see little harm in this; but *whilst* is an unnecessary word and many people, including all Americans, pass blamelessly from cradle to grave without ever using it.

and the verb's meaning depends on it, they form together a phrasal verb (see p. 64)—*put up with* for instance—and to separate them makes nonsense. It is said that Churchill once made this marginal comment against a sentence that clumsily avoided a prepositional ending: 'This is the sort of English up with which I will not put.' The ear is a pretty safe guide. Over a hundred years ago Dean Alford protested against this so-called rule. 'I know', he said, 'that I am at variance with the rules taught at very respectable institutions for enabling young ladies to talk unlike their elders. But that I cannot help.' The story is well known of the nurse who performed the remarkable feat of getting four* prepositions at the end of a sentence by asking her charge: 'What did you choose that book to be read to out of for?' She said what she wanted to say perfectly clearly, in words of one syllable, and what more can one ask?

(ii) Cannibalism by prepositions.

Cannibalism is the name given by Fowler to a vice that prepositions are specially prone to, though it may infect any part of speech. One of a pair of words swallows the other:

> Any articles for which export licences are held or for which licences have been applied . . .

The writer meant 'or for which export licences have been applied for', but the first *for* has swallowed the second.

The converse also occurs. A preposition may be wrongly repeated:

> The saturated fat contained in the milk *from* which the yoghurt was made *from* has been shown to raise the cholesterol.

The writer has forgotten that he has written the first *from*.

For circumlocutory prepositions (*in regard to* and the like) see pp. 54–6.

(iii) *Between* and *among*.

The *OED* tells us—and no one needs to be told twice—to ignore those who say that *between* must only be used of two things and that

---

* There are really only three. *Out* is an adverb, forming, with *of*, a composite preposition. Even the improved variant 'What did you bring that book I don't like to be read aloud to out of from up for?' cannot fairly be credited with more than the same three—*to, out of* and *for. From* is a mere repetition of *out of* and *up* is an adverb going with *bring*.

when there are more the preposition must be *among*. It goes on to say (and again we shall all agree):

> *Between* is still the only word available to express the relation of a thing to many surrounding things severally and individually, *among* expressing a relationship to them collectively and vaguely: we should not say 'the space lying among the three points' or 'a treaty among three powers' or 'the choice lies among the three candidates in the select list' or 'to insert a needle among the closed petals of a flower'.

(iv) *Between each.*

Grammarians generally condemn the common use of *between* with *each* or *every*, as in 'there will be a week's interval between each sitting'. It is arguable that this can be justified as a convenient way of saying 'between each sitting and the next', and that, considering how common it is, only pedantry can object. But those who want to be on the safe side can say either 'weekly intervals between the sittings' or 'a week's interval after each sitting'.

(v) *Between . . . or* and *between . . . and between.*

If *between* is followed by a conjunction, this must always be a simple *and*. It is wrong to say 'the choice lies between Smith or Jones', or to say 'we had to choose between taking these offices and making the best of them and between perhaps finding ourselves with no offices at all'. If a sentence has become so involved that *and* is not felt to be enough, it should be recast. This mistake is not unknown in high places:

> It is thought that the choice lies between Mr Trygve Lie continuing for another year or the election of Mr Lester Pearson.

And in the following, more exotic, example we find *as opposed to* being used instead of *and*:

> There is a distinction between giving local authorities a share in the proceeds of a local tax as opposed to making them free to fix their own tax rates for their own areas.

Between . . . and, like *both . . . and* (see p. 101–2), requires proper balancing:

> There is often a difference between doing research in universities and in private industry.

We must adjust the balance in this way:

There is often a difference between doing research in universities and doing research in private industry.

(vi) For *between you and I* see *I* and *me* (p. 115).

(vii) *Due to.*

Owing to long ago established itself as a prepositional phrase. But the orthodox still keep up the fight against the attempt of *due to* to do the same: they maintain that *due* is an adjective and should not be used otherwise. That means that it must always have a noun to agree with. You may say: 'Floods due to a breach in the river bank covered a thousand acres of land'. But you must not say: 'Due to a breach in the river bank, a thousand acres of land were flooded'. In the first *due to* agrees properly with floods, which were in fact due to the breach. In the second it can only agree with a thousand acres of land, which were not due to the breach, or to anything else except the Creation.

Due to is rightly used in:

The closing of the telephone exchange was due to lack of equipment. (*Due to* agrees with *closing*.)
The delay in replying has been due to the fact that it was hoped to call upon you. (*Due to* agrees with *delay*.)

Due to is wrongly used in:

We must apologise to listeners who missed the introduction to the talk due to a technical fault.
There was no play at Trent Bridge today due to the rain.
Not all students receive such instruction due to the lack of specialised staff.

Many readers feel very strongly against the 'incorrect' use of *due to*, common though it is. Sensible writers should therefore try to form a habit of using it correctly, though they may well feel that there are many points more worth their attention. If you are in doubt, you may prefer to use *owing to* or *because of*, which are always safe.

(viii) *Following.*

Grammarians do not admit *following* as a preposition, though its use as one is becoming so common that they may soon have to give it *de facto* recognition. The orthodox view is that it is the participle of the verb *follow*, and must have a noun to agree with, as it has in:

Such rapid promotion, following his exceptional services, was not unexpected.

But as a preposition it is unnecessary when it usurps the place of *in consequence of*, *in accordance with*, *because of*, or *as a result of*, as in:

> Following judgments of the High Court, Ministers of Religion are not regarded as employed under a contract of service.
>
> It has been brought to my notice following a recent visit of an Inspector of this Ministry to the premises of . . . that you are an insured person under the Act.
>
> Following heavy rain last night the wicket is very wet.

Still less can there be any justification for it with a merely temporal significance. It might perhaps put in a plea for a useful function as meaning something between the two—between the *propter hoc* of those prepositional phrases and the *post hoc* of *after*. This announcement might claim that justification:

> A man will appear at Bow Street this morning following the destruction of Mr Reg Butler's statue of the Political Prisoner.

But the word shows little sign of being content with that rather subtle duty. More and more, under the strong lead of BBC announcers, it is becoming merely a pretentious substitute for *after*.

> Following the orchestral concert, we come to a talk by . . .
>
> Following that old English tune, we go to Latin America for the next one.

(ix) Prior to.

There is no good reason to use *prior to* as a preposition instead of *before*. *Before* is simpler, better known and more natural, and therefore preferable. It is moreover at least questionable whether *prior to* has established itself as a preposition. By all means use the phrase a *prior engagement*, where *prior* is doing its proper job as an adjective. But do not say that you made an engagement *prior to* receiving the second invitation.

> Mr X has requested that you should submit to him, immediately prior to placing orders, lists of components . . .

In sentences such as these *prior to* cannot have any advantage over the straightforward *before*.

The same objections apply to *previous to* instead of *before*, and *subsequent to* instead of *after*.

11

The handling of words: troubles with pronouns

'The use of pronouns', said Cobbett, 'is to prevent the repetition of nouns, and to make speaking and writing more rapid and less encumbered with words.' In more than one respect they are difficult parts of speech to handle.

(i) Be sure that a pronoun has a true antecedent.
It is an easy slip to use a pronoun without a true antecedent.

He offered to resign but it was refused.

Here *it* has no true antecedent, as it would have had if the sentence had begun 'He offered his resignation'. The antecedent would then have been *his resignation*. In the next example, there is an absurd possible connection of *they* with *abortion laws*, though nobody is likely to be misled by it:

Experience shows that when abortion laws are liberalised, they skyrocket.

There is no antecedent for *they*, which should be replaced by *abortions*. The error in these sentences is purely grammatical, but unless care is taken over it a verbal absurdity may result. Cobbett gives this example from Addison:

There are indeed but very few who know how to be idle and innocent, or have a relish of any pleasures that are not criminal; every diversion they take is at the expense of some one virtue or other, and their very first step out of business is into vice or folly.

As Cobbett points out, the only possible antecedent to *they* and *their* is the 'very few who know how to be idle and innocent', and that is the opposite of what Addison means.

(ii) Be sure that there is no real ambiguity about the antecedent.
This is more than a grammatical point; it affects the intelligibility of what you write. Care is needed with the pronouns *he* and *him* or *she* and *her* when more than one person has been mentioned. We must not make our readers guess, even though it may not be difficult to guess

right. As Jespersen points out, a sentence like 'John told Robert's son that he must help him' is theoretically capable of six different meanings. It is true that Jespersen would not have us trouble overmuch when there can be no real doubt about the antecedent, and he points out that there is little danger of misunderstanding the theoretically ambiguous sentence:

> If the baby does not thrive on raw milk, boil it.

Nevertheless, he adds, it is well to be very careful about one's pronouns.

Here are several examples, to show how difficult it is to avoid ambiguity:

> Mr S told Mr H he was prepared to transfer part of his allocation to his purposes provided that he received £10,000.

The *his* before *purposes* refers, it would seem, to Mr H and the other three pronouns to Mr S.

> Mr H F saw a man throw something from his pockets to the hens on his farm, and then twist the neck of one of them when they ran to him.

Here the change of antecedent from a *man* to *Mr H F* and back again to a *man* is puzzling at first.

> The plans must be assessed in the light of their contributions to the effectiveness of defence expenditure. This is achieved by the decisions of Ministers advised by their staffs, both military and civilian.

What does *This* refer to? The obvious antecedent is 'the effectiveness', but it is odd to say that the effectiveness is achieved by the decisions of Ministers. Perhaps *This* is intended to refer to 'their contributions', but if so *This* is an error for *These*.

The word *They* in the second of the two following sentences is a particularly disreputable example of a pronoun with doubtful antecedents.

> The possibilities of following subjects and activities in school through to youth organisations and adult education are too numerous to be explored in detail. They may represent the only contact with non-commercial interests a young person will have.

There are several possible ways of removing ambiguities such as these. Let us take by way of illustration the sentence, 'Sir Henry

Ponsonby informed Mr Gladstone that the Queen had been much upset by what he had told her' and let us assume that the ambiguous *he* refers to Mr Gladstone. We can make the antecedent plain by

1. Not using a pronoun at all, and writing 'by what Mr Gladstone had told her'.
2. Parenthetic explanation—'by what he (Mr Gladstone) had told her'.
3. The *former–latter* device—'by what the latter had told her'.
4. By rewriting the sentence—'The Queen was much upset by what Mr Gladstone told her, and Sir Henry Ponsonby so informed him'.
5. The device that Henry Sidgwick called 'the polite alias' and Fowler 'elegant variation', and writing (say) 'by what the Prime Minister had told her', or 'the G.O.M.' or 'the veteran statesman'.

It may safely be said that the fifth device should seldom if ever be adopted, and the third only when the antecedent is very close.

(iii) Do not be shy of pronouns.

So far we have been concerned in this section with the dangers that beset the user of pronouns. But we should be concerned also with the danger of not using them when we ought. Legal language, which must aim above all things at removing every possible ambiguity, is more sparing of pronouns than ordinary prose, because of an ever-present fear that the antecedent may be uncertain. For instance, an Act of Parliament reads:

> The Secretary of State may by any such regulations allow the required notice of any occurrence to which the regulations relate, instead of being sent forthwith, to be sent within the time limited by the regulations.

Anyone not writing legal language would have avoided repeating *regulations* twice; he would have put *they* in the first place and *them* in the second.

Ordinary writers should not allow themselves to become infected with pronoun-avoidance. If they do, the result is that what they write is often, in Cobbett's phrase, more 'encumbered with words' than it need be.

> The examiner's search would in all cases be carried up to the date of the

filing of the complete specification, and the examiner (he) need not trouble his head with the subject of disconformity.

The Ministry of Agriculture and Fisheries are anxious that the Rural Land Utilisation Officer should not in any way hinder the acquisition or earmarking of land for educational purposes, but it is the duty of the Rural Land Utilisation Officer (his duty) to ensure . . .

Arrangements are being made to continue the production of these houses for a further period, and increased numbers of these houses (them) will, therefore, be available.

Often the repeated word is embroidered by *such*:

. . . the admission of specially selected Public Assistance cases, provided that no suitable accommodation is available for such cases (them) in a home . . .

This also is no doubt due to infection by legal English, where this use of *such* is an indispensable device for securing economy of words. The draftsman, whose concern is to make his meaning certain beyond the possibility of error, avoids pronouns lest there should be an ambiguity about their antecedents, but escapes the need for repeating words of limitation by the use of *such* or *such* . . . *as aforesaid*. The rest of us need not usually be so punctilious.

But using *such* in the way the lawyers use it is not always out of place in ordinary writing. Sometimes it is proper and useful.

One month's notice in writing must be given to terminate this agreement. As no such notice has been received from you . . .

Here it is important for the writer to show that in the second sentence he is referring to the same sort of notice as in the first and the *such* device is the neatest way of doing it.

(iv) Try to put the pronoun after the antecedent.

It is usually better not to allow a pronoun to precede what it refers to. If the pronoun comes first, readers may not know what it refers to until they reach the relevant words.

I regret that it is not practicable, in view of its size, to provide a list of the agents.

Here, it is true, the readers are only momentarily left guessing what *its* refers to. But they would have been spared even that if the sentence had been written:

I regret that it is not practicable to provide a list of the agents; there are too many of them.

(v) *Each other*.

Grammarians used to say that *each other* is the right expression when only two persons or things are referred to and *one another* when there are more than two. But Fowler, quoted with approval by Jespersen, says of this so-called rule, 'This differentiation is neither of present utility nor based on historical usage'.

(vi) *Former* and *latter*.

Do not hesitate to repeat words rather than use *former* or *latter* to avoid doing so. Readers probably have to look back to see which is which, and so you annoy them and waste their time. And there is no excuse at all for using *latter* merely to serve as a pronoun, as in:

In these employments we would rest our case for the exclusion of young persons directly on the grounds of the latter's moral welfare. (Their moral welfare.)

Remember that *former* and *latter* can refer to only two things and if you use them of more than two you may puzzle your readers. If you want to refer otherwise than specifically to the last of more than two things, say *last* or *last-mentioned*, not *latter*.

(vii) *I* and *me*.

About the age-long conflict between *it is I* and *it is me*, no more need be said than that, in the present stage of the battle, most people would think 'it is I' pedantic in talk and 'it is me' improper in writing.

What calls more for examination is the practice of using *I* for *me* in combination with some noun or other pronoun, e.g. 'between you and I', 'let you and I go'. Why this has become so prevalent is not easy to say. Perhaps it comes partly from an excess of zeal in correcting the opposite error. When Mrs Elton said 'Neither Mr Suckling nor me had ever any patience with them', and Lydia Bennet 'Mrs Forster and me are such friends', they were guilty of a vulgarism that was, no doubt, common in Jane Austen's day, and is not unknown to-day. One might suppose that this mistake was corrected by teachers of English in our schools with such ferocity that their pupils are left with the conviction that such combinations as *you and me* are in all circumstances ungrammatical.

It is the combination of oneself with someone else that proves fatal.

The official who wrote 'I trust that it will be convenient to you for my colleague and I to call upon you next Tuesday' would never, if he had been proposing to come alone, have written 'I trust that it will be convenient to you for I to call upon . . .'. A sure and easy way of avoiding this blunder is to ask oneself what case the personal pronoun would have been in—would it have been *I* or *me?*—if it had stood alone. It should remain the same in partnership as it would have been by itself.

The association of someone else with oneself sometimes prompts the use of *myself* where a simple *I* or *me* is all that is needed, e.g. 'The inspection will be made by Mr Jones and myself'. *Myself* should be used only for emphasis ('I saw it myself') or as the reflexive form of the personal pronoun ('I have hurt myself').

(viii) *It.*

This pronoun is especially troublesome because the convenient English idiom of using *it* to anticipate the subject of a sentence tends to produce a plethora of *its*. A correspondent sent in this example:

> It is to be expected that it will be difficult to apply A unless it is accompanied by B, for which reason it is generally preferable to use C in spite of its other disadvantages.

This, he justly said, could be put more effectively and tersely by writing:

> C is generally preferable, in spite of its disadvantages, because application of A without B is difficult.

(ix) Unnecessary use of *one.*

One has a way of intruding in such a sentence as 'The problem is not an easy one'. 'The problem is not easy' may be a neater way of saying what you mean.

(x) Pronouns with *one.*

What pronoun should be used with *one*? *His* or *one's*, for example? That depends on what sort of a *one* it is, whether 'numeral' or 'impersonal', to use Fowler's labels. Fowler illustrates the difference thus:

> One hates *his* enemies and another forgives them (numeral).
> One hates *one's* enemies and loves *one's* friends (impersonal).

But any sentence that needs to repeat the impersonal *one* is bound to be inelegant, and you will do better to rewrite it.

(xi) *One of those who.*

A common error in sentences of this sort is to use a singular verb instead of a plural, as though the antecedent of *who* were *one* and not *those*—to write, for instance, 'It is one of the exceptional cases that *calls for* (instead of *call for*) exceptional treatment'. In some instances, however, the antecedent of *who* is *one* and then the singular is correct: 'Leslie is the only one of the secretaries in this office who *types* accurately'.

(xii) *Same.*

Four hundred years ago, when the Thirty-nine Articles were drawn up, it was good English idiom to use *the same* as a pronoun where we should now say *he* or *she*, *him* or *her*, *they* or *them*, or *it*.

The riches and goods of Christians are not common, as touching the right title and possession of the same, as certain Anabaptists do falsely boast.

This is no good reason for the present pronominal use of *the same* and *same*, which survives robustly in commercialese and still occasionally appears in official writing. This use of *same* is now by general consent reprehensible because it gives an air of artificiality and pretentiousness.

Example

As you have omitted to insert your full Christian names, I shall be glad if you will advise me of same.

With reference to the above matter, and my representative's interview of the 12th October, relative to same . . .

I enclose the necessary form for agreement and shall be glad if you will kindly complete and return same at your early convenience.

Alternative version

As you have omitted to insert your full Christian names, I shall be glad if you will let me know what they are.

With reference to this matter and my representative's interview of the 12th October about it . . .

(For *same* substitute *it*.)

In the following sentence,

I am informed that it may be decided by X Section that this extra will not be required. I await therefore their decision before taking further action in an attempt to provide.

it would be pleasing to think that the writer stopped abruptly after *provide*, leaving it objectless, in order to check himself on the brink of writing *same*. But he might harmlessly have written *it*.

(xiii) *They* for *he or she*.

It is common in speech, and not unknown in serious writing, to use *they*, *them*, or *their* as the equivalent of a singular pronoun of a common sex, as in 'Each insisted on their own point of view, and hence the marriage came to an end'. This is stigmatised by grammarians as a usage grammatically indefensible. The Judge ought, they would say, to have said 'He insisted on his own point of view and she on hers'. Jespersen says about this:

> In the third person it would have been very convenient to have a common-sex pronoun, but as a matter of fact English has none and must therefore use one of the three makeshift expedients shown in the following sentences:
> The reader's heart—if he or she have any. (Fielding)
> He that hath ears to hear let him hear. (AV)
> Nobody prevents you, do they? (Thackeray)

Current usage is in disarray on this matter. You will be wise for the present not to be tempted by the greater convenience of the third expedient, though it may eventually become fully accepted in all serious writing. Many will be disconcerted or irritated to be confronted with the switch from singular *your partner* to plural *them* in this question on a form:

> Does your partner use any of the money that you give them to pay for any of the things on this list?

It would satisfy all if the writer replaced *them* by *him or her*. But frequent repetition of such combinations in the same sentence or in adjoining sentences is clumsy and unpleasing. The abbreviated device of *he/she*, *him/her*, and *his/her* is ugly, suitable only for forms. (The abbreviation *s/he* is even uglier and in any case is available only when the pronouns are the subject.) You may sometimes find it least clumsy to follow the traditional use of *he*, *him* and *his* to include both sexes, but you should then make it unmistakably clear that you are using these pronouns in this way. Very often, however, you can evade the problem by rephrasing your sentences. Consider replacing the singulars by plurals throughout. Instead of this:

No blame should be attached to a member of staff who has acted in good faith and in accordance with the guidance and training he has received.

you might write this:

No blame should be attached to members of staff who have acted in good faith and in accordance with the guidance and training they have received.

In some instances you might find it possible to jettison the pronouns:

Sometimes a violent individual has to be escorted from his home to hospital.

Here you might replace *his home* by *home*.

If you are referring to people of both sexes, it is also better to avoid where possible nouns that seem to specify only males. If there are established common-sex nouns, prefer them. You will avoid giving offence by using *human accomplishments* instead of *man's accomplishments* and *working hours* instead of *man hours*.

Whatever justification there may be for using *themselves* as a singular common-sex pronoun, there can be no excuse for it when only one sex is referred to, as in:

The female manipulative jobs are of a type to which by no means everyone can adapt themselves with ease.

There is no reason why *herself* should not have been written instead of *themselves*.

(xiv) *What*.

What, in the sense of *that which*, or *those which*, is an antecedent and relative combined. Because it may be either singular or plural in number, and either subjective or objective in case, it needs careful handling.

Fowler says that its difficulties of number can be solved by asking the question 'what does it stand for?'

What is needed is more rooms.

Here Fowler would say that *what* means *the thing that*, and the singular verbs are right. On the other hand, in the sentence 'He no doubt acted with what are in his opinion excellent reasons', *are* is right because *what* is equivalent to *reasons that*. But this is perhaps over-subtle, and there is no great harm in treating *what* as plural in such a construction whenever the complement is plural. It sounds more natural.

Because *what* may be subjective or objective, writers may find themselves making the same word do duty in both cases, a practice condemned by grammarians. For instance:

This was what came into his head and he said without thinking.

What is here being made to do duty both as the subject of *came* and as the object of *said*. If we want to be punctiliously grammatical we must write either:

This is what (subjective) came into his head and what (objective) he said without thinking.

or, preferably:

This is what came into his head, and he said it without thinking.

(xv) *Which.*

The *New Yorker* of the 4th December 1948 quoted a question asked of the *Philadelphia Bulletin* by a correspondent:

My class would appreciate a discussion of the wrong use of *which* in sentences like 'He wrecked the car which was due to his carelessness'.

and the answer given by that newspaper:

The fault lies in using *which* to refer to the statement '*He wrecked the car*'. When *which* follows a noun it refers to that noun as its antecedent. Therefore in the foregoing sentence it is stated that the car was due to his carelessness, which is nonsense.

What is? Carelessness? is the *New Yorker*'s query.

Which shows how dangerous it is to dogmatise about the use of *which* with an antecedent consisting not of a single word but of a phrase. *Punch* has also provided an illustration of the same danger ('from a novel'):

Mrs Brandon took the heavy piece of silk from the table, unfolded it, and displayed an altar cloth of her own exquisite embroidery . . . upon which everyone began to blow their nose . . .

In the following example (which finds its place here because *whereupon* might as easily have been *upon which*) the antecedent is a phrase rather than a single word, but it is not the phrase that has actually been used: it is a phrase vaguely implied by what has gone before.

The number of permissible absences by a member of the governing body [should] be only two per annum, whereupon the member shall be deemed to have vacated his office as Governor.

If this writer had thought out what he was trying to say he would have written:

A Governor shall be deemed to have vacated his office if he is absent from more than two meetings in a year.

The fact is that this is a common and convenient usage, but needs to be handled discreetly to avoid ambiguity or awkwardness.

The required statement is in course of preparation and will be forwarded as soon as official records are complete, which will be in about a week's time.

Here it is unnecessary; the sentence can be improved by omitting the words 'which will be', and so getting rid of the relative altogether.

The long delay may make it inevitable for the authorities to consider placing the order elsewhere which can only be in the United States which is a step we should be anxious to avoid.

Here the writer has used *which* in this way twice in a single sentence, and shown how awkward its effect can be. He might have put a full stop after *elsewhere* and continued 'That can only be in the United States and is a step we should be anxious to avoid'.

(xvi) *Which* and *that.*

On the whole it makes for smoothness of writing not to use the relative *which* where *that* would do as well, and not to use either if a sentence makes sense and runs pleasantly without. But that is a very broad general statement, subject to many exceptions.

That cannot be used in a 'commenting'* clause; the relative must be *which.* With a 'defining'* clause either *which* or *that* is permissible. When in a 'defining' clause the relative is in the objective case, it can often be left out altogether. Thus we have the three variants:

This case ought to go to the Home Office, *which* deals with police establishments. (Commenting relative clause.)

The Department *that* deals with police establishments is the Home Office. (Defining relative clause.)

This is the case you said we ought to send to the Home Office. (Defining

* These terms are explained on p. 158.

relative clause in which the relative pronoun, if it were expressed, would be in the objective case.)

There are still some people who try to insist that to use *which* or *who* in a defining clause is wrong, and that every such clause must have *that* (except of course where a preposition precedes the relative). There is no justification for this. There are some sentences in which *that* comes more naturally, others in which it does not.

Who is more usual in a defining clause where the antecedent is personal and the relative is subject of the clause. At the beginning of the preceding paragraph 'There are still some people *that* try to insist . . .' would not be wrong, but *who* is more natural. On the other hand, *that* or no relative is more common where the relative is not the subject: 'There are still some people that I have not met'. (Similarly: '. . . some people that I have not talked to'.) Perhaps the reason is that we can then avoid having to choose between *who* and *whom*.

That is more usual in a defining clause even where the antecedent is not personal if the antecedent is rather short: 'I have sent the papers *that* you need for tomorrow's meeting'; 'You can choose anything *that* is of interest to you'. You may also leave out the relative in the first example ('I have sent the papers you need for tomorrow's meeting'), but not in the second, since there the relative is the subject and is needed to mark the beginning of the clause.

We indicate that the relative clause is commenting by putting it within commas. (See pp. 158–9 for the punctuation of relative clauses.) Sometimes there is little or no difference whether you treat the clause as commenting or defining:

The fire fighters battled for three hours to control a factory fire, which was fuelled by toxic chemicals from a storage tank.

Here the comma indicates that the clause should be read as commenting, but it would be possible to omit the comma and read the clause as defining. Often, however, there is a sharp difference of meaning. You would be insulting all teenagers if you wrote:

Teenagers, who drive carelessly, should not be allowed to have a driving licence.

Here the commenting clause implies that all teenagers drive careless-ly. If there is any danger that people will misunderstand your defining clause as a commenting clause, it is safer to use *that* as your relative, since *that* occurs only with defining clauses.

There are some relative clauses that are best described neither as defining nor as commenting:

> It is the drug dealers that we need to prosecute.
> There are some other items that I wish to place on the agenda.

The sentences involve an emphatic re-arrangement of the normal patternings 'We need to prosecute the drug dealers' and 'I wish to place some other items on the agenda'. In these relative clauses *that* is always more natural than *who*, *whom*, or *which*, but it is often equally natural to leave out the relative.

That is an awkward word because it may be one of three parts of speech—a conjunction, a relative or demonstrative pronoun and an adjective. 'I think that the paper that he wants is in that box' illustrates the three in the order given.

It is a sound rule that *that* should be dispensed with whenever this can be done without loss of clarity or dignity. For instance, the sentence just given might be written with only one *that* instead of three: 'I think the paper he wants is in that box'. Some verbs seem to need a conjunctive *that* after them more than others do. *Say* and *think* can generally do without. The more formal words like *state* and *assert* cannot.

The conjunctive *that* often leads writers into error, especially in long sentences.

> It was agreed that, since suitable accommodation was now available in a convenient position, and that a move to larger offices was therefore feasible, Treasury sanction should be sought for acquiring them.

And here links with *since* and not with *that*. It would be possible, but unnecessary, to replace *that* by *since*.

> All removing residential subscribers are required to sign the special condition, that if called upon to share your line that you will do so.

The second *that* is another case of careless duplication.

> The Ministry allow such demonstrations only if the materials used are provided by the staff and that no food is sold to the public.

In this sentence the use of *that* for *if* is less excusable because the writer had less time to forget how he had begun.

Their intention was probably to remove from the mind of the native that he was in any way bound to work and that the Government would protect him from bad employers.

This example shows the need of care in sentences in which *that* has to be repeated. If you do not remember what words introduced the first *that*, you may easily find yourself, as here, saying the opposite of what you mean. What this writer meant to say was that the intention was to remove the first idea from the native's mind and to put the second into it, not, as he has accidentally said, to remove both.

(xvii) *Who* and *whom*.

Who is the subjective case and *whom* the objective. The proper use of the two words should present no difficulty. But we are so unaccustomed to different case-formations in English that when we are confronted with them we are liable to lose our heads. In the matter of *who* and *whom* good writers have for centuries been perverse in refusing to do what the grammarians tell them. They will insist on writing sentences like 'Who should I see there?' (Addison), 'Ferdinand whom they suppose is drowned' (Shakespeare), 'Whom say men that I am?' (translators of the Bible). Now it is obvious that, by the rules, *who* in the first quotation, being the object of *see*, ought to be *whom*, and that *whom* in the second and third quotations, being in the one the subject of *is*, and in the other the complement of *am*, ought to be *who*. What then is the average person to believe? There are some who would have us do away with *whom* altogether, as nothing but a mischief-maker. That might be a useful way out, but *whom* will take some killing. Shakespeare and the translators of the Bible have their followers today, not only among journalists but also among distinguished writers.

The problem is particularly acute when expressions such as *I know*, *we see*, or *they think* intervene and seem to capture *whom* as their object ('He was not the man whom the police think may be able to help them').

Sometimes, though more rarely, the opposite mistake is made:

A Chancellor who, grudging as was the acknowledgement he received for it, everyone knew to have saved his party.

It has not yet become pedantic—at any rate in writing—to use *who* and *whom* in what grammarians would call the correct way, and the

ordinary writer should so use them, ignoring the vagaries of the great.
You should be specially careful about such sentences as:

The manager should select those officers *who* he thinks will be ready for
promotion next year. ('He thinks that *they* will be ready.')
The manager should select those officers *whom* he wants to promote next
year. ('He wants to promote *them*.')
There has been some argument about *who* should be promoted next year.
('*They* should be promoted.')

Whoever baits a slightly different trap:

If the front door swings open for Mr Wilson it opens too for whomever else
can hang on to those charismatic coat-tails.

The writer has been misled by the preposition *for*, which is normally
followed by the objective case ('It opens for them'). But here *for*
introduces a clause, and the subject of that clause should be *whoever*,
not *whomever*. There is no doubt that *whomever else* is wrong here. It is
equivalent to *anyone else who*, and *whoever* is necessary.

(xviii) *Whose*.

There used to be a grammarians' rule that *whose* must not be used
of inanimate objects: we may say 'authors whose books are famous',
but we must not say 'books whose authors are famous'; we must fall
back on an ugly roundabout way of putting it, and say 'books the
authors of which are famous'. This rule, even more than that which
forbids the split infinitive, is a cramping one, productive of ugly
sentences and a temptation to misplaced commas.

There are now a large number of direct controls, the purpose of which is to
allocate scarce resources of all kinds between the various applicants for their
use.

Here the writer, having duly respected the prejudice against the
inanimate *whose*, finds that *controls the purpose* is an awkward
juxtaposition, with its momentary flicker of a suggestion that *controls*
is a verb governing *purpose*.* So he separates them by a comma,

---

* Care should be taken to avoid the 'false scent' that comes from grouping words in a
way that suggests a different construction from the one intended, however fleeting the
suggestion may be. In the sentence:
'Behind each part of the story I shall tell lies an untold and often unsuspected story
of hard work . . .'
the words 'I shall tell lies' irresistibly group themselves together until the eye has passed

although the relative clause is a 'defining' one (see pp. 158–9), and the comma therefore misleading. In his effort to avoid one ambiguity he has created another. But sensible writers have always ignored the rule, and sensible grammarians have now abandoned it. You may use *whose* of an inanimate object without any feeling of guilt, as in:

The hospital whose characteristics and associations link it with a particular religious denomination . . .

That revolution the full force of whose effects we are beginning to feel . . .

There has been built up a single centrally organised blood-transfusion service whose object is . . .

---

on. Never try to correct this sort of thing with a comma; always reconstruct. Consider also the mask of the bizarre behind in a sentence quoted by Walter Salant in the *Journal of Political Economy*:

. . . there is more to California than the mask of the bizarre behind which the state hides.

12

The handling of words: troubles with verbs

(i) Singular or plural verb.

The rule that a singular subject requires a singular verb, and a plural subject a plural verb, is an easy one to remember and generally to observe. But the rule has its difficulties. (See also pp. 187–8.)

(*a*) Collective words.

In using collective words or nouns of multitude (*Department, Parliament, Government, Committee* and the like), should we say 'the Government have decided' or 'the Government has decided'; 'the Committee are meeting' or 'the Committee is meeting'? There is no rule; either a singular or a plural verb may be used. The plural is more suitable when the emphasis is on the individual members, and the singular when it is on the body as a whole. 'A committee *was* appointed to consider this subject'; 'the committee *were* unable to agree'. Sometimes the need to use a pronoun settles the question. We cannot say 'The committee leaves its hats in the hall', nor, without risk of misunderstanding, 'The committee were smaller when I sat on them'. But the number ought not to be varied in the same document without good cause. Accidentally changing it is a common form of carelessness:

The firm *has* given an undertaking that in the event of *their* having to restrict production . . .

The industry *is* capable of supplying all home requirements and *have* in fact been exporting.

Any representative body must retain the right to represent *their* fellows as *it* thinks right.

The Corporation *has* not asked for any advice . . . and I do not doubt *its* ability to deal with the immediate situation *themselves*.

Conversely a subject plural in form may be given a singular verb if it signifies a single entity such as a country (the United States has agreed) or an organisation (the United Nations has resolved) or a measure (six miles is not too far; twelve months is a long time to wait).

(*b*) Words linked by *and*.

To the elementary rule that two singular nouns linked by *and* should be given a plural verb, justifiable exceptions can be found where the linked words form a single idea. The stock example is Kipling's 'The tumult and the shouting dies'; 'the tumult and the shouting', it is explained, are equivalent to 'the tumultuous shouting'. But *die* would not have rhymed with *sacrifice*. Rhyming poets must be allowed some licence.

It is safer to observe the rule, and not to use the singular verb except where the linked words are so closely associated that they might almost be hyphened. 'Cut and thrust is the essence of good debating' is unobjectionable. Sometimes the singular verb is needed for clarity. 'Bread and butter is good for you' does not mean quite the same as 'Bread and butter are good for you'.

Other instances of singular verbs with subjects linked by *and* cannot be so easily explained away. They are frequent when the verb comes first. Shakespeare has them ('Is Bushy, Green and the Earl of Wiltshire dead?') and so have the translators of the Bible ('Thine is the kingdom, the power and the glory'). If we may never attribute mere carelessness to great writers, we must explain these by saying that the singular verb is more vivid, and should be understood as repeated with each noun—'Is Bushy, (is) Green and (is) the Earl of Wiltshire dead?' Those who like to have everything tidy may get some satisfaction from this, but writers of official English should forget about these refinements. They should stick to the simple rule. Its unjustified breach is exemplified in successive paragraphs of an important White Paper (*The Reorganisation of Central Government*, 1970, Cmnd. 4506):

> Public administration and management in central government has stood up to these strains.
>
> The systematic formulation of policy and the presentation to Ministers of defined options for decision provides them with the opportunity for . . .

And when Mr Anthony Grey was nominated for a National Press Award as 'Journalist of the Year' one would not expect the formal citation to say that

> his refusal to submit to sustained pressures on mind and spirit were worthy of the highest traditions of journalism.

The rule does not apply when the part introduced by *and* is parenthetic and the main subject is singular. A singular verb is then required:

The Prime Minister—and perhaps her husband too—is likely to attend the function.

The chairman of the company, and not the other directors, is attending the meeting.

But if it is convenient to do so, it may be better to rearrange the sentence to avoid the awkwardness of the parenthesis in this position: 'The Prime Minister is likely to attend the function, and perhaps her husband too'; 'The chairman of the company is attending the meeting, and not the other directors'.

It is curious that we have to choose a singular verb when singular nouns linked by *and* are accompanied by *each* or *every*:

Every school and college was closed that day.
Each boy and each girl has been given a medical examination.

It seems that *each* and *every* focus on the singularity of the nouns.

(*c*) Words linked by *with*.

If the subject is singular the verb should be singular. 'The Secretary of State together with the Under-Secretary is coming.' The same applies when other prepositions link a singular subject to another noun; for example *as well as* and *in addition to*.

(*d*) Alternative subjects.

Either and *neither* must always have a singular verb unless one of the alternative subjects is a plural word. It is a very common error to write such sentences as:

I am unable to trace that either of the items have been paid.
Neither knowledge nor skill are needed.

If one of the alternative subjects is a plural word and the other is a singular word, it is best to choose the number of the verb by whichever word is nearer to the verb:

Neither my letters nor my report on the case is in the file.
Neither my report on the case nor my letters are in the file.

You may apply the same principle when the alternative subjects differ in person:

Neither you nor anyone else from the Department has been invited.
Either the manager or I have to sign the letter.

But this or any other choice may jar, and it is safer to rephrase the sentence if you can do so: 'Neither you have been invited, nor anyone else from the Department'; 'Either the manager or I should sign the letter'.

(*e*) *Either or both.*

Phrases like *either or both* cause difficulty. *Either* needs a singular verb and *both* a plural one. But it would be absurd to write 'unless either or both of his parents is or are dead'; and still more so to write 'When either or both of his parents is or are away, he writes daily to him or her or them, as the case may be'. Unless the difficulty can be conveniently avoided by rearranging the sentence, it is best to let the matter be settled by whichever word is nearer to the verb, and write 'If either or both are dead' and 'Is either or both dead?'

(*f*) *Each.*

When *each* is the subject of a sentence the verb is singular and so is any pronoun:

Each has a room to himself.

When a plural noun or pronoun is the subject, with *each* in apposition, the verb is plural.

They have a room each.

(*g*) Attraction.

The verb must agree with the subject, and not allow itself to be attracted into the number of the complement. Modern grammarians will not pass 'the wages of sin is death'. The safe rule for the ordinary writer in sentences such as this is to regard what precedes the verb as the subject and what follows it as the complement, and so to write 'the wages of sin are death' and 'death is the wages of sin'.

A verb some way from its subject is sometimes lured away from its proper number by a noun closer to it, as in:

We regret that assurances given us twelve months ago that a sufficient supply of suitable local labour would be available to meet our requirements *has* not been fulfilled. (The main subject is *assurances*.)

So far as the heating of buildings in permanent Government occupation *are* concerned. . . . (The main subject is *heating*.)

Comprehensive information about the work of the Ministry examiners and the results *are* already published by HMSO in the annual reports of the licensing authorities. (The main subject is *information*.)

Sometimes the weight of a plural pushes the verb into the wrong number, even though they are not next to one another:

Thousands of pounds' worth of damage *have* been done to the apple crop.

In these sentences the italicised words are blunders. So is the common attraction of the verb into the plural when the subject is *either* or *neither* in such sentences as 'Neither of the questions have been answered' or 'Either of the questions were embarrassing'. But in one or two exceptional instances the force of this attraction has conquered the grammarians. With the phrase *more than one* the pull of *one* is so strong that the singular is always used (e.g. 'more than one question was asked'), and owing to the pull of the plural in such a sentence as 'none of the questions were answered' *none* has come to be used indifferently with a singular or a plural verb. Conversely, owing to the pull of the singular *a* in the expression *many a*, it always takes a singular verb. 'There's many a slip twixt cup and lip' is idiomatic English. In *a great many, a good many, a few, a good few,* and similar expressions, the *a* has not prevailed; they require a plural verb ('a few win, a great many lose'). See Number, p. 133.

Other plural phrases of quantity are also introduced by *a* or *another*: 'a happy five years', 'a surprising 253 votes', 'another three days', 'another ten miles'. These phrases and other plural phrases of quantity are often treated as singular when they are considered as single entities: 'A happy five years is as much as you can expect', 'Another three days is all that I can manage', 'Ten pounds is all that we have left', 'Twenty years represents a generation'. Other contexts require a plural verb: 'A surprising 253 votes were cast for the independent candidate', 'Another three days have passed'. If we say 'Ten pounds are all that we have left' we seem to refer to the individual pound coins rather than to the total amount.

(*h*) *There is, there was.*

It is a common slip to write *there is* or *there was* where a plural subject requires *there are* or *there were*.

There was available one large room and three small ones.

Was should be *were*.

It is true that Ophelia said 'there is pansies'. But she was not herself at the time.

(*i*) Nouns that pose a problem.

Agenda, though in form plural, has been admitted to the language as a singular word. Nobody would say 'the agenda for Monday's meeting *have* not yet reached me'. If a word is needed for one of the components of the agenda, say 'item No. so-and-so of the agenda', not 'agendum No. so-and-so', which would be the extreme of pedantry. If one is wanted for the plural of the word itself it must be *agendas* or *agenda papers*.

Data, like *agenda*, remains the plural word that it is in Latin.

> Unless firm data is available at an early date . . .
> Data that is four to twelve years old is of limited use.

These are wrong. *Is* should be *are*.

If a singular is wanted, it is usually *one of the data*, not *datum*. The ordinary meaning of *datum* is:

> Any position or element in relation to which others are determined: chiefly in the phrases: *datum point*, a point assumed or used as a basis of reckoning, adjustment or the like—*datum line*, a horizontal line from which heights and depths of points are reckoned, as in a railroad plan . . . (Webster.)

The press is a medium of mass communication; so is radio; so is television. They are often collectively called 'the media'. The singular *medium*, unlike *agendum*, is in constant and unpedantic use; its plural can only be *media*, and *media* can only be plural.

Criteria is always plural. Its singular is *criterion*. Some people wrongly treat *criteria* as singular and compound the error by forming the new plural *criterias*.

Phenomena has been subjected to the same mishandling as *criteria*. *Phenomena* is plural and its singular is *phenomenon*. It is wrong to treat *phenomena* as singular or to make the plural *phenomenas*.

Means in the sense of 'means to an end' is a curious word; it may be treated either as singular or as plural. Supposing, for instance, that you wanted to say that means had been sought to do something, you may if you choose treat the word as singular and say 'a means was sought' or 'every means was sought'. Or you may treat it as plural and say 'all means were sought'. Or again, if you use just the word *means* without any word such as *a* or *every* or *all* to show its number, you may give it a singular or plural verb as you wish: you may say either 'means was sought' or 'means were sought'; both are idiomatic.

Perhaps on the whole it is best to say 'a method (or way) was sought' if there was only one, and 'means were sought' if there was more than one.

Means in the sense of monetary resources is always plural.

Number. Like other collective nouns, *number* may take either a singular or a plural verb. Unlike most of them, it admits of a simple and logical rule. When all that it is doing is forming part of a composite plural subject, it should have a plural verb, as in:

A large number of people are coming today.

But when it is standing on its own legs as the subject, it should have a singular verb, as in:

The number of people coming today is large.

The following are accordingly unidiomatic:

There is a number of applications, some of which were made before yours.
There is a large number of outstanding orders.

The true subjects are not 'a number' and 'a large number' but 'a-number-of-applications' and 'a-large-number-of-outstanding-orders', and both these subjects require the plural verb *are*. Those who find these distinctions difficult to observe have an obvious way out of their difficulty—they should write *many* instead of *a large number of*. And even those to whom all is crystal-clear would often be well advised to do the same.

Of the following examples the first has a singular verb that should be plural and the second a plural verb that should be singular.

There was also a number of conferences calling themselves peace conferences which had no real interest in peace.
The number of casualties in this disaster are thought to be about five hundred.

Majority and *minority* are best treated as plural when they are part of a composite plural subject. In the following example the singular verb should be plural:

The majority of us has made proposals which will remove the present inconsistencies in the powers to arrest without warrant.

See also page 243.

Those kind of things. The use of the plural *these* or *those* with the singular *kind* or *sort* is common in conversation, and instances of it could be found in good authors. But it has not yet quite established itself as a permissible idiom in good writing, and until it does so it is as well to humour the purists by writing *things of that kind*.

(ii) *ing*-words.

Most words ending in *ing* have traditionally been called either present participles or gerunds. The two terms label these words in different uses. But the distinction is not always clear, and for our purpose the more general term is adequate.

Numerous pitfalls beset the use of *ing*-words. Here are some of them.

(*a*) Absolute construction.

This is, in itself, straightforward enough. The absolute construction, in the words of the *OED*, is a name given to a phrase 'standing out of grammatical relation or syntactical construction with other words'. In the sentence 'The chairman having restored order, the committee resumed', the phrase 'the chairman having restored order' forms an absolute construction.

But there is no absolute construction in the sentence 'The chairman, having restored order, called on the last speaker to continue'. Here *the chairman* is the subject of the sentence.

Because of a confusion with that type of sentence, it is a curiously common error to put a comma in the absolute construction. See Comma (iv), p. 159.

(*b*) Unattached (or unrelated) *ing*-word.

This blunder is rather like the last. A writer begins a sentence with an *ing*-word and then forgets to give it its noun, thus leaving it 'unattached'.

Arising out of a collision between a removal van and a fully loaded bus in a fog, E.C.F., removal van driver, appeared on a charge of manslaughter.

Grammatically in this sentence it was the van-driver, not the charge against him, that arose out of the collision. He probably did; but that is not what the writer meant.

While requesting you to furnish the return now outstanding, you are advised that in future it would greatly facilitate . . .

Requesting is unattached. If the structure of this rather clumsy sentence is to be retained it must run 'While requesting you . . . I advise you that . . .'.

Many letters to the press start with an unattached *ing*-word, like *disagreeing* in the following example:

Sir,

While not disagreeing with the authors of the *London and Cambridge Economic Bulletin*, present conditions require that emphasis be given for the need for direct Government action to restore profitability.

What the writer means is, 'I do not disagree with . . ., but what really needs emphasising in present conditions is the need for . . .'.

Some *ing*-words have won the right to be treated as prepositions. Among them are *regarding, considering, owing to, concerning, according to, including* and *failing*. When any of these is used as a preposition, there can be no question of its being unattached. There is nothing wrong with:

Considering the attack that had been made on him, his speech was moderate in tone.

If, however, *considering* were used not as a preposition, it could be unattached. It is so in:

Considering the attack on him beneath his notice, his speech was moderate in tone.

When purchasing a nominal amount of stock a signed transform with the amount left blank is preferred because the total stock cannot be known in advance.

As the sentence stands, a signed transform is said to be doing the purchasing. The sentence appeared in instructions accompanying an application for government stock. A more recent version corrects the error of the unattached *ing*-word and improves the sentence in other ways:

If you are buying a specific amount of stock, called 'nominal stock', please complete the cheque as usual but in this case leave the amount blank because the total cost cannot be known in advance.

The next example comes from a company booklet addressed to employees:

The Company will encourage a participative style and an open, trusting and collaborative relationship between supervisor and supervised by exchanging information regularly on a face-to-face basis.

Grammatically, 'by exchanging information' means that the Company will exchange information, but what seems to be intended is that the supervisor and supervised will do so. The sentence needs radical rephrasing to avoid the unattached *ing*-word and to remove other stylistic blemishes.

Past participles, which usually end in *ed*, may also become unattached:

Administered at first by the National Gallery, it was not until 1917 that the appointment of a separate board and director enabled a fully independent policy to be pursued.

The writer must have started with the intention of making the Tate Gallery (about which he was writing) the subject of the sentence but changed his mind, and so *administered* is left unattached.

Formal application is now being made for the necessary wayleave consent, and as soon as received the work will proceed.

Grammatically *received* can only be attached to work; and that is nonsense. The writer should have said 'as soon as this is received'.

Words other than verbs may be unattached:

Upon importation into the United Kingdom, an importer or his authorised agent is required to declare details of goods on a specified form.

It is not the importer or his authorised agent who is being imported into the United Kingdom. The writer should have said 'Upon importing goods into the United Kingdom'.

When out of work, the state requires you to register for unemployment benefit.

The state is not out of work. The sentence should read 'When you are out of work'.

Weak from their long ordeal, the rescuers carried the survivors to the waiting ambulances.

Weak is unattached. This sentence must run 'The rescuers carried the survivors, weak from their long ordeal, to the waiting ambulances'.

The sentence reads more smoothly if the phrase is turned into a subordinate clause ('since they were weak from their long ordeal') and the clause is put at the end.

The use of unattached *ing*-words and the like is becoming so common that grammarians may soon have to throw in their hand and recognise it as idiomatic. But they have not done so yet; so it should be avoided.

(*c*) *ing*-word versus infinitive.

In what seems to be a completely arbitrary way, some nouns, adjectives and verbs like to take an infinitive, and some an *ing*-word with a preposition. For instance:

Aim at doing	Try to do
Dislike of doing	Reluctance to do
Capable of doing	Able to do
Shrink from doing	Hesitate to do
Prohibit from doing	Forbid to do

Instances could be multiplied indefinitely. There is no rule; it can only be a matter of observation and consulting a dictionary when in doubt.

Some verbs permit either an *ing*-word or an infinitive. For instance:

Try doing	Try to do
Like doing	Like to do
Prefer doing	Prefer to do
Continue doing	Continue to do
Intend doing	Intend to do
Can afford doing	Can afford to do

There is sometimes a difference in meaning. 'They tried to withhold the information from the public' is not the same as 'They tried withholding the information from the public'.

(*d*) Possessive with *ing*-word.

All authorities agree that it is idiomatic English to write 'the *Bill's* getting a second reading surprised everyone'; that is to say, it is correct for *Bill's* to be in the possessive. What they are not agreed about is whether it is also correct to write 'the *Bill* getting a second reading surprised everyone'. If that is a legitimate grammatical construction, the subject of the sentence, which cannot be *Bill* by itself, or *getting* by itself, must be a fusion of the two.

Sometimes we feel one construction to be the more idiomatic, and sometimes the other. Proper names and personal pronouns seem to demand the possessive, particularly when the construction is the subject of the sentence. Nobody would prefer 'He coming (or Smith coming) surprised me' to 'His coming (or Smith's coming) surprised me'. That is sure ground.

For the rest, it is always possible, and generally wise, to be on the safe side by turning the sentence round, and writing neither 'the Bill getting, etc.' (which offends some purists) nor 'the Bill's getting, etc.' (which sounds odd to some ears) but 'everyone was surprised that the Bill got a second reading'.

(iii) Subjunctive.

The subjunctive is the mood of imagination or command. Apart from the verb *to be*, it has no form separate from the indicative, except in the third person singular of the present tense, where the subjunctive form is the same as the indicative plural (*he have*, not *he has*; *he go*, not *he goes*). Generally therefore, in sentences in which the subjunctive might be fitting, neither the writer nor the reader need know or care whether the subjunctive is being used or not.

But the verb *to be* spoils this simple picture. The whole of the present tense is different, for the subjunctive mood is *be* throughout— *I be, he be, we be, you be* and *they be*. The singular (but not the plural) of the past tense is also different—*I were* and *he were* instead of *I was* and *he was*. In the subjunctive mood what looks like the past tense does not denote pastness; it denotes a greater call on the imagination. Thus:

'If he is here' implies that it is as likely as not that he is.
'If he be here' is an archaic way of saying 'if he is here'.
'If he were here' implies that he is not.

Thirty years ago one would have said that the subjunctive was dying, being superseded more and more by the indicative, and that its only remaining regular uses were:

(*a*) In certain stock phrases: 'Be it so', 'God bless you', 'come what may', 'if need be' and others.

(*b*) In legal or formal language: 'I move that Mr Smith be appointed Secretary', 'I suggest that Mrs Jones lead the delegation'.

(*c*) In conditional sentences where the hypothesis is not a fact:

Were this true, it would be a serious matter.
If he were here I would tell him what I think of him.

(*d*) With *as if* and *as though*, if the hypothesis is not accepted as
true, thus:

He spoke of his proposal as if it were a complete solution of the difficulty.

In America usage (*b*) has never been confined to formal language; it
is usual in such sentences as 'I ask that he be sent for', 'It is important
that he be there', and even in the negative form 'he insisted that the
statement not be placed on record'; in all these the custom in this
country is to insert a *should*.

It is remarkable—for it seems contrary to the whole history of the
development of the language—that under the influence of American
English the use of the subjunctive is creeping back into British
English. The following examples from British writing are thirty years
old:

No one would suggest that a unique, and in the main supremely valuable,
work be halted.
Public opinion demands that an inquiry be held.
He is anxious that the truth be known.

The subjunctive is now even more common in sentences like these,
but it is still felt to give an air of formality. Except in legal or formal
language, you should prefer *should* to the subjunctive.

The past subjunctive *were* is less common, but many writers still
feel it to be the only correct form. Be careful to use this subjunctive
only where you view the situation as unlikely or where you rule it out:

If I were elected to the committee, I will support your proposals.

Here the subjunctive *were* conflicts with *will*. If the election is viewed
as quite possible, you should say 'If I am elected'. On the other hand,
if it is viewed as unlikely you should say 'I would support your
proposals'. The same error results from combining *will* with the past
indicative *was* ('If I was elected to the committee, I will support your
proposals'), but this error is perhaps less likely to occur.

(iv) Misuse of the passive.

Grammarians condemn such constructions as the following, which
indeed condemn themselves by their contorted ugliness:

The report that is proposed to be made.
Several amendments were endeavoured to be inserted.
A question was threatened to be put on the paper.
A sensational atmosphere is attempted to be created.

Anyone who finds that he has written a sentence like this should recast it, e.g. 'the proposed report', 'attempts were made to insert several amendments', 'a threat was made to put a question on the paper', 'an attempt is being made to create a sensational atmosphere'. 'Motion made: that the words proposed to be left out stand part of the question' is an ancient and respectable Parliamentary formula, but should not be allowed to infect ordinary writing. Even the House of Commons has now abandoned it in favour of 'that the amendment be made'—though on grounds of convenience rather than grammar.

Hope should not be used in the passive except in the impersonal phrase *it is hoped*. We may say 'It is hoped that payment will be made next week', or 'payment is expected to be made next week', but not 'payment is hoped to be made next week'. The phrasal verb *hope for*, being transitive, can of course be used in the passive.

Overuse of the passive may render a sentence impenetrable. This monstrosity appeared in a list of parking offences:

The vehicle was left in a parking place without payment of the charge indicated by a parking token duly affixed to a valid permit/parking card displayed on the vehicle/by the display on the vehicle of a valid season ticket/daily ticket.

The symbols for alternatives contribute their share to the complexity of the sentence. The unfortunate driver who finds this notice on his car may well be intimidated into pleading guilty. We might rewrite the sentence in plain words:

You left the vehicle in a parking place and did not show that you had paid the charge by displaying on the vehicle either a parking token fixed to a valid permit or parking card, or a valid season ticket or daily ticket.

(v) Omission or duplication of verb.

Where a verb is used with more than one auxiliary (e.g. 'he must and shall go') make sure that the main verb is repeated unless, as in this example, its form is the same. It is easy to slip into such a sentence as:

The steps which those responsible can and are at present taking to remedy this state of affairs.

Can taking makes no sense. The proper construction is shown in:

The board must take, and are in fact taking, all possible steps to maintain production.

The opposite fault is that of duplicating either the future or the past.

The most probable thing will be that they will be sold in a Government auction.

This should be 'The most probable thing is that they will be'.

The Minister said he would have liked the Government of Eire to have offered us butter instead of cream.

This should be 'he would have liked the Government of Eire to offer . . .'.

(vi) *Shall* and *will*.

English text-books used to begin by stating the rule that to express the 'plain' future *shall* is used in the first person and *will* in the second and third:

I shall go
You will go
He will go

and that if it is a matter not of plain future but of volition, permission or obligation it is the other way round:

I will go (I am determined to go, or I intend to go)
You shall go (You must go, or you are permitted to go)
He shall go (He must go, or he is permitted to go)

But the idiom of the Celts is different. They have never recognised 'I shall go'. For them 'I will go' is the plain future. The story is a very old one of the drowning Scot who was misunderstood by English onlookers and left to his fate because he cried, 'I will drown and nobody shall save me'.

American practice follows the Celtic, and in this matter, as in so many others, the English have taken to imitating the American. If we go by practice rather than by precept, we can no longer say dogmatically that 'I will go' for the plain future is wrong, or smugly with Dean Alford:

> I never knew an Englishman who misplaced *shall* and *will*; I hardly ever have known an Irishman or Scotsman who did not misplace them sometimes.

The Irish and the Scots are having their revenge for our bland assumption that English usage must be 'right' and theirs 'wrong'.

In England *shall* continues to express the plain future for the first person, though it is frequently replaced by *will* or other verbs. *Shall* is also used for the first person for other meanings, particularly in questions:

> Shall I send you both forms?
> What shall we tell them?

In the first sentence, *will* cannot replace *shall*, which expresses something like obligation. We might say for the first sentence 'Should I send you both forms?' or 'Would you like me to send you both forms?', and similar substitutes are possible for the second sentence.

Official writers who are accustomed to using *shall* in the first person should follow the traditional usage in their formal writing. Others need not feel guilty if they fail to do so.

Shall is still normal with the third person in legal or quasi-legal language to stipulate regulations or legal requirements:

> The Underwriters shall in no case be bound to accept notice of any transfer of interest.
>
> Every contract made by the Council which is estimated to exceed £15,000 in value or amount shall comply with these Standing Orders.

Otherwise, the use of *shall* with the second or third person is old-fashioned:

> You shall write exactly as I have set out in my last letter to you.
> She shall receive her pension as soon as she has reached the age of 60.

In the first sentence, *must* would now be normal. In the second, *will* is possible, although perhaps a nearer equivalent is 'I shall arrange for her to receive her pension'.

(vii) *Would* and *should*.

The various shades of meaning of *would* and *should* derive in the main from the primary ideas of resolve in *will* and of obligation in *shall*: ideas illustrated in their simplest form by 'he would go' (he was determined to go, or he made a habit of going) and 'he should go' (he ought to go).

Should and *would* may be colourless auxiliaries, merely accompanying a hypothesis that is not accepted as true. For this use the textbooks once prescribed *should* in the first person and *would* in the second and third. *Should* resumes its tinge of *ought* in the second and third persons: in 'If you tried you should succeed' it has a nuance not present in 'If I tried I should succeed'. But the rule requiring *should* in the first person is now largely ignored (compare *shall* and *will*); *would* and *should* are used indifferently. Even a Professor of Poetry could use them for what seems to be merely elegant variation:

> If we could plot each individual poet's development, we would get a different pattern with each and we would see the pattern changing. . . . We should notice Mr Auden, for example, breaking suddenly away from the influence of Thomas Hardy. . . .

In such a phrase as 'In reply to your letter of . . . I would inform you . . .' *would* is not a mere auxiliary expressing the conditional mood; it retains the now archaic meaning of 'I should like to'. In general, however, avoid using this expression on the ground that, since it is archaic, it cannot help being stiff.

'It would appear' and 'I should think' are less dogmatic, and therefore more polite, ways of saying 'it appears' and 'I think'.

(viii) Split infinitive.

The grammarians' well-known rule against splitting an infinitive means that nothing must come between *to* and the infinitive. It is a bad name because we have many infinitives without *to*, as in 'We helped him start the car', 'I let them go', 'I made her apologise'. Since *to* is not an essential part of the infinitive, broadminded grammarians see no grammatical reason for the rule.

It is also a bad rule, which many people (including good writers) reject. It increases the difficulty of writing clearly and makes for ambiguity by inducing writers to place adverbs in unnatural and even misleading positions.

Some of the stones . . . must have been of such a size that they failed completely to melt before they reached the ground.

Did the hailstones reach the ground completely frozen or incompletely melted? The second is probably what the writer meant, and he probably committed the ambiguity because he was scared of the split infinitive (*failed to completely melt*). In this example, however, he could have avoided the ambiguity if he had expressed the second meaning by *failed to melt completely* and the first by *completely failed to melt*.

It is right therefore to record our view that the time we were given was sufficient to allow us properly to consider the issues raised by our terms of reference.

Here fear of the split infinitive (*allow us to properly consider*) has persuaded the writer to put *properly* in an unnatural position before *to consider*. When it comes before the verb, the adverb *properly* generally has a different meaning from the one that this writer presumably intended: 'We properly considered all the issues' (We did the right thing in doing so) is not the same as 'We considered all the issues properly' (in a proper manner). Both the possible alternative positions for *properly* are also awkward. If we put it after *consider*, it interrupts between the verb and the direct object; if we put it at the end of the sentence, it is too far from the verb. To escape the problem of the split infinitive, we would need to abandon the infinitive: '. . . the time we were given was sufficient for proper consideration of the issues raised by our terms of reference'. We have at the same time improved the sentence by omitting the redundant *to allow us*.

The split infinitive taboo, leading as it does to the putting of adverbs in awkward places, is so potent that it produces an impulse to put them there even though there is not really any question of avoiding a split infinitive. The infinitive can be split only by inserting something between *to* and the infinitive. *To really understand* is a split infinitive, and so is *to really have understood*. But *to have really understood* is not, because the adverb *really* comes between the infinitive *have* and the main verb *understood*. The writer of the sentence 'They appeared completely to have adjusted themselves to it' almost certainly put the adverb in that uncomfortable position because he thought that to write 'to have completely adjusted' would be to split an infinitive. The same fear may also be presumed to account for the unnatural placing of the adverb in 'so tangled is the web that I cannot pretend for a moment that we have succeeded entirely in unweaving it', though there is no infinitive here. But the split infinitive taboo leads some people to think it wrong to put an adverb between any auxiliary and any part of a verb ('should really understand'), or between any preposition and any part of a verb ('by really understanding'), even where there is no infinitive in the sentence.

Opposition to the split infinitive remains powerful. It is therefore wiser to avoid splitting your infinitives. There is nearly always an easy and natural way of doing so.

Even the most vigorous rebel against the taboo could hardly condone such a crescendo of splitting as this:

The tenant hereby agrees:
  (i)   to pay the said rent;
 (ii)   to properly clean all the windows;
(iii)   to at all times properly empty all closets;
(iv)   to immediately any litter or disorder shall have been made by him or for his purpose on the staircase or landings or any other part of the said building or garden remove the same.

13

The handling of words: troubles with negatives and other matters

(i) Double negatives.

It has long been settled doctrine among English grammarians that two negatives cancel each other and produce an affirmative. As in mathematics $-(- x)$ equals $+ x$, so in language 'he did not say nothing' must be regarded as equivalent to 'he said something'.

It is going too far to say, as is sometimes said, that this proposition is self-evident. The ancient Greeks did not think that two negatives made an affirmative. Nor do the modern French. Nor did Chaucer think so when he wrote:

> He never yit no vileineye ne sayde
> In al his lyf, unto no maner wight.
> He was a verray parfit gentil knyght.

Nor did Shakespeare, who made King Claudius say of Hamlet:

> Nor what he said, though it lacked form a little,
> Was not like madness.

Nor do the many thousands of people who find it natural today to deny knowledge by saying 'I don't know nothing at all about it'.

In all these examples the two or more negatives combine to make a forceful negative.

Still, the grammarians' rule should be observed in English today. This extract from a formal memorandum to a Select Committee of the House of Commons must be condemned as illiterate:

> The time is not being used neither adequately nor efficiently.

Breaches of the rule are commonest with verbs of surprise or speculation ('I shouldn't wonder if there wasn't a storm'; 'I shouldn't be surprised if he didn't come today'). Indeed this is so common that it is classed by Fowler among his 'sturdy indefensibles'. A speech in the House of Lords affords a typical instance of the confusion of thought bred by double negatives:

Let it not be supposed because we are building for the future rather than the present that the Bill's proposals are not devoid of significance.

What the speaker meant, of course, was 'Let it not be supposed that the Bill's proposals *are* devoid of significance'.

Another example is:

There is no reason to doubt that what he says in his statement . . . is not true.

Here the speaker meant, 'There is no reason to doubt that his statement *is* true'.

Avoid multiple negatives when you can. Even if you dodge the traps they set and succeed in saying what you mean, you give your reader a puzzle to solve in sorting the negatives out. Indeed it is wise never to make a statement negatively if it could be made positively.

The elementary ideas of the calculus are not beyond the capacity of more than 40 per cent of our fifth-year students.

It is hard to say whether this asserts that two-fifths or three-fifths of the class could make something of the ideas. If the writer had said that the ideas were within the capacity of at least sixty per cent, all would have been clear.

The reader has good reason to be offended at the obscurity of this sentence:

The Government does not accept that the higher direction of naval ship procurement is not seized of the fact that time is money.

Here there are other faults apart from the double negative that force the reader to work at disentangling the meaning.

In the next example the writer has ended by saying the opposite of what he intended:

Anyone with even a superficial knowledge of railways can hardly fail to be unaware of the constant negotiations between . . .

We would uncover his intention if we replaced 'can hardly fail to be unaware', by 'can hardly fail to be aware', or by 'can hardly be unaware', or (clearest of all) by 'must surely be aware'.

It is usually easy to avoid multiple negatives. This instruction appears on a form:

Do not delay returning this form because you do not know your National Insurance number.

Members of the public would be more likely to follow the instruction if it went like this:

> Send this form back at once even if you do not know your National Insurance number.

(ii) *Neither . . . nor.*

Some books tell you that *neither . . . nor* should not be used where the alternatives are more than two. That is, you may write 'Neither blue nor red' but must not write 'Neither blue nor red nor yellow'. This is untenable. The famous passage

> . . . neither death, nor life, nor angels, nor principalities, nor powers, nor things present, nor things to come, nor height, nor depth, nor any other creature, shall be able to separate us from the love of God . . .

is as good English today as it was three hundred years ago.

(iii) *Nor* and *Or.*

When should *nor* be used and when *or*? If a *neither* or an *either* comes first there is no difficulty; *neither* is always followed by *nor* and *either* by *or*. There can be no doubt that it is wrong to write 'The existing position satisfies neither the psychologist, the judge, or the public'. It should have been 'neither the psychologist, nor the judge, nor the public'. But when the initial negative is a simple *not* or *no*, it is often a puzzling question whether *nor* or *or* should follow. Logically it depends on whether the sentence is so framed that the initial negative runs on into the second part of it or is exhausted in the first; practically it may be of little importance which answer you give, for the meaning will be clear.

> He did not think that the Bill would be introduced this month, nor indeed before the recess.

'He did not think' affects everything that follows *that*. Logically therefore *nor* produces a double negative, as though one were to say 'he didn't think it wouldn't be introduced before the recess'.

> The blame for this disorder does not rest with Parliament, or with the bishops, or with the parish priests. Our real weakness is the failure of the ordinary man.

Here the negative phrase 'does not rest' is carried right through the sentence, and applies to the bishops and the parish priests as much as to Parliament. There is no need to repeat the negative, and *or* is logically right. But *nor* is so often used in such a construction that it would be pedantic to condemn it: if logical defence is needed one might say that 'did he think it would be introduced' in the first example, and 'does it rest' in the second were understood as repeated after *nor*. But if the framework of the sentence is changed to

The blame for this disorder rests not with Parliament, nor with the bishops, nor with the parish priests, but with the ordinary man,

it is a positive verb (*rests*) that runs through the sentence; the original negative (*not*) is attached not to the verb but to *Parliament*, and exhausts itself in exonerating Parliament. The negative must be repeated, and *nor* is rightly used.

(iv) *And* and *But*.
Similar difficulties may occur with *and* or *but*:

He blamed the police because they did not attempt to establish good relations with the community and learned how to control crowds firmly but fairly.

Here the negative does not reach into the second part of the sentence, although the writer obviously intends it to do so. There are two ways of carrying the negative over, and they differ somewhat in meaning. We might change *learned* to *learn*, and then 'did not attempt to' is understood as repeated after *and*. Or we might repeat the negative by beginning the second part 'and did not learn'.

It is possible to make the reverse mistake. You may unintentionally carry over the negative to the second part of the sentence:

They must not be allowed to brush aside the concerns of ordinary people but tackle the problems of crime and unemployment.

As the sentence stands, 'must not be allowed to' is understood as repeated after *but*. We may make the second part positive by adding *must* after *but*:

They must not be allowed to brush aside the concerns of ordinary people but must tackle the problems of crime and unemployment.

In the next example the two parts are not explicitly linked by *but*:

The New Ulster Movement may be non-sectarian: it is playing straight into the hands of those who are.

As the sentence stands, the end must mean 'those who are

non-sectarian', but it was intended to mean 'those who are sectarian'. To extract that meaning, we must rewrite the first part 'may not be sectarian'.

In selection procedures little weight was attached to good manners. Why on earth not?

Here again the writer has said the opposite of what he meant. The first part should read 'not much weight'.

(v) *Not.*

(*a*) *Not all.*

It is idiomatic English, to which no exception can be taken, to write 'all officials are not good draftsmen' when you mean that only some of them are. Compare 'All that glisters is not gold'. But some people might understand the sentence to mean that none of the officials are good draftsmen. It is therefore clearer to write 'Not all officials are good draftsmen', if that is what you mean. Similarly, write 'Not every member of the committee was present' rather than the ambiguous 'Every member of the committee was not present'.

(*b*) *Not . . . but.*

It is also idiomatic English to write 'I did not go to speak but to listen'. It is pedantry to insist that, because logic demands it, this ought to be 'I went not to speak but to listen'. But if the latter way of arranging a 'not . . . but' sentence runs as easily and makes your meaning clearer, as it often may, it should be preferred.

(*c*) *Not . . . because.*

Not followed by *because* sometimes leads to ambiguity. 'I did not write that letter because of what you told me' may mean either 'I refrained from writing that letter because of what you told me' or 'It was not because of what you told me that I wrote that letter'. Avoid this ambiguity by rewriting the sentence. You can conveniently present the first meaning unambiguously by rearranging the order of the sentence: 'Because of what you told me, I did not write the letter'. The difference is usually clear in speech, since we can easily convey through intonation what we intend *not* to include.

(vi) *Qualification of absolutes.*

Certain adjectives and adverbs cannot properly be qualified by such words as *more, less, very, rather*, because they do not admit of degrees. *Unique* is the outstanding example. When we say a thing is *unique* we mean that there is nothing else of its kind in existence; *rather unique* is meaningless. But we can of course say *almost unique*.

It is easy to slip into pedantry here, and to condemn the qualification of words which are perhaps strictly absolutes but are no longer so treated—*true*, for instance, and *empty* and *full*. We ought not to shrink from saying 'very true', or 'the hall was even emptier today than yesterday' or 'this cupboard is fuller than that'. But this latitude must not be abused. It is strained when an official circular defines 'draining a bulk tank' as 'removing the liquid contents that remain after emptying'; it is certainly carried too far in this quotation:

It may safely be said that the design of sanitary fittings has now reached a high degree of perfection.

We should not condone the expression *more or less wholly*. And the comparative does not seem a happy choice in *more virgin*, which has been seen in an advertisement.

(vii) Repetition.

Pronouns were invented to avoid the necessity of repeating nouns. The chapter on Pronouns (pp. 111–26) deals with this subject, and also with the device known as 'the polite alias' or 'elegant variation'.

Unnecessary repetition of a word is irritating to a reader. If it can be avoided in a natural way it should. For instance, in the sentence 'The Minister has considered this application, and considers that there should be a market in Canada', the repetition of 'consider' gives the sentence a clumsy and careless air. The second one might just as well have been 'thinks'. It would have been easy also to avoid the ugly repetition of *essential* in the sentence 'It is essential that the Minister should have before him outline programmes of essential works'; or of *further* in the sentence 'Meanwhile I do not think there is anything further we can do to further the project at this stage'. But where the same thing or act is repeatedly mentioned, it is better to repeat a word than to avoid it in a laboured and obvious way.

Irritating repetition of a sound (assonance) is usually mere carelessness.

The controversy as to which agency should perform the actual contractual work of erection of houses . . .

Reverting to the subject of the letter, the latter wrote . . . (This is indefensible because it could so easily be avoided by calling 'the latter' by name.)

Since a certain amount of uncertainty still appears to exist . . .

14
Punctuation

That learned men are well known to disagree on this subject of punctuation is in itself a proof, that the knowledge of it, in theory and practice, is of some importance. I myself have learned by experience, that, if ideas that are difficult to understand are properly separated, they become clearer; and that, on the other hand, through defective punctuation, many passages are confused and distorted to such a degree, that sometimes they can with difficulty be understood, or even cannot be understood at all.

Aldus Manutius, *Interpungendi ratio*, 1466. From the translation in
Punctuation, its Principles and Practice by T. F. and M. F. A. Husband,
Routledge, 1905.

This is a large subject. Whole books have been written about it, and it is still true, as it apparently was 500 years ago, that no two authorities completely agree. Taste and common sense are more important than any rules; you put in stops to help your readers to understand you, not to please grammarians. And you should try to write in such a way that they will understand you with a minimum of help of that sort. Fowler said:

It is a sound principle that as few stops should be used as will do the work. . . . Everyone should make up his mind not to depend on his stops. They are to be regarded as devices, not for saving him the trouble of putting his words in the order that naturally gives the required meaning, but for saving his reader the moment or two that would sometimes, without them, be necessarily spent on reading the sentence twice over, once to catch the general arrangement, and again for the details. It may almost be said that what reads wrongly if the stops are removed is radically bad; stops are not to alter the meaning, but merely to show it up. Those who are learning to write should make a practice of putting down all they want to say without stops first. What then, on reading over, naturally arranges itself contrary to the intention should be not punctuated, but altered; and the stops should be as few as possible consistently with the recognised rules.

The symbols we shall have to consider in this chapter are the apostrophe, colon, comma, dash, full stop, hyphen, inverted commas, question mark, semicolon. It will also be a suitable place to say something about capital letters, paragraphs, parentheses and sentences.

Apostrophe

The only uses of the apostrophe that call for notice are (*a*) its use to denote the possessive of names ending in *s* and of pronouns, (*b*) its use before a final *s* to show that the *s* is forming the plural of a word or symbol not ordinarily admitting of a plural and (*c*) its use with a defining plural (e.g. *Ten years' imprisonment*).

(i) Names ending in *s*.

There is no universally accepted code of rules governing the formation of the possessive case of names ending in *s*. Logic would insist on adding another *s* as well as an apostrophe; and this is certainly the commonest practice with monosyllables—Mr Jones's room, St James's Street, not Mr Jones' room, St James' Street. But with longer names many people let an apostrophe do the job alone, even though they may sound the *s* when they pronounce the names. It is now quite usual to write *Jesus' parables, Moses' rod, Dickens' novels.* Greek names with more than one syllable are always written with an apostrophe alone when they end with an *s* sound: *Socrates' teaching, Xerxes' expeditions.*

Many pronouns dispense with an apostrophe in their possessive cases—*hers, yours, theirs, ours* and *its. It's* is not the possessive of *it* but a contraction of *it is* or *it has*. The apostrophe is performing its normal duty of showing that one or more letters have been omitted.

The pronoun *one* and compound pronouns in *-one* and *-body* take an apostrophe in their possessive cases. So we must write *one's, someone's, everybody's, nobody's* for the possessives.

(ii) *P's* and *Q's*, etc.

Whether an apostrophe should be used to denote the plural of a word or symbol that does not ordinarily make a plural depends on whether the plural is readily recognisable as such. Unless the reader really needs help it should not be thrust upon him. It is clearly justified with single letters: 'there are two o's in woolly'; 'mind your p's and q's'. Otherwise it is rarely called for. It should not be used with contractions (e.g. MPs) or merely because what is put into the plural is not a noun. Editors of Shakespeare do without it in 'Tellest thou me of ifs', and Rudyard Kipling did not think it necessary in:

> One million Hows, two million Wheres,
> And seven million Whys.

(iii) *Ten years' imprisonment*, etc.

Whether one should use an apostrophe in such expressions as 'ten years' imprisonment' is a disputed and not very important point. The answer seems to be that if *ten years* is regarded as a descriptive genitive (like *busman's* in *busman's holiday*) we must write *years'*; if as an adjectival phrase there must be no apostrophe but the words must be hyphenated (see Hyphen, p. 167–9). In the singular (*a year's imprisonment*), *year's* can only be a descriptive genitive.

In such phrases as *games master* and *customs examination*, *games* and *customs* are clearly adjectival, and need no apostrophe.

Capitals

No one needs telling that capitals are used for the first letter in every sentence, for proper names, for the names of the months and days and for the titles of books and newspapers. The only difficulty is with words that are sometimes written with capitals and sometimes not. Here there can be no general rule; everyone must do what he thinks most fitting. But two pieces of advice may perhaps be given:

(i) The particular and the general.

Use a capital for the particular and a small letter for the general. Thus:

It is a street leading out of Oxford Street.

I have said something about this in Chapter 1; I shall have more to say in later chapters.

In this case the Judge went beyond a judge's proper functions.

Many parliaments have been modelled on our Parliament.

(ii) Consistency.

Whatever practice you adopt, be consistent throughout any document you are writing.

Colon

About the use of the colon there is even less agreement among the authorities than about the use of other stops. All agree that its systematic use as one of a series of different pause-values has almost died out. But some hold that it is still useful as something less than a full stop and more than a semicolon; others deny it. Into this we need not enter; it will be enough to note that the following two uses are generally recognised as legitimate, the second being by far the more common:

(i) Antithesis.
To mark the antithesis between two sentences more sharply than a semicolon would.

In some cases the executive carries out most of the functions: in others the delegation is much less extensive.

(ii) Explanation, particularisation, or list.
To precede an explanation or particularisation or to introduce a list or series: in the words of Fowler 'to deliver the goods that have been invoiced in the preceding words'.

The design of the school was an important part of the scheme: Post Office counters with all the necessary stores were available and maps and framed specimens of the various documents in use were exhibited on the walls of light and cheerful classrooms.
News reaches a national paper from two sources: the news agencies and its own correspondents.

For the second purpose the dash is the colon's weaker relative. But for this purpose the semicolon is no relative at all. The next sentence comes from an information sheet issued by a Government Department:

The selector switch, mounted below the volume control, has 3 positions; microphone (M), pick-up coil (T) and off (O).

There should be a colon after *positions*, not a semicolon.

Comma

The use of commas cannot be learned by rule. Not only does conventional practice vary from period to period, but good writers of the same period differ among themselves. Moreover, stops have two kinds of duty. One is to show the construction of sentences—the 'grammatical' duty. The other is to introduce nuances into the meaning—the 'rhetorical' duty. 'I went to his house and I found him there' is a colourless statement. 'I went to his house, and I found him there' hints that it was not quite a matter of course that he should have been found there. 'I went to his house. And I found him there.' This indicates that to find him there was surprising. Similarly you can give a different nuance to what you write by encasing adverbs or adverbial phrases in commas. 'He was, apparently, willing to support you' throws a shade of doubt on his bona fides that is not present in 'He was apparently willing to support you'.

The correct use of the comma—if there is such a thing as 'correct' use—can only be acquired by common sense, observation and taste. Present practice is markedly different from that of the past in using commas much less freely. The fifteenth-century passage that heads this chapter is peppered with them with a liberality not approved by modern practice.

This section will attempt no more than to point out some traps that commas set for the unwary, and those who want to know more about the subject should consult Carey's *Mind the Stop*,* a little book which has the rare merit of explaining the principles of punctuation without getting lost in its no-man's-land. We shall first look at some uses of the comma that are generally regarded as incorrect, and then at uses which, though they may not be incorrect, need special care in handling, or are questionable.

Incorrect uses

(i) Between two independent sentences not linked by a conjunction.

The common practice is to use a heavier stop in this position, usually a semicolon. 'Tom is handsome; Dick is clever.' (See also under Semicolon, pp. 173–4.)

We wrote on the 12th May asking for an urgent report regarding the above contractor's complaint, this was followed up on the 24th May by a telephone call.

You may not be aware that a Youth Employment Service is operating throughout the country, in some areas it is under the control of the Ministry of Labour and National Service and in others of the Education Authorities.

There should be a semicolon after *complaint* in the first quotation and *country* in the second.

* Cambridge University Press, 2nd edition, 1958.

The Department cannot guarantee that a licence will be issued, you should not therefore arrange for any shipment.

I regret the delay in replying to your letter but Mr X who was dealing with it is on leave, however, I have gone into the matter . . .

There should be a semicolon or a full stop after *issued* in the first quotation and a full stop after *leave* in the second.

In most cases this will be a C12, however, at some ports/airports where a computerised entry system does not operate, a form C10 will be required.

Certain areas in general hospitals have potential for violence due to the risk of burglary and robbery, staff within these areas seem particularly vulnerable to attacks from members of the general public.

There should be a semicolon or a full stop in the first quotation (which would be improved if the alternatives were 'some ports or airports'), and a semicolon or a full stop in the second. The first sentence of the second quotation also urgently needs amending to rid it of the clumsy 'have potential for' and to avoid the nonsensical interpretation that the possible violence is due to the risk of burglary and robbery. The writer might recast the sentence like this: 'There is a danger of violence occurring in those areas in general hospitals where there is a risk of burglary or robbery'.

Where three or more independent sentences are combined into one sentence and the last two of these parts are linked by a conjunction, it is permissible to insert merely commas between the parts. Here is an example:*

Barley has taken the place of scrub on the chalk hills of Dorset, conifers have been planted on the heath, barbed wire has supplanted hawthorn and pylons stretch across the plains, corrugated iron barns and silos have appeared in well-drained farmyards, and everywhere there are chemical fertilizers and pesticides.

(ii) One instead of either a pair or none.

This very common blunder is more easily illustrated than explained. It is almost like using one only of a pair of brackets. Words that are parenthetical may be able to do without any commas, but if there is a comma at one end of them there must be one at the other end too.

---

* Asa Briggs, *A Social History of England*. Penguin Books, 1985.

Against all this must be set considerations which, in our submission are overwhelming. (Omit the comma.)

We should be glad if you would inform us for our record purposes, of any agency agreement finally reached. (Either omit the comma or insert one after *us*.)

It will be noted that for the development areas, Treasury-financed projects are to be grouped together. (Either omit the comma or insert one after *that*.)

The first is the acute shortage that so frequently exists, of suitable premises where people can come together. (Omit the comma.)

(iii) With 'defining' relative clauses.

Relative clauses fall into two main classes. Grammarians give them different labels, but *defining* and *commenting* are the most convenient and descriptive. If you say, 'The man who was here this morning told me that', the relative clause is a defining one; it completes the subject 'the man', which conveys no definite meaning without it. But if you say, 'Jones, who was here this morning, told me that', the relative clause is commenting; the subject 'Jones' is already complete and the relative clause merely adds a bit of information about him which may or may not be important but is not essential to the definition of the subject. A commenting clause should be within commas; a defining one should not. This is not an arbitrary rule; it is a utilitarian one. If you do not observe it, you may fail to make your meaning clear, or you may even say something different from what you intend. For instance:

A particular need is provision for young women, who owing to war conditions have been deprived of normal opportunities of learning homecraft, . . .

Here the comma announces that the relative clause is 'commenting'; it is added by way of explanation why young women in general had this need after the war. Without the comma the relative clause would be read as a 'defining' one, limiting the need for this provision to those particular young women who had in fact been deprived of those opportunities. Conversely:

Any expenditure incurred on major awards to students, who are not recognised for assistance from the Ministry, will rank for grant. . . .

Here the comma is wrong. The relative clause must be 'defining'. The commas suggest that it is 'commenting' and imply that no students are recognised for assistance.

I have made enquiries, and find that the clerk, who dealt with your enquiry, recorded the name of the firm correctly.

The relative clause here is a defining one. The comma turns it into a commenting one and implies that the writer has only one clerk. The truth is that one of several is being singled out; and this is made clear if the commas after *clerk* and *enquiry* are omitted.

The same mistake is made in:

The Ministry issues permits to employing authorities to enable foreigners to land in this country for the purpose of taking up employment, for which British subjects are not available.

The grammatical implication of this is that employment in general is not a thing for which British subjects are available.

An instruction book called 'Pre-aircrew English', supplied during the war to airmen in training in a Commonwealth country, contained an encouragement to its readers to 'smarten up their English'. This ended:

Pilots, whose minds are dull, do not usually live long.

The commas convert a truism into an insult.

(iv) In an 'absolute phrase'.

An absolute phrase (e.g. 'then, the work being finished, we went home') always has parenthetic commas round it. But there is no sense in the comma that so often carelessly appears inside it.

The House of Commons, having passed the third reading by a large majority after an animated debate, the bill was sent to the Lords.

The insertion of the first comma leaves the House of Commons in the air waiting for a verb that never comes. (See pp. 134.)

(v) To clarify faultily constructed sentences. (See also p. 92.)

It is instructive to compare the following extracts from two documents issued by the same Department:

It should be noted that an officer who ceased to pay insurance contributions before the date of the commencement of his emergency service, remained uninsured for a period, varying between eighteen months and two-and-a-half years, from the date of his last contribution and would, therefore, be compulsorily insured if his emergency service commenced during that period.

Officers appointed to emergency commissions direct from civil life who were not insured for health or pensions purposes at the commencement of emergency service are not compulsorily insured during service.

Why should the first of these extracts be full of commas and the second have none? The answer can only be that, whereas the second sentence is short and clear, the first is long and obscure. The writer tried to help the reader by putting in five commas, but all he did was to give him five jolts. The only place where there might have been a comma is after *last contribution*, and there the writer has omitted to put one.

Another example of the same abuse of a comma is:

Moreover, directions and consents at the national level are essential pre-requisites in a planned economy, whereas they were only necessary for the establishment of standards or for grant-aid and borrowing purposes, in the comparatively free system of yesterday.

The proper place for 'in the comparatively free system of yesterday' is after *whereas*, and it is a poor second-best to try to throw it back there by putting a comma in front of it. (Note also the superfluous adjective in *essential pre-requisites*.)

A barefaced attempt to correct a slovenly sentence by a comma was perpetrated by a Colonial bishop, who wrote to *The Times* a letter containing the sentence:

I should like to plead with some of those men who now feel ashamed to join the Colonial Service.

After the publication of the letter the bishop wrote again to *The Times*, saying:

The omission of a comma in my letter makes me seem to suggest that men might feel ashamed of joining the Colonial Service. My typescript reads, 'I should like to plead with some of those men who now feel ashamed, to join the Colonial Service'.*

(vi) To mark the end of the subject of a verb, or the beginning of the object.

It cannot be said to be always wrong to use a comma to mark the end of a composite subject, because good writers sometimes do it deliberately.

---

* Quoted in Gowans Whyte, *An Anthology of Errors*, Chaterson, 1947.

But to use commas in this way is a dangerous habit; it encourages a writer to shirk the trouble of so arranging his sentences as to make their meaning plain without punctuation.

I am however to draw your attention to the fact that goods subject to import licensing which are despatched to this country without the necessary licence having first been obtained, are on arrival liable to seizure . . .

If the subject is so long that it seems to need a boundary post at the end, it would be better not to use the slovenly device of a comma but to rewrite the sentence in conditional form.

. . . if goods subject to import licensing are despatched . . . they are on arrival . . .

In the following sentences the comma merely interrupts the flow:

The French shopkeeper appears to misunderstand the procedure and I can only suggest that you write to the shopkeeper again with a request that the yellow copies certified by UK Customs, be forwarded to the Bureau des Douanes for them to process and then authorise the shop to refund the tax charged.

Those involved, should be encouraged to examine the reasons why they feel the incident occurred.

Postponement of the object may get a writer into the same trouble.

In the case of both whole-time and part-time officers, the general duties undertaken by them include the duty of treating without any additional remuneration and without any right to recover private fees, patients in their charge who are occupying Section 5 accommodation under the proviso to Section 5 (1) of the Act.

This unlovely sentence obviously needs recasting. One way of doing this would be:

The general duties undertaken by both whole-time and part-time officers include the treating of patients in their charge who are occupying Section 5 accommodation under the proviso to Section 5(1) of the Act, and they are not entitled to receive additional remuneration for it or to recover private fees.

(vii) Before a clause beginning with *that*.

A comma was at one time always used in this position:

It is a just though trite observation, that victorious Rome was itself subdued by the arts of Greece. (Gibbon.)

The true meaning is so uncertain and remote, that it is never sought. (Johnson.)

The author well knew, that two gentlemen . . . had differed with him. (Burke.)

We are more sparing of commas nowadays, and this practice has gone out of fashion. 'Indeed it is safe to say that immediately before the conjunction *that* a comma will be admissible more rarely than before any other conjunction.'*

Correct uses

If we turn from uses of the comma generally regarded as incorrect to those generally regarded as legitimate, we find one or two that need special care.

(i) With adverbs and adverbial phrases.

(*a*) At the beginning of sentences.

In their absence, it will be desirable . . .
Nevertheless, there is need for special care . . .
In practice, it has been found advisable . . .

Some writers put a comma here as a matter of course. But others do it only if a comma is needed to emphasise a contrast or to prevent the reader from going off on a wrong scent, as in:

A few days after, the Minister of Labour promised that a dossier of the strike would be published.
Two miles on, the road is worse.

On the principle that stops should not be used unless they are needed, this discrimination is in general to be commended. But on the principle that the meaning should wherever possible be clear without stops, these particular sentences are blameworthy. It would have been better to dispense with the commas by writing 'A few days afterwards' and 'The road is worse two miles on'.

(*b*) Within sentences.

To enclose an adverb in commas is, as we have seen, a legitimate and useful way of emphasising it. 'All these things may, eventually, come to pass' is another way of saying 'All these things may come to pass—eventually'. Or it may serve to emphasise the subject of the

---

* Carey, *Mind the Stop*.

sentence: 'He, however, thought differently'. The commas underline *he*. But certain common adverbs such as *therefore, however, perhaps, of course*, present difficulties because of a convention that they should always be enclosed in commas, whether emphasised or not. This is dangerous; the only safe course is to treat the question as one not of rule but of common sense, and to judge each case on its merits. Lord Dunsany blames printers for this convention:

> The writer puts down 'I am going to Dublin perhaps, with Murphy'. Or he writes 'I am going to Dublin, perhaps with Murphy'. But in either case these pestilent commas swoop down, not from his pen, but from the darker parts of the cornices where they were bred in the printer's office, and will alight on either side of the word *perhaps*, making it impossible for the reader to know the writer's meaning, making it impossible to see whether the doubt implied by the word *perhaps* affected Dublin or Murphy. I will quote an actual case I saw in a newspaper. A naval officer was giving evidence before a Court, and said, 'I decided on an alteration of course'. But since the words 'of course' must always be surrounded by commas, the printer's commas came down on them . . . and the sentence read, 'I decided upon an alteration, of course'!

The adverb *however* is especially likely to stand in need of clarifying commas. For instance, Burke wrote:

> The author is compelled, however reluctantly, to receive the sentence pronounced on him in the House of Commons as that of the Party.

The meaning of this sentence would be different if the comma after *reluctantly* were omitted, and one inserted after *however*.

> The author is compelled, however, reluctantly to receive . . .

(ii) The 'throw-back' comma.

A common use of the comma as a clarifier is to show that what follows it refers not to what immediately precedes it but to something further back.

> The National Health Service (Injury Benefits) Regulations 1974 SI 1974 No. 1547, provides for the payment of injury benefits to, or in respect of any person engaged in the NHS who suffers permanent reduction in earning ability of more than 10% or is on sick leave with reduced pay, or dies, as a result of an injury suffered during the course of his duties . . .

The comma after 'dies' brings the reader to a bewildering halt. It is intended to show that the final phrase applies to the catalogue of reasons for the payment. The device is clumsy. If words are arranged in the right order these artificial aids will rarely be necessary. The sentence should be recast and three other comma errors corrected. The comma after 'No. 1547' wrongly separates the subject from the verb and should be omitted. On the other hand, a second comma is required for the parallel expressions 'the payment of injury benefits to, or in respect of, any person'. And if there is a comma after 'pay', there should also be a comma after '10%'. Here is the corrected version, which incorporates some other improvements:

The National Health Service (Injury Benefits) Regulations 1974 SI 1974 No. 1547 provides for the payment of injury benefits to, or in respect of, any person engaged in the NHS if as a result of an injury suffered during the course of his duties that person experiences a permanent reduction in earning ability of more than 10%, or is on sick leave with reduced pay, or dies.

(iii) Years in commas.

Printers and typists used to be taught that, in dates, the year must be encased in commas. ('On the 2nd August, 1950, a committee was appointed; on the 6th December, 1951, it reported.') No usefulness can be claimed for this practice to offset its niggling and irritating appearance, and it has now been generally abandoned.

(iv) Commas in series.
(*a*) Nouns and phrases.
In such a sentence as:

The company included ambassadors, cabinet ministers, bishops and judges.

commas are always put after each item in the series up to the last but one, but practice varies about putting a comma between the last but one and the *and* introducing the last. Neither practice is wrong. Those who favour a comma (a minority, but gaining ground) argue that, since a comma may sometimes be necessary to prevent ambiguity, there had better be one there always. Supposing the sentence were:

The company included the Bishops of Winchester, Salisbury, Bristol, and Bath and Wells.

the reader unversed in the English ecclesiastical hierarchy needs the comma after 'Bristol' in order to sort out the last two bishops. Without it they might be, grammatically and geographically, either (*a*) Bristol and Bath and (*b*) Wells, or (*a*) Bristol and (*b*) Bath and Wells. Ambiguity cannot be justified by saying that those who are interested will know what is meant and those who are not will not care.

(*b*) Adjectives.

Where the series is of adjectives preceding a noun, it is a matter of taste whether there are commas between them or not. The following are equally correct:

A silly verbose pompous letter
A silly, verbose, pompous letter

The commas merely give a little emphasis to the adjectives. Where the final adjective is one that describes the species of the noun, it must of course be regarded as part of the noun, and not be preceded by a comma. Thus:

A silly, verbose, pompous official letter.

Dash

The dash is seductive; it tempts the writer to use it as a punctuation-maid-of-all-work that saves him the trouble of choosing the right stop. We all know letter-writers who carry this habit to the length of relying on one punctuation mark only—a nondescript symbol that might be a dash or might be something else. Moreover the dash lends itself easily to rhetorical uses that may be out of place in humdrum prose. The examples of its recognised uses therefore come appropriately from Churchill's war speeches.

(i)   In pairs for a parenthesis.

No future generation of English-speaking folks—for that is the tribunal to which we will appeal—will doubt that we were guiltless.

(ii) To introduce an explanation, amplification, paraphrase, particularisation, or correction of what immediately precedes it.

They were surely among the most noble and benevolent instincts of the human heart—the love of peace, the toil for peace, the strife for peace, the pursuit of peace, even at great peril.

Overhead the far-ranging Catalina air-boats soared—vigilant protecting eagles in the sky.

The end of our financial resources was in sight—nay, had actually been reached.

(iii) To gather up the subject of a sentence when it is a very long one.

After the long loose canter of the subject you need to collect your horse for the jump to the verb.

The formidable power of Nazi Germany, the vast mass of destructive munitions that they have made or captured, the courage, skill and audacity of their striking forces, the ruthlessness of their central war direction, the prostrate condition of so many people under their yoke, the resources of so many lands which may to some extent become available to them—all these restrain rejoicing and forbid the slightest relaxation.

Similarly with the jump from the verb.

I would say generally that we must regard all those victims of the Nazi executioners in so many lands, who are labelled Communists and Jews—we must regard them just as if they were brave soldiers who die for their country on the field of battle.

(iv) To introduce a paradoxical, humorous, or whimsical ending to a sentence.

He makes mistakes, as I do, though not so many or so serious—he has not the same opportunities.

(v) With a colon to introduce a substantial quotation or a list (e.g. *as follows:–*).

At one time it was common to combine the colon with a dash (:–), but this is no longer the usual practice and is unnecessary, since either the colon or the dash can do all that is needed by itself.

Full stop

The full stop is an exception to the rule that stops should be few. If you follow the advice already given that sentences should be short, you will use the full stop plentifully. That is not to say that good prose never contains long sentences. On the contrary, the best prose is a judicious admixture of the long with the short. Mark Twain, after advising young authors to write short sentences as a rule, added:

At times he may indulge himself with a long one, but he will make sure that there are no folds in it, no vaguenesses, no parenthetical interruptions of its view as a whole; when he has done with it, it won't be a sea-serpent with half of its arches under the water; it will be a torch-light procession.*

If you can write long sentences that you are satisfied really merit that description, by all means surprise and delight your readers with one occasionally. But the short ones are safer. See pp. 13–4 and 174–5.

Always use a full stop to separate statements between which there is no true continuity of thought. For example, *and* is too close a link in these sentences:

There are 630 boys in the school and the term will end on April 1st.

As regards Mr Smith's case, a report was made on papers AB 340 and I understand he is now dead.

Hyphen

The author of the style-book of the Oxford University Press of New York (quoted in Perrin's *Writer's Guide*) says 'If you take hyphens seriously you will surely go mad'. You should not take hyphens seriously.

It seems natural to use a hyphen in 'hair-remover', but Fowler pointed out that 'superfluous hair-remover' can only mean a hair-remover nobody wants. Neither 'superfluous-hair remover' nor 'superfluous-hair-remover' is quite satisfactory, and some of us might settle for 'superfluous hair remover'. But it seems odd that the addition of the adjective should lead us to abandon the hyphen that is natural in the compound noun standing by itself. The truth is that there is no satisfactory answer. The same sort of difficulty presents itself in 'fried fish merchant'.

It is not possible to lay down rules for hyphens without being misleading, since the general practice is often contradicted in specific instances. But here are a few elementary warnings.

(i) Unnecessary hyphen.

If, for instance, you must use *overall* as an adjective (though this is not recommended) write it like that, and not *over-all*.

But if you do split a word with a hyphen, make sure you split it at the main break. Though you may write *self-conscious*, if you wish to have a hyphen in the word, you must not write *unself-conscious* but *un-selfconscious*.

---

* Quoted in Earle's *English Prose, its Elements, History and Usage, 1890.*

(ii) Hyphen after a prefix.

Use a hyphen after a prefix to prevent the word being mistaken for another word. For example, the hyphen distinguishes between the contrasting pairs *re-form*, *reform*; *re-cover*, *recover*; *re-creation*, *recreation*; *co-op*, *coop*. We need a hyphen in *co-op*, since otherwise readers may be puzzled whether *coop* is something to put a hen in or a profit-sharing association. But the absence of a hyphen in *cooperate* and similar words does not result in ambiguity.

At one time a hyphen was regularly inserted in words like *pre-eminent* and *non-effective*, where the absence of the hyphen might suggest a wrong pronunciation. But there is a growing tendency to write such words solid, perhaps following the American practice. You will still need a hyphen to avoid doubling the vowel *i* (*semi-illiterate*, *anti-intellectual*) or tripling the consonant *l* (*shell-like*).

(iii) Hyphens in compound adjectives.

To prevent ambiguity, a hyphen should be used in a compound adjective (e.g. *first-class*, *six-inch*, *copper-coloured*, *water-cooled*). The omission of a hyphen between *government* and *financed* in the following sentence throws the reader on to a false scent:

> When Government financed projects in the development areas have been grouped. . . .

And we might puzzle the reader if we omitted the hyphens in *long-dead relatives*, *light-blue dress*, and *cheap baby-food*. But it is unnecessary to insert a hyphen after an adverb in -*ly* (*happily married couple*) since the relationship is then clear. The hyphen is correct in *well-developed plan*, but would be superfluous in *carefully developed plan*.

Remember that words which form parts of compound adjectives when they precede a noun may stand on their own feet when they are doing a different duty, and then they must not be hyphenated. 'A first-class compartment' needs a hyphen, but 'to travel first class' does not. There must be hyphens in 'the balance-of-payment difficulties' but not in 'the difficulties are over the balance of payments'. A worth-while job is one that is worth while.

(iv) Suspended hyphens.

Avoid as far as possible the practice of separating a pair of hyphenated words, leaving a hyphen in mid-air. To do this is to misuse the hyphen (whose proper function is to link a word with its immediate neighbour) and it has a slovenly look. The saving of one word cannot justify writing

Where chaplains (whole- or part-time) have been appointed

instead of 'where chaplains have been appointed, whole-time or part-time'.

In a passage quoted on p. 237

. . . the Committee will meet at three or four monthly intervals . . .

the meaning would have been clearer with hyphens after *three* and *four*, but the suspended hyphen would have looked clumsy. The writer could have avoided leaving the first in the air (*three-* or *four-monthly*) by writing *three-monthly or four-monthly*. But, as suggested on p. 237, it would be better still to recast the sentence.

Inverted commas

Some people bemoan the invention of inverted commas and wish that they could be abolished. Certainly the Bible is clear enough without them. But they seem unlikely to disappear, and we must learn to live with them.

Two points are worth making.

One is to give a warning against over-indulgence in the trick of encasing words or phrases in inverted commas to indicate that they are being used in a slang or technical or facetious or some other unusual sense. This is a useful occasional device; instances may be found in this book. But it is a dangerous habit, as has been pointed out on p. 4.

The second question is whether punctuation marks (including question and exclamation marks) should come before or after the inverted commas that close a quotation. The general British practice is to put the stops in their logical positions. If the question and exclamation marks are part of the sentence quoted, put them within the inverted commas. If they are part of a longer sentence within which the quotation stands, put them outside the inverted commas. If the quotation and the sentence embracing it end together, so that each needs a stop at the same time, do not carry logic to the lengths of putting one inside and one out, but be content with the one outside. To give three simple examples of the application of this advice to question marks:

> I said to him 'Why worry?'
> Why did you say to him 'Don't worry'?
> Why did you say to him 'Why worry'? (Strictly 'Why worry?'?)

Do not, however, put a full stop at the end of the sentence when the question or exclamation mark is merely inside the inverted commas.

If your quotation is part of a dialogue and is a sentence, put the full stop inside the inverted commas.

> 'I suppose,' she said, 'that he admires your work.'

But if you are giving only a partial quotation or merely citing expressions as examples, put the full stop outside, as in this sentence that appeared on p. 168:

> There must be hyphens in 'the balance-of-payment difficulties' but not in 'the difficulties are over the balance of payments'.

Paragraphs

Letters, reports, memoranda and other documents would be unreadable if they were not divided into paragraphs, and much has been written on the art of paragraphing. But little of it helps the ordinary writer; the subject does not admit of precise guidance. The chief thing to remember is that, although paragraphing loses all point if the paragraphs are excessively long, the paragraph is essentially a unit of thought, not of length. Every paragraph must be homogeneous in subject matter, and sequential in treatment of it. If a single sequence of treatment of a single subject goes on so long as to make an unreasonably long paragraph, it may be divided into more than one. But you must not do the opposite, and combine into a single paragraph passages that have not this unity, even though each by itself may be below the average length of a paragraph.

Parenthesis

The purpose of a parenthesis is ordinarily to insert an illustration, explanation, definition, or additional piece of information of any sort into a sentence that is logically and grammatically complete without it. A parenthesis may be marked off by commas, dashes or brackets. The degree of interruption of the main sentence may vary from the almost imperceptible one of explanatory words in apposition,

Mr. Smith, the secretary, read the minutes.

to the violent one of a separate sentence complete in itself:

A memorandum (six copies of this memorandum are enclosed for the information of the Board) has been issued to management committees.

If the sentence contains other commas or if the parenthesis itself contains commas, use dashes or brackets for marking the boundaries of the parenthesis:

The fee due should be attached to the appropriate Land Registry application form and payment made by cheque or, for small amounts, if preferred, by Land Registry adhesive stamps obtainable at any Head Post Office in denominations of 5p, 10p, 15p and 50p.

Brackets should replace the commas after *or* and *preferred* to enclose the parenthesis 'for small amounts, if preferred'.

Parentheses should be used sparingly. Their very convenience is a reason for fighting shy of them. They enable the writer to dodge the trouble of arranging his thought properly; but he does so at the expense of the reader, especially if the thought that he has spatchcocked into the sentence is an abrupt break in it, or a long one, or both. The second of the three examples just given shows an illegitimate use of the parenthesis. The writer had no business to keep the reader waiting for the verb by throwing in a parenthesis that would have been put better as a separate sentence. The following examples are even worse:

. . . to regard day nurseries and daily guardians as supplements to meet the special needs (where these exist and cannot be met within the hours, age-range and organisation of nursery schools and nursery classes) of children whose mothers are constrained by individual circumstances to go out to work . . .

If duties are however declined in this way, it will be necessary for the Board to consider whether it should agree to a modified contract in the particular case, or whether—because the required service can be provided only by the acceptance of the rejected obligations (e.g. by a whole-time radiologist to perform radiological examinations of paying patients in Section 5 beds in a hospital where the radiologists are all whole-time officers)—the Board should seek the services of another practitioner . . .

These are intolerable abuses of the parenthesis, the first with its interposition of 21 words in the middle of the phrase 'needs of children', and the second with its double parenthesis, more than 40 words long, like two snakes eating each other. There was no need for either of these monstrosities. In both examples the main sentence should be allowed to finish without interruption, and what is now in the parenthesis, so far as it is worth saying, should be added at the end:

> . . . to regard day nurseries and daily guardians as supplements to meet the special needs of children whose mothers are constrained . . . and whose needs cannot be met . . .
>
> . . . or whether the Board should seek the services of another practitioner, as they will have to do if the required service can be provided only . . .

Here is a parenthesis that keeps the reader waiting so long for the verb that he has probably forgotten what the subject is:

> Close affiliation with University research in haematology—and it may be desirable that ultimately each Regional Transfusion Officer should have an honorary appointment in the department of pathology in the medical school—will help to attract into the service medical men of good professional standing.

In former days, when long and involved sentences were fashionable, it was customary after a long parenthesis to put the reader on the road again by repeating the subject with the words 'I say'. Thus the writer of the last example would have continued after 'medical school' with the words 'close affiliation with University research in haematology, I say, will help to attract, etc.'. Now that this handy device has fallen into disuse, there is all the more need not to keep the reader waiting. There was no necessity to do so here. What is said as a parenthesis might just as well have been said as an independent sentence following the main one.

It is not only the reader who may forget where he was when the parenthesis started. Sometimes even the writer does, as in the letter quoted on p. 15.

> . . . owing to a shortage of a spare pair of wires to the underground cable (a pair of wires leading from the point near your house back to the local exchange and thus a pair of wires essential to the provision of a telephone service for you) is lacking. . . .

The writer thought he had entered the parenthesis with the words 'Owing to the fact that a spare pair of wires to the underground cable' and he continued conformably when he emerged.

Question mark

Only direct questions need question marks; indirect ones do not. There must be one at the end of 'Have you made a return of your income?' but not at the end of 'I am writing to ask whether you have made a return of your income'.

It is usual but not necessary to put question marks at the end of requests cast into question form for the sake of politeness. 'Will you please let me know whether you have made a return of your income?'

For the position of question marks in relation to inverted commas see pp. 169–70.

Semicolon

Do not be afraid of the semicolon; it can be most useful. It marks a longer pause, a more definite break in the sense, than the comma; at the same time it says 'Here is a clause or sentence too closely related to what has gone before to be cut off by a full stop'. The semicolon is a stronger version of the comma.

The scheme of work should be as comprehensive as possible and should include gymnastics, games, boxing, wrestling and athletics; every endeavour should be made to provide facilities for swimming.

If these arrangements are made in your factory you should take any difficulty which you may have to these officers when they call; you need not write to the Tax Office or call there.

These two sentences illustrate the common use of the semicolon. Each consists of two clauses. If these had been linked by the conjunction *and*, a comma might have been enough after *athletics* and *call*. But where there is no conjunction, a comma is not enough; the stop must be either a semicolon or a full stop. (See pp. 156–7.) The writers of these sentences felt that the clauses were not closely enough linked to justify a conjunction but too closely linked to admit of a full stop. They therefore rightly chose the middle course of a semicolon.

Each of the following sentences needs a semicolon in place of the comma:

The Company is doing some work on this, it may need supplementing.

If it is your own pension please say what type it is, if it is your mother's then it need not be included in your income.

Even where the clauses are linked by a conjunction, a semicolon may nevertheless be kinder to readers than a comma. If either or both clauses are long, and still more if they contain commas of their own, a semicolon may be helpful to readers by directing them to the major break in the sentence and enabling them to catch their breath:

> The Government do not want to amend trade union laws just before the bye-elections, since they fear that the controversy will lose them many votes; and trade union leaders themselves are said not to be eager to announce their views on the proposals until after the elections.

Similarly, a semicolon may be needed to separate phrases that have their own commas:

> The long-term commitments of the research council include hospital laboratories in London, Birmingham and Edinburgh; research institutes in London, Glasgow and Manchester; and eight University Departments that specialise in cancer treatment.

The semicolon is also useful for avoiding the rather dreary trailing participles with which writers often end their sentences:

> The postgraduate teaching hospitals are essentially national in their outlook, their geographical situation being merely incidental.
> An attempt to devise permanent machinery for consultation was unsuccessful, the initial lukewarm response having soon disappeared.

There is nothing faulty in the grammar of these sentences, and the meaning of each is unambiguous. But they have a tired look. They can be wonderfully freshened by using the semicolon, and rewriting them:

> The postgraduate teaching hospitals are essentially national in their outlook; their geographical situation is merely incidental.
> An attempt to devise permanent machinery for consultation was unsuccessful; the initial lukewarm response soon disappeared.

Sentences

A sentence is not easy to define. Many learned grammarians have tried, and their definitions have been torn in pieces by other learned grammarians. But what most of us understand by a sentence is what the *OED* calls the 'popular definition': 'such a portion of composition or utterance as extends from one full stop to another'. That definition is good enough for our present purposes, and the question we have to consider is what general guidance can be given to writers about what they should put between one full stop and the next.

The two main things to be remembered about sentences by those who want to make their meaning plain is that they should be short and should have unity of thought. Here is a series of 84 words between one full stop and another, which violates all the canons of a good sentence. In fact it might be said to explode the definition, for it would be flattering to call it a 'sentence'. It is better described as gibberish.

Forms are only sent to applicants whose requirements exceed one ton, and in future, as from tomorrow, forms will only be sent to firms whose requirements exceed five tons, and as you have not indicated what your requirements are, I am not sending you forms at the moment because it is just possible that your requirements may be well within these quantities quoted, in which case you may apply direct to the usual suppliers, of which there are several, with a view to obtaining your requirements.

If we prune this of its verbiage, and split it into three short sentences, a meaning will begin to emerge.

Only firms whose requirements exceed five tons now need to apply to us for forms. Others can apply direct to the suppliers. As you do not say what your requirements are, I will not send you a form unless I hear that you need one.

The following is an even worse example of a meandering stream of words masquerading as a sentence:

Further to your letter of the above date and reference in connection with an allocation of . . . , as already pointed out to you all the allocations for this period have been closed, and I therefore regret that it is not possible to add to the existing allocation which has been made to you and which covers *in toto* your requirements for this period when originally received, by virtue of the work on which you are engaged, a rather higher percentage has been given to you, namely 100 per cent of the original requirements and at this stage I am afraid it is not practicable for you to increase the requirement for the reasons already given.

The fault here is excessive verbiage rather than of combining into one sentence thoughts that ought to have been given several. The thought is simple, and can be conveyed in two sentences, if not in one:

Your original application was granted in full because of the importance of your work. I regret that the amount cannot now be increased, as no more allocations for this period will be made.

15

Some recent trends

It is quite impossible to stop the progress of language—it is like the course of the Mississippi, the motion of which is at times scarcely perceptible yet even then it possesses a momentum quite irresistible. Words and expressions will be forced into use in spite of all the exertions of all the writers in the world.

Webster

Like all living languages, our language continues to change. The most conspicuous changes since the earlier editions of this book were published have occurred in vocabulary: new words have joined the language and new meanings have become established for old words. The revisions in earlier chapters have taken account of particular points of usage and of attitudes to them. This chapter looks in general at developments in the language in the last few decades.

The trend towards informality

The previous edition noted that since the second world war there has been a steady trend towards much greater informality of expression. Contributing to this trend have been the growth of literacy, some lowering of social barriers and a consequent increasing sense of egalitarianism, and the informal style adopted in most of the language put out for popular consumption by the press, broadcasting and television.

The trend has affected most kinds of writing, particularly writing addressed to the general public. Forms, notices, advertisements, news reports and feature articles are written in a far more informal style. Sometimes the style is quite casual in its use of conversational forms like *don't* and *he's* and in its punctuation of phrases or words as separate sentences.

The trend towards greater informality has also affected business writing and official writing. There is an increasing awareness that people often do not understand formal language and are intimidated by it. Official and business letters tend now to sound more personal; they use *I* or *we* for the writer and *you* for the recipient. They are less likely to include unexplained technical terms or uncommon words and phrases.

Most people will agree that the trend towards greater informality in the use of the written word is to be welcomed rather than deplored. But it sets some problems for officials, whether they are writing a letter or drafting a document for publication. Remembering the advice 'Be human', they do not want their letters to seem stuffy or condescending by modern standards, but if they use too informal a style they risk being thought impertinent or facetious; their readers do not want a pompous reply, but they do expect a serious one. Similarly, in a formal statement of important Government policy a certain degree of dignity is necessary if the desired impact is to be made. A modern official will almost certainly avoid 'Her Majesty's Government have been driven to the conclusion, after long and earnest consideration, that this proposition cannot be brought within the realms of practicability in the foreseeable future'. But 'Her Majesty's Government don't think this is on' will not quite do either.

People expect official writing to be dignified. There is no justification for the pomposities that are characteristic of what is sometimes called the 'mandarin prose' of the Civil Service. But official writing should not be conversational and certainly not slangy. Conversational contractions like *can't*, *won't* and *they're* convey an inappropriate chattiness, and may indeed be less intelligible to some readers than the full forms. Readers need to feel that they have received an important communication that requires their serious attention.

The objections to sexist language

It is perhaps only within the last ten years (though certainly earlier across the Atlantic) that vigorous attacks have been made on certain features or uses of the language that are allegedly biased against women. It is asserted that when we use the masculine pronouns *he*, *him*, and *his* and expressions such as *man*, *chairman* and *mankind* to include both sexes we confirm the stereotype of men as dominant in society. Such expressions, it is said, reinforce tendencies to exclude women from consideration for certain occupations and posts. Their occurrence in written material is resented because they seem to assume that the reader is a man and that the subject matter primarily concerns men. *Ms* is advocated as a term of address for women in place of *Miss* and *Mrs* to avoid a distinction in the marital status of women that we do not make for men.

The suggestions for changes have by no means received unanimous support, even from women. The proposed changes have been dismissed as trivial, the concerns of a radical fringe; and they have been ridiculed as clumsy or incorrect, offences against the spirit of the language and its history.

Present usage on such matters is unstable. In particular, *chairperson* and other new words ending in *person* have yet to win general approval. Meanwhile, it is safer for official writers to be cautiously conservative, and to take evasive action where possible. (See p. 11.)

The influence of science and technology

Science and technology have developed more rapidly during the last twenty years than ever before, and correspondingly they have introduced multitudes of new terms to express new concepts, new techniques, new discoveries, and inventions. Most of this terminology remains within the closed world of the experts. Those of us who are not experts encounter some of these terms when scientists and technologists attempt to explain their work to us in popular books or articles, and in programmes or interviews on radio and television. And we may start using such terms ourselves, both literally and metaphorically.

The computer is a recent technological advance that has affected the ordinary language. Computers have produced a new vocabulary of their own, as they are entitled to do, but it is not a graceful one; and computer experts seem to take less trouble than most experts to express themselves grammatically or to make themselves plain to ordinary readers. This is a pity, for as the years go by ordinary people are having more and more to do with computers. Young children are already becoming as accustomed to handling computers as their predecessors were to using electronic calculators.

An interesting feature of computer language is that the American spelling *program* has been adopted to denote a sequence of instructions fed into a computer and designed to solve a problem or attain a specific result. It would now be as contrary to British usage to use *programme* in this special sense as to use *program* in any other. Other familiar words have been given special meanings and new words have been coined. For instance, *hardware* means the physical components of a computer and *software* the programs written for a computer. *Input* means data introduced into a computer and *output* data produced by a computer. There is no harm in any of this in its place, but *input* in particular has become an overworked vogue word in its metaphorical uses, for example to mean merely suggestion, contribution, or reaction:

Before coming to a decision, the Board would like some input from members of the staff.

Another vogue word is *user-friendly*, which means that the computer or the computer programs are simple to use. It has started to spread outside the field of computers, for example to books.

Here is an illustration of unhelpful writing from a manual for beginners:

Tabs in this program are absolute, so tabbing to column 10 for example will always cause the next character to print in that column. This means that when a proportional font is being used it is possible that tabs will cause overprinting, and they should be used with care.

Some years ago Sir Lawrence Bragg (then Cavendish Professor of Experimental Physics at Cambridge) wrote as follows:

I will try to define what I believe to be lacking in our present courses for science undergraduates. They do not learn to write clearly and briefly, marshalling their points in due and aesthetically satisfying order, and eliminating inessentials. They are inept at those turns of phrase or happy analogy which throw a flying bridge across a chasm of misunderstanding and make contact between mind and mind. They do not know how to talk to people who have had a very different training from them, and how to carry conviction when decisions on plans for action of vital importance to them are made. . . . The gift of expression is important to them as scientists; the best research is wasted when it is extremely difficult to discover what it is all about. . . . It is even more important when scientists are called upon to play their part in the world of affairs, as is happening to an increasing extent.

No doubt these strictures still apply to much that is written on scientific or technical subjects. But there is enough good, clear writing to make it evident that if writers know their subject and take trouble they can get their meaning across to the ordinary reader without torturing the language. Many scientific journalists do this extremely well, and so do some experts.

Here is a passage by one of the finest scientific journalists.* It describes, and comments on, an experiment that provided support for Einstein's formula on mass and energy: $E = mc^2$.

Cockcroft and Ernest Walton built an electrical accelerator for atomic particles and used it to shoot protons, the nuclei of hydrogen atoms, at a target of lithium metal. On hitting the nucleus of a lithium atom, a proton would merge with it and cause it to split into two new nuclei—of helium, in fact. The masses of two helium nuclei, added together, are slightly less than the combined masses of the hydrogen nucleus (proton) and the lithium nucleus, which made them. So matter disappeared in this nuclear reaction.

The experimenters could 'see' the pairs of helium nuclei that flew out from the target in opposite directions. Each flying nucleus caused a small flash of light when it hit a fluorescent screen, like a miniature TV screen. Cockcroft and Walton estimated the energy of motion of the helium nuclei by seeing how far they could travel through the air. To within an experimental accuracy of just a few per cent, the energy of motion of the helium nuclei gauged by Cockcroft and Walton fully accounted for the missing matter, in accordance with Einstein's formula $E = mc^2$.

You could say (and many people do) that a certain amount of mass has been abolished and converted into the energy of motion of the helium fragments. But that is a rather sloppy way of talking about events in Einstein's universe. Mass and energy are not just interconvertible, in the way that I can convert dollars into gold or vice versa. They are the same thing—mass-energy. In the Cambridge atom-splitting experiment the flying helium fragments together possess, for a moment at least, exactly the same mass as the combined mass of the particles that produced them. Their mass-energy of motion is added to their conventional mass. They lose it as they slow down, handing over their energy of motion to other atoms in their neighbourhood, which share out their 'excess' mass as well; the energy is converted into heat. The mass-energy then remaining with the helium nuclei is often called the 'rest mass', and it corresponds to the traditional idea of mass—an amount of matter. But as matter is just a particular, frozen form of mass-energy, I prefer the term

* Nigel Calder, *Einstein's Universe*, p.14. Viking Press, 1979.

'rest-energy' for conventional mass. Every other form of energy has mass associated with it. For example, a pressing iron is slightly heavier when it is hot than when it is cold, and a car has more mass when in motion than when at rest.

Contrast the lucidity of the previous passage with the difficulty of the sentence quoted just below. The sentence comes from an article in a book on science and technology that is ostensibly aimed at non-experts.

Dicke estimated how fast the core ought to slow down on the assumption that viscous shear stresses provide the only vehicle for angular momentum transfer beneath the outer convection zone.

The social sciences, including education, are notorious for obscure and pretentious writing, particularly in their academic journals. But some social scientists strive for convoluted sentences filled with technical terms even when they are writing for ordinary people. Perhaps they feel that their subjects have not gained as much academic esteem as they would like and are afraid that if they write simply their readers will think that the subject matter is simple too. Here are two examples written for ordinary people.

The national significance of the distributive sector must be assessed also in the light of its high visibility and integration into the physical and social fabric of the community.

This means that shops are important in the life of the nation because they are easy to see and are part and parcel of our daily life.

The main quantitative thresholds (necessitating new works) should not be crossed in any of the towns with the exception of St Boswells, which is the only place where the substantial expenditure necessary for the implementation of new public utility networks is justified from the economic viewpoint.

This means that only at St Boswells can expenditure on new public utility systems be justified.

One could multiply quotations. These perhaps suffice to suggest that if by precept and by example a few academic writers could persuade fellow professionals in their own disciplines to write decently, the direct and indirect benefits to academic and official writing would be immense.

The influence of other varieties of English

Since the second world war, English has become firmly established as the foremost language for international communication. It is the first language for over 300 million people. Most of them live in our country and the United States of America (56 million and 222 million respectively), but there are also substantial numbers in other countries, principally Canada (17 million) and Australia (14 million). In addition, English is the second language in many countries where it has official status as a means of communication and where people have usually learned it in school. Estimates of numbers of second-language speakers of English vary wildly, depending on the level of competence that estimators recognise as sufficient for this purpose. Almost all the countries where English has official status are former British colonies that gained their independence after the second world war. The most heavily populated are India (700 million) and Pakistan (85 million). Finally, English is the first foreign language in most other countries of the world.

States where English is a second language have always looked to British or American English (that is, the English of the United States) for their standards. Until recently the same was true for the other countries where English is a first language, but some, especially the Canadians and the Australians, are beginning to assert their linguistic independence. Foreign learners generally learn British or American English, although some countries in the Far East are turning to Australia.

American English differs from British English not only in pronunciation but also in some points of spelling, punctuation, syntax and (above all) vocabulary. It would be absurd for us to assume that an American word, expression, or construction is necessarily better just because it seems novel, or that it is necessarily worse just because we have not encountered it before. Occasionally what seems an American innovation is in fact an old English usage that has survived across the Atlantic but has been generally abandoned in the land of its origin. Older usages preserved in American English include *fall* meaning 'autumn', *mad* meaning 'angry', the verb form *gotten*, and *loan* as a verb.

Resentment against American importations is longstanding. In earlier times the verbs *utilise*, *advocate* and *belittle* and the adjectives *lengthy*, *talented* and *reliable* were ridiculed, but these have now established themselves in British English and are not recognised as originally American. Numerous American words made their way into Britain earlier this century; the American source is not obvious in such words as *cafeteria* and *cereal*, or in such verb phrases as *stay put*, *turn down* and *sit up and take notice*. In more recent years American English has been invading these islands with ever-increasing force and persistence through films, magazines, books, radio and television. American entertainers and politicians are frequently interviewed on British morning television programmes, and American films and soap operas are regularly shown on television. New words and phrases are rapidly disseminated through the press, radio, and television. Americans are now encountered in this country in increasing numbers: tourists, participants in conventions, and personnel from multi-national corporations and international agencies. We may well marvel that popular British usage has continued to maintain a measure of independence. *Autumn*, *pavement*, *underground* (or *tube*), *queue* and (potato) *crisps* have not surrendered to *fall*, *sidewalk*, *subway*, *line* and *chips*. Earlier chapters mention other examples of common American usages which are not, or at least not yet, accepted as British usage. But other American usages have either supplanted local usages or exist side by side with them. *Radio* has virtually ousted *wireless*; and we can now hear or see both British and American words with the same meaning: both *tin* and *can*, *lift* and *elevator*, *stones* and *rocks*.

We are concerned here with the extent to which those who write British English and who 'use words as tools of their trade in administration or business' should allow themselves to be influenced by the assaults of American English. They should not put up any resistance to words which aptly fill a real need—as did *teenager*, *doodle* and *commuter*, now well established in British English. There can be no objection to allowing *update* to do the work of *bring up to date*, or *host* the work of *be host at*. The American *round-trip* is preferable to the ambiguous *return journey*. Though still an over-used vogue word, *meaningful* can be useful. And so is *guesstimate*, meaning an estimate so rough that it is little better than a guess. The numerous scientific and technological words entering the ordinary language are necessary additions, whether they are first introduced here or across the Atlantic.

But those who write British English should not lightly allow a newcomer to supplant a perfectly good British word. Thus, there is no reason for preferring *envision* to *envisage* or (when they have the same meaning) *transportation* to *transport*. Nor should they be seduced by such ungainly temptresses as *in the event that* (if), *at this time* and *at this point of time* (now), *in this day and age* (now), or *as of now* (now). We must view with suspicion the tendency to add to simple verbs strings of adverbs and prepositions which make little or no difference to the meaning; the danger is that the simple verb will eventually be robbed of its right to mean anything by itself. In Britain boy meets girl and should continue to do so, even though in America he meets with her, or even meets up with her. (*Meet with*, in British English, is properly used only where what is met is abstract—a man can meet with opposition and an expedition can meet with disaster—and even there *meet* is often used alone. Of course one can meet force with sweet reason or disaster with courage but those are different constructions.) *Consult with* and *visit with* are other Americanisms which should be made unwelcome; *consult* and *visit* should not be rendered impotent.

But these differences in usage do not present nearly so serious a menace as the tortured, polysyllabic style of much American official and academic writing—what has been stigmatised as 'gobbledygook'. Here the British resistance has been by no means as sturdy as one could wish.

If pearls of wisdom reach us in a copious wrapping of cotton wool and corrugated cardboard, it is no ingratitude to enjoy the pearls and discard the wrapping. Many British writers seem to think that unless they display the wrapping they will be suspected of not having received the pearls. The previous section of this chapter provides some examples of British gobbledygook, and there is no need to multiply examples.

The American assault is made not only directly through American English but also indirectly through 'United Nations English'. Many of the publications of the United Nations, of their specialised agencies and of other international bodies bear eloquent witness to the prominent and influential part played in their activities by the United States. Another reason why United Nations English differs from British English is that it often emanates from men and women on the staff of these bodies who use English rather than any of the other official languages but whose native tongue is not English at all. These publications are usually seen in draft by British officials or delegates, but however good their use of their own tongue may be they cannot insist that a draft should always be translated into good British English, and it is not always tactful for them to try.

Here are just two examples of United Nations English. They illustrate the influence of American English rather than that of English used as a second language.

At present many factors lead to a serious public health problem in the form of protein calorie malnutrition and other forms of malnutrition resulting from dietary deficiencies of vitamins and minerals which affect particularly infants, pre-school children and expectant and nursing mothers.

With respect to the question whether the financial communities in the donor and recipient countries should be widely alerted or not, the confidentiality of the warnings should be maintained.

Just as we cannot reasonably object to the use of American English by Americans, so we cannot reasonably object to the use of United Nations English by the United Nations. But that is not to say that we should allow either to influence British English for the worse.

There has been relatively little influence on British English from other English-speaking countries. We now hear Australian accents, for example, from announcers and presenters on radio and television where once only BBC English was allowed for these roles. The same tolerance has been extended to educated pronunciations that mark the speakers as coming from particular regions in the British Isles. But there is little, if anything, from either the other national varieties or the British regional varieties that is likely to affect those who write British English.

The most recent threat to British English has developed since we joined the European Economic Community, and the threat is particularly menacing for official writers. They are exposed to a flood of documents in English from the European Commission and other Community institutions. The English in the Community's publications, which has been derisively called Euro-English, is distorted under the influence of other European languages and displays a bureaucratic jargon of its very own. The impositions of Euro-jargon should be firmly opposed and the Europeanisms resisted. It is foreign to our natural usage to call fully grown cattle *adult bovine animals*, and live sheep and goats and their meat *sheepmeat*. Euro-English is clotted with impenetrable terms, such as *co-responsibility levy* meaning a tax on excessive production, *denaturing* a method of identifying an agricultural product (for example as fit only for animal consumption), *derogation* temporary suspension of the application of a clause in a Community decree, and *regime* the Community rules for individual commodity markets (as in the 'sheepmeat regime').

But more pernicious than the jargon is the clotted style. Here are two illustrations from publications of the Community.

At present, both the traditional form of apprentice training and full-time school-based vocational training are in many respects inadequate. The former is too rigidly aligned to the short-term needs of the undertakings and, in many cases, to specific jobs or mono-occupations. The latter is not in a position to react quickly to the changing vocational requirements, job contents and production processes and is unable to adapt the training programmes accordingly. In brief: the first-mentioned form of vocational training has a deficit in respect of theoretical instruction in that the various elements of training do not relate to occupational fields and do not incorporate pedagogical objectives. School-based training, on the other hand, shows a deficit from the practical point of view; the pupils are unable to verify their newly-gained knowledge under practical conditions on the job.

The European Council considers that the structural Funds should become effective Community policy instruments aimed at reducing regional development lags and converting regions in industrial decline; promoting dynamic and competitive agriculture by maintaining and developing effective agricultural structures, in particular in the less-favoured regions; combating unemployment, in particular youth unemployment.

The dangers for official writing are certain to increase as our ties with the European Community become closer. Official writers must therefore be on their guard not to allow Euro-English to infect their writing.

16
Some selected passages

Words are meant to convey thought; if you take trouble in the use of words you are bound to clarify the thought which you wish to convey.

Anonymous diplomat

It may be useful to select a few pieces for detailed study—not so much of their literary merit as of their practical efficiency. This will enable us to pick up some of the points made in earlier chapters and note how easy it usually is to convert the bad into the acceptable.

We have chosen neither the best nor the worst. It would be of little use to present ordinary readers with the brilliant writing of highly gifted writers and invite them to emulate it. Of the following seven specimens of plain writing by sensible and educated people, the first four seem to fall below the standard that we could all successfully aim at; the next one more or less attains it; the last two are particularly good examples of simple, lucid English by a scientist and a novelist respectively.

Specimen 1

Our first specimen is a memorandum formally submitted to a House of Commons Select Committee. The writer is urging various improvements in the arrangements for training teachers, but the general effect is spoilt by carelessness, clichés and flaccidity.

It may seem a little unfair to take an eight-page memorandum and quote only its blemishes, or rather some of its blemishes. A much less unfavourable impression would have been given if it had been quoted in full, for the author can clearly write efficiently if he tries. But that is, of course, precisely the point: most sensible people can.

We find, in consecutive sentences, *a significantly higher level of expenditure* and *significant improvements are urgent*, meaning respectively *much more expenditure* and *big improvements are urgently needed*.

Within a few lines of each other are no fewer than three plural subjects with singular verbs:

The activities of the Pooling Committee, which does not include representation from those who are actually responsible for and/or engaged in the work of the colleges, *is* likely to restrict . . .

There can be no justification for the widely different standards applied to universities and non-university institutions in the provision made for students' leisure activities and which *applies* both to premises and recurrent expenditure.

. . . it is through active participation in such activities in their colleges that they build up the interests and the expertise which *allows* them to do so.

In the first of these sentences we also find *and/or*. This phrase is occasionally useful, particularly to a lazy writer, but is much better avoided (see p. 16). It is always ugly, usually unnecessary and sometimes downright wrong. It is also discourteous, because it nearly always forces readers to read the sentence twice, which they would not have had to do if the writer had taken a little more trouble. Here it is easily avoided, for instance by writing 'which includes no college teachers or administrators'. All that *and/or* does is to note that some people both teach and administer and that the Committee has none of them either.

In the second sentence, not only should *applies* be *apply* but *and which* is wrong too (see pp. 98–9). The *and* should go. But the whole sentence clearly needs recasting. We need something like:

The standard of provision, both capital and recurrent, for students' leisure activities is much lower in non-university institutions than in universities. There can be no justification for this.

We find fashionable but unsatisfactory phrases like:

. . . all institutions concerned must do everything possible to maximise their cost effectiveness.

. . . this is impossible in the context of a binary system of administration and control.

The words *do everything possible to* are quite unnecessary, for *maximise* by itself means to make as big as possible. It would be better to say 'must do all they can to increase', for *maximise* is still a word to be avoided if possible. *Cost effectiveness* (which would be better with a hyphen) is a vogue word which is lasting well. In the second example, *in the context of* means *under* or *if there is*. (*Binary system* is a technical term in education and is not to be objected to.)

There are trailing, flaccid sentences like:

It would be desirable for all universities to be involved in this kind of development to allow for smaller and more intimate groupings of colleges so improving communication within each group and promoting variety of course provision.

This would be good management practice and would avoid the frustrating delays which occur under current procedures which in some cases also leave decisions over particular expenditures in the hands of those least competent to make them.

(Note incidentally the tendency to *make a decision over* something rather than to *take a decision about* it.)

We find also a good example of the evil influence exerted by vague abstract nouns like *measure*.

Initially the university might expect to exercise a fairly tight measure of control over the colleges but as they gained in experience they could be given an increasing measure of independence.

These *measures*, whether tight or increasing, destroy the virility of the writing. Let the university simply exercise 'fairly tight control', and later give 'more independence'. *Level, degree, character, nature* are other words of the same kind, useful on occasions but too often reached for by writers who shun direct and simple language (cf. pp. 84–6). For instance, this same writer has:

It is right for those directly responsible to the taxpayer to determine the overall level of expenditure.

This simply means 'total expenditure'. We have already noted his 'significantly higher level of expenditure'.

Finally, the following sentence will interest the student of 'commenting' and 'defining' relative clauses (see pp. 158–9):

The thing to aim for is a flexible programme that allows for changes of mind as the course progresses but which also satisfies the vocational drive of those who already have a commitment to teaching on entry.

There are three relative clauses here, all 'defining'. So *that* and *which* (or *who*) are equally permissible. But the first two have the same antecedent, and it is careless and inconsistent to write 'a programme *that* allows . . . but *which* also satisfies'. Admittedly, the repetition of *that* would sound a bit awkward. The best answer here is to omit the second relative pronoun altogether ('a programme that allows . . . but also satisfies'). But the third relative clause defines quite a different antecedent, and whether *that* or *which* has been used for the first two the writer has a free choice between *that* and *who* for the third. He chose *who*, and so would we. (Incidentally, *aim for* is presumably a confusion between *go for* and *aim at*.)

These blunders and inelegances are surely plain enough. With the possible exception of the *that* and *which* in the last quotation, they must obtrude themselves on almost all readers and divert their attention from the merits of the arguments to the demerits of the writing. Yet this was the work of a highly educated man. He had failed to make the best of his case by omitting to acquire elementary good habits as a writer.

Specimen 2

The next specimen is not so bad. Thousands of pages of writing like this are produced every year, particularly in the annual reports of both public and private bodies. This paragraph comes from an Annual Report of the defunct National Ports Council. The Report as a whole is neither better nor worse than most.

The large development programme which is still continuing, the likely demands for progressive improvement of facilities, coupled with the very high interest rates now ruling, and the comprehensive reconstruction of manning structures, wages and terms of employment, confront the ports with a situation in which, giving all due weight to the benefits to be expected from increased management and operating efficiency, disposal of out-of-date assets and other measures within the control of management, it appears clear to the Council that it will be difficult to achieve a satisfactory and continuing financial net surplus.

There is nothing wrong here with the grammar, and the vocabulary, though rather stilted, is by no means outrageous. A more sensitive writer would have avoided the *reconstruction of structures*; *situation* is, as so often, a bad sign; and *financial net surplus* seems to be just a grand way of saying *profit*. But what is chiefly wrong is that this is flat, tired, perfunctory, inconsiderate writing: inconsiderate, because the reader has to plough through a lot of words, perhaps more than once, before getting a clear idea of what this long and stodgy sentence is leading up to.

It would have been much easier if the writer had broken up the sentence a bit and used fewer abstract words. There is plenty of choice. Here is one possible redraft:

> The ports face heavy costs. A large development programme is not yet complete and still further improvements in facilities are likely to be demanded; interest rates are very high; and manning, wages and terms of employment are all being completely overhauled. The ports can take various steps to help their finances, for instance by disposing of out-of-date assets and improving their own efficiency. But, even so, they will clearly find it difficult to make and sustain satisfactory profits.

This does not seem to omit anything that the writer wanted to put in, but if it does the saving of fifteen words can be drawn on to repair the omission.

The lesson here is one which constantly recurs in this book. Think what you want to say before putting pen to paper; let your writing follow your thought; revise what you have written, with the reader's feelings in mind. The result may not be inspiring but it will be readable.

Specimen 3

Here is an extract from a paper that was prepared for a meeting in 1985 of the Health Authority of a London borough. The paragraph comments on a point made in another document.

> Current regional and district policy within the health service places emphasis on shifting patient care away from hospitals and out into the community. This applies primarily to patients with long term health problems (e.g. elderly, mentally ill and handicapped patients). It is necessary that policies are prepared to ensure the smooth transition of these potentially more highly dependent patients from hospital to community care, and that arrangements are made to monitor the impact of this change in care patterns on the community services. The transfer in the location of care should be complemented by a similar transfer of resources, and it is necessary that the concept of the Primary Care Team and current attachment policies be jointly reviewed by the FPC and DHA in the light of these changes.

Several phrases are verbose or stilted. In the first sentence we might prefer to use the more forceful *emphasises* instead of the circumlocutory *places emphasis on*, and to replace the compressed *patient care* with the more natural *the care of patients*. Initial *this* in the second sentence is troublesome. Is its antecedent *policy* or *emphasis* or *shifting patient care?* The writer should not force his readers to guess. The third sentence is pompous and inflated. We can say the same in fewer words and far more clearly:

> We must ensure that when these more dependent patients leave hospital they will be cared for at once by community services, and we must observe how the transfer from hospital to home care affects the services.

The final sentence will surely horrify readers. It is clogged with abstract nouns and unnecessary passives. The first half means no more than 'We shall therefore divert money and staff from caring for patients in hospital to caring for them at home'. Why should the reader be made to excavate this meaning?

Specimen 4

This is an extract from the Government reply to a report from the Home Affairs Committee (1981–82) on police complaints procedures. We have numbered the sentences for convenient reference.

(1) The most important proposal is for the introduction of an independent assessor for serious complaints, at the investigation stage. (2) This is in addition to the independent elements provided by the Director of Public Prosecutions and the Police Complaints Board in the consideration of the outcome of complaints investigations. (3) The assessor's function will be to ensure that investigations carried out under his supervision are conducted expeditiously, thoroughly and impartially. (4) He will have the necessary powers for this purpose and will be actively involved from the appointment of the investigating officer right through the investigation to its completion. (5) Only when he has signified his satisfaction with the investigation will decisions be made on what action, if any, should be taken. (6) Under the arrangements described, in any case not referred to the assessor he will be able, in effect, to call it in and determine whether by reason of the gravity of the allegation or other exceptional circumstances it should be investigated under his supervision.

(1) The first sentence contains a glaring use of the 'throw-back' comma (see pp. 163–4). The final phrase *at the investigation stage* properly belongs after *introduction*, but if it is put there it will disrupt the equally close connection of *introduction* with *of an independent*

assessor. The clumsy device of the 'throw-back' comma is intended to deter readers from connecting the final phrases *serious complaints at the investigation stage.* But many readers will be misled, at least at first reading, despite the intervening comma. If we recast the sentence, we can resolve the problem that induced the writer to insert the comma:

The most important proposal is that an independent assessor be introduced when serious complaints are investigated.

The change gives us the added bonus of ridding the sentence of the abstract words *introduction* and *investigation stage.*

(2) What does *This* refer to? The most likely candidate is *an independent assessor.* If so, the sentence should begin *The independent assessor,* since (apart from the ambiguity about the antecedent) it is odd to use *this* to refer back to a person in such a way.

Provided is also ambiguous. Do the Director of Public Prosecutions and the Police Complaints Board appoint 'the independent elements' or (more probably) are they themselves the 'independent elements'? And we surely must get rid of the empty word *elements.*

The reader is likely to be confused by the last words of the sentence. The sentence ends with a string of prepositional phrases that are loosely attached to what precedes them. We should clarify the connection. The Director of Public Prosecutions and the Police Complaints Board consider only the results of the investigations. This important difference is obscured in the original.

We may now attempt a translation:

The independent assessor serves in addition to the independent Director of Prosecutions and the independent Police Complaints Board, both of whom consider only the results of investigations into complaints.

(3) The sense requires that the assessor's function is to supervise investigations. The sentence reads better like this:

The assessor's function is to supervise investigations to ensure that they are conducted expeditiously, thoroughly and impartially.

(4) This is the best sentence of the passage.

(5) We may wish to get rid of the abstract word *satisfaction*:

Only when he has signified that he is satisfied with the investigation . . .

(6) The sentence starts badly. The word *described* is unnecessary if

we replace *the* by *these*; *Under these arrangements* is more succinct and more natural. But *Under this proposal* is better still, since the details so far described do not include the assessor's power to deal with cases that are not referred to him.

The position of *in any case* may start a false trail, and suggest the meaning 'whatever else is done'. Also, the arrangement of words makes it harder for readers to work out the antecedents of *he* and *it*.

The phrase *in effect* is superfluous, adding nothing to a sentence that is already longwinded. We may similarly wish to omit *by reason of the gravity of the allegation or other exceptional circumstances*, since *in any case* indicates that the assessor can decide to take up any complaint; he does not have to justify doing so.

Here is a translation, which also gets rid of the unnecessary passive at the end of the sentence. We have made the sentence far clearer, and at the same time exactly halved the number of words.

> Under this proposal, the assessor can call in any complaint not referred to him and decide whether he should supervise the investigation.

Specimen 5

Our next specimen consists of the opening paragraphs of a Government presentation to Parliament in 1978. The document details the Government's guidance to British companies with interests in South Africa. The passage is an example of official writing that does its job competently enough despite some minor blemishes.

1. At their meeting in Brussels on 20 September 1977 the Foreign Ministers of the Nine Member States of the European Community approved the text of a Code of Conduct for companies with interests in South Africa, which is at Annex 1.

2. The Government urges United Kingdom companies with interests in South Africa to make every effort to promote the adoption of the policies and practices recommended in the Code of Conduct to the fullest possible extent. It is in the interests of companies themselves that they should maintain the best employment practices in South Africa and be seen to do so. Many United Kingdom companies have already demonstrated their commitment to this policy. In South Africa, and elsewhere, it remains Her Majesty's Government's policy that United Kingdom companies and their affiliates should act in accordance with the laws of the countries within which they operate. In urging adoption of the policies and practices recommended in the Code at Annex 1, including those in Section 1, the Government is not asking companies to act contrary to South African law. These

policies and practices are in many respects already incorporated and recommended in other international codes, for example, the OECD Guidelines for Multinational Enterprises, and the ILO Tripartite Declaration of Principles Concerning Multinational Enterprises and Social Policy. Whilst welcoming the initiative taken by the Urban Foundation in Johannesburg in conjunction with employers' organisations in South Africa to adopt an enlightened code of employment practice, the Government emphasises that it is the Code of Conduct of the Nine which it commends for adoption by United Kingdom companies.

The first paragraph is clear and direct. In the first sentence of the second paragraph, the final phrase *to the fullest possible extent* is too far from the verb *promote*, and the series *make every effort to promote the adoption of* might well be shortened without appreciable loss. The second part of this sentence reads more smoothly like this:

. . . to adopt as fully as possible the policies and practices recommended in the Code of Conduct.

The third sentence (beginning *In South Africa*) seems out of place, although not sufficiently to baffle the reader. Its logical place is after the sentence that follows it (*In urging adoption of the policies*). The order is clearer like this: the Government urges companies to follow its advice; tells them that it is not asking them to do anything against South African order; and notes that it never asks companies to act against the law of foreign countries.

There is one minor punctuation fault. In the sentence beginning *These policies and practices*, the phrase *for example* is enclosed in commas. At a first reading *for example* may seem to refer backwards to *other international codes*, though it becomes clear that the writer intends it to refer forwards to *the OECD Guidelines*, etc. We ensure that readers understand the correct direction if we put a semicolon before *for example* or if we leave out the second comma.

Specimens 6 and 7

To cap these run-of-the-mill specimens of official writing, we append two very different ones. The first is by the scientist and Nobel prizewinner Sir Peter Medawar;* the second by the novelist and literary critic Dan Jacobson.† What these two good passages have in common (besides their medical subject-matter) is that neither is in the least elevated or bombastic

* Peter Medawar, *Pluto's Republic*, pp. 62–63. Oxford University Press, 1984.
† Dan Jacobson, *Time and Time Again*, pp. 205–206. André Deutsch, 1985.

in style: they say what they have to say in simple, graceful modern prose. The first is expository, the second narrative. This is the first passage (Specimen 6):

I must begin by making it clear that my criticism of psychoanalysis is not to be construed as a criticism of psychiatry or psychological medicine as a whole. People nowadays tend to use 'psychoanalysis' to stand for all forms of psychotherapy, much as 'Hoover' is used as a generic name for all vacuum cleaners and 'Vaseline' for all ointments of a similar kind. By psychoanalysis I understand that special pedigree of psychological doctrine and treatment which can be traced back, directly or indirectly, to the writings and work of Sigmund Freud. The position of psychological medicine today is in some ways analogous to that of physical or conventional medicine in the middle of the nineteenth century. The physician of a hundred and thirty years ago was confronted by all manner of medical distress. He studied and tried to cure his patients with great human sympathy and understanding and with highly developed clinical skills, by which I mean that he had developed to a specially high degree that form of heightened sensibility which made it possible for him to read a meaning into tiny clinical signals which a layman or a beginner would have passed over or misunderstood. The physician's relationship to his patient was a very personal one, as if healing were not so much a matter of applying treatment to a 'case' as a collaboration between the physician's guidance and his patient's willingness to respond to it. But—there was so little he could do! The microbial theory of infectious disease had not been formulated, viruses were not recognised, hormones were unheard of, vitamins undefined, physiology was rudimentary and biochemistry almost non-existent.

The psychiatry of today is in a rather similar position, because we are still so very ignorant of the mind. But the best of its practitioners are people of great skill and understanding and apparently inexhaustible patience; people whose humanity reveals itself just as much in the way they recognise their limitations as in their satisfaction when a patient gets better in their care. I am emphasising this point to make it clear that to express dissatisfaction with psychoanalysis is not to disparage psychological medicine as a whole.

In these two paragraphs, Medawar begins with a definition and goes on to draw an analogy between the conventional medicine of the past and modern psychiatry. The structure is clear, the sentences manageable in length, and the vocabulary appropriate. Note the delicate shifts of level between the formal *construed* and *analogous*, the technical *microbial*, and the simple *when a patient gets better*. There is nothing here that we could improve.

This is the second passage (Specimen 7):

The hours seemed to go by even more slowly than they had the previous night. Before a patient was taken down to the theatre, I had been told, a 'pre-med' was administered, to make him drowsy. Then the preparations would be complete, and darkness would supervene. When the staff-nurse finally approached me, well after midday, I sat up almost eagerly, to take my medicine like a man. Or rather, like a child. At that point there took place the only 'mishap' I have to report, as far as my own treatment is concerned. The nurse had not come to give me my 'pre-med'; far from it. She had come to tell me that I would not, after all, be operated on that afternoon; indeed, the operation would not take place until the next Monday. (It was then Thursday.) They had miscalculated the time needed in the theatre by the two patients who had preceded me there.

All that apprehension for nothing? All of it to go through again? These last days of strenuous waiting, and these last hours of preparation, utterly without point? The shock of that announcement was in its own way quite as painful as anything I had felt since I had fallen ill; in some respects it was even worse than any of the other pains I had suffered or was still to go through, for it had not come about through an act of nature, as it were, but as a result of human misjudgement and mismanagement. Anger, incredulity, paranoid suspicion (I *knew*, I'd always known, they were capable of pulling something like this on me; I'd always known *I'd* be the one they would do it to), shame, impotence, even a tiny, sneaking flicker of relief—it does not take long, no more than a second it seems, for such conflicting and mutually exacerbating emotions to fill one's breast. To get them to settle down is a more protracted business.

In the end, however, the torment-by-anti-climax I had been put through did produce two incidental benefits. The first was that the wintry weekend I found myself unexpectedly spending at home (two long black nights and three brown days, accompanied throughout by the sound of leaves creeping and crackling in the streets) turned out to be surprisingly enjoyable. The second was that when I did return to the hospital on Sunday, to be prepared all over again for the operation, I felt none of the apprehension I had gone through on the previous occasion. I did not give a damn about anything but getting the whole performance over and done with; I certainly was not going to let them make a fool of me again by investing emotion in it beforehand.

This comes from a collection of autobiographical episodes, and deals vividly with the author's reactions to a particular experience. The passion of the middle paragraph contrasts with the calm of the two other paragraphs. This is not a kind of writing that most of us are called upon to attempt. Let it serve to remind us, however, that although the field of good English prose writing is much wider than the little patch that we cultivate, the rules are everywhere much the same.

17

A checklist: words and phrases to be used with care

Words and phrases appear in this alphabetic list for a variety of reasons. Some are often used in senses generally regarded as incorrect. For example, *disinterested* is frequently intended to mean 'uninterested' and *verbal* to mean 'oral'. Certain pairs of words are repeatedly confused, such as *alternately* and *alternatively*. Some words are wrongly constructed; for example, *hardly* must be followed by *when*, not by *than*.

We have also included words and phrases that tend to be used unsuitably rather than incorrectly. We frequently suggest replacements that follow the rules 'Be short, be simple, be human'. *Ongoing* and *feedback* are vogue words that are better replaced by synonyms; *said* (*in the said document*) and *pursuant to* are legal jargon; the verbose *with the result that* should give way to the concise *so that*, the pretentious *deem* to *think*, and the Latinism *per annum* to *a year*; we prefer the more human *Thank you for your letter* to *I acknowledge receipt of your letter*.

We sometimes point to changes in usage. *Agree* is now commonly used without a preposition, as in *I must agree your figures*; and *under the circumstances* has established itself despite the objections of purists. And we give advice on variants, such as the choice between *ise* and *ize*.

Accede to

Do not use this expression where *grant, allow, agree, or consent to* will do. To accede to someone's demands may imply a yielding of one's own wishes in giving consent, but that is not what most writers of officialese mean by it.

Accommodation

While we stay in the same place we can still call our house our house, or our flat our flat, or our lodgings our lodgings. But if Authority arranges to move us, it will not be to another house, or a different flat, or new lodgings. It will always be to alternative accommodation. This cliché has run wild, and its versatility is astonishing. Sometimes it means no more than *houses*:

> The real cause of bad relations between landlord and tenant is the shortage of alternative accommodation.

Or it may mean something less than houses:

> Experience has shown that many applications have been received for exemption certificates [sc. from the obligation to provide sanitary conveniences] on the ground that alternative accommodation is available. . . . Public sanitary conveniences should not be considered satisfactory alternative accommodation.

Do not use *accommodation* where *home* will do.

Accompanying

If possible, rephrase your sentence so as to be able to replace *accompanying* by *with*.

Accordingly

Prefer *so* or *therefore*.

According to

You can replace 'According to our records' by 'Our records show', and it is simpler and more direct to do so.

Accountability

This popular vogue word means the area for which someone is responsible:

> to distinguish their individual accountabilities from their joint accountabilities.

For a change, use *responsibility*. To be accountable for something is to be personally answerable for it, so that the expression can scarcely be used of things. It is reasonable to say 'I am accountable to your parents for your safety', but not 'The appalling weather was accountable for their failure'.

Achieve

This word implies successful effort, and should not be treated as merely the equivalent of *getting* or *reaching*, as in the phrase, which is not unknown, 'Officers achieving redundancy'. There is an air of dignity about *achieve* which may lead writers to prefer misguidedly such sentences as 'this was impossible of achievement' to the simpler 'this could not be done'. It is not sensible to say that a weapon 'has achieved good accuracy' instead of 'has proved to be (very) accurate' or to describe an unsuccessful student as 'a low achiever' or 'an underachiever'.

Acknowledge

It is pleasanter to write 'Thank you for your letter' than merely to *acknowledge* it.

Acquaint

Prefer *tell* or *inform*. To acquaint oneself is to *find out*, and to be acquainted with something is to *know* it. *Acquaint* is a starchy word.

Acquire

Use *get* or *buy* or *win* according to which you mean.

Action

In managerial jargon, *action* is used as a verb, as in 'Please action this report'. This is a convenient piece of shorthand for *take action on*, but the longer phrase should be preferred for public pronouncements.

Adequate

Where possible, use *enough*. To have an adequate standard of living is, in simple parlance, to have enough money.

Adjacent

Use *near* or *next to*.

Adjust, Adjustment

If you mean *change*, say so.

Adumbrate

Try using *outline* or *foreshadow*.

Advantageous

Prefer *useful* or *helpful*.

Advert to

Use *refer to* or *mention*.

Affect

This word has won an undeserved popularity because it is colourless—a word of broad meaning that saves a writer the trouble of thought. It is a useful word in its place, but not when used from laziness. It may be easier to say 'The progress of the building has been *affected* by the weather', but it is better to use a more precise word—*hindered*, perhaps, or *delayed* or *stopped*. Elsewhere, *affected* may be better replaced by *changed*.

Affirmative

An *affirmative* reply, or one that is in *the affirmative*, is one that says yes. Rephrase your sentence to get rid of this pompous word.

Affluent

Use the simpler word *rich*.

Afford

Use *give* or *provide* if that is what you mean, as in 'afford shelter'. To most people, *afford* means 'be able to pay for'.

Aforementioned, Aforesaid

These are lawyers' words. In ordinary writing, 'the aforesaid notice' can usually become 'the notice' or 'this notice' or 'it'.

Agree

Following the example set by *approve*, *agree* is showing a disposition to shake off its attendant prepositions *to*, *on* and *with*, and to pose as a transitive verb, particularly in the past participle: 'I agree your figures', 'We must agree the arrangements for this', 'I agree your draft', 'an agreed statement'. Some would castigate this, but there seems to be no great harm in it. After all, the Chairman of the meeting says 'Is that agreed?' not 'Is that agreed to?' and his dutiful hearers murmur 'Agreed, agreed' rather than 'Agreed with, agreed with'. It is true that established idiom requires 'I agree with your figures', 'We must agree on the arrangements' and 'I agree with' or (if from a superior) 'I agree to your draft'. But the change has surely come to stay, and is now absorbed into English idiom.

Aid

This is the appropriate word for money and resources provided for a public cause, as in 'overseas aid'. Where there is no need to strike this impersonal note, use *help*.

Alibi

The Victorians allowed great scope to individuality and masculinity, strong passions and high spirits, and other alibis for over-weening egomania, insecurity and aggression.

Members of the timber trade, like members of any other trade, are glad of any alibi to explain any particular increases in price.

Either we accept the bare facts or we go down to a lower standard of living. The day of alibis is gone.

Alibi is used in these examples in the sense of *excuse*, or of an admission of guilt with a plea of extenuating circumstances, or of throwing the blame on someone else. But *alibi* is the Latin for *elsewhere*. To plead an alibi is, strictly, to rebut a charge by adducing evidence that the person charged was elsewhere at the time of the crime. The vogue of detective stories may have stimulated the corruption. So many of them rely on an alibi for their plot that the word has come to be used for any means of rebutting a charge. It is probably too late to resist the establishment of this enlarged use.

Allergic

Allergic is a useful word. It gives us a convenient alternative to the stilted 'I have a subconscious antipathy to' and the slang 'I have a thing about'. But it should not be allowed too often to displace common words that might be more suitable, such as *dislike*, *repugnance* and *aversion*.

Alter

Prefer the simpler word *change* where that will do.

Alternate(ly), Alternative(ly)

These are sometimes confused. *Alternate(ly)* means by turn, or every other. *Alternative(ly)* means in a way that offers a choice. 'The journey may be made by rail or alternately by road' means, if it means anything, that every other journey may be made by road. It does not mean, as the writer intended, that for every journey the traveller has a choice between the two means of transport. Conversely, 'alternatively they sat and walked in the moonlight, talking of this and that' cannot have been intended to mean that they sat and walked in the moonlight as an alternative to doing something else; what must have been intended is that they sat and walked alternately. *Alternate* can also be a verb meaning, in popular language, to 'take it in turns'.

The use of *alternative* for such words as *other*, *new*, *revised* or *fresh* is rife. Perhaps this is due to infection spread by the cliché *alternative accommodation*.

The Minister regrets that he will not be able to hold the Conference arranged for the 15th March. Members will be informed as soon as alternative arrangements have been made.

Alternative must imply a choice between two or more things. *Other* is the right word here. It is pedantry to say that, because of its derivation, *alternative* must not be used where the choices are more than two.

In certain contexts *alternative* has developed a specific social and political sense which cannot be paraphrased. The hippie youth culture of the late 1960s spoke of itself as the *alternative* society, and now we have alternative newspapers and alternative cinema, independent of commercial financing; alternative energy derived from windmills and the sun; and alternative technology, using small cheap tools and human muscles. It would be churlish to object to this extension of meaning.

Ambivalent

Ambivalent is overworked. It is sometimes even treated as if it meant *ambiguous*. It is a psychoanalytical term applicable to the simultaneous operation in the mind of two irreconcilable wishes. The condition it describes must be as old as humanity, and it would be a pity if so pretentious a usurper were allowed to displace the expression *mixed feelings*, which has served us so well and so long.

Ameliorate

Prefer *improve*. It means make better, and is sometimes confused with *counteract* or *mitigate*. You can ameliorate conditions, but not hardships.

Amenity

This is overused as a word for anything useful or convenient. Roads, power and sewage are now urban amenities, and a rubbish dump is an amenity site. We might like to confine the use of *amenity* to environmental pleasures of no economic value, such as woodland not harvested for timber or lakes used for boating rather than for civic water supplies; but the battle is probably lost.

Analogous

You can avoid this starchy word by recasting the sentence to use *like*.

Analysis

Instead of writing 'in the ultimate, the final, or the last analysis', consider saying *in the end*.

Anticipate

The use of this word as a synonym for *expect* is now so common, despite persistent opposition from lovers of the language, that some faint-hearts are beginning to give up the fight. But it is still worth while to urge that *anticipate* should convey the idea of forestalling an event, as in the time-honoured reply of Chancellors of the Exchequer, 'I cannot anticipate my budget statement'. A safe rule is to use it only with a noun or pronoun, never with an infinitive or a *that*-clause. Here are two examples, the first of its right use and the second of its wrong.

Remember, in conducting, that your thought and gesture will almost certainly be too late rather than too early. Anticipate everything.

It is anticipated that a circular on this and other matters will be issued at an early date.

Here is a remarkable example of its incorrect and correct use in consecutive sentences.

The 'after-care' effort is concentrated on all large cases and cases where difficulty is anticipated. By this method most of the more serious problems are anticipated and action can be taken timeously.

Antithetical

Replace it by *against* or *opposite* or *opposed* if you can.

Apparent

If you mean *clear, plain, obvious*, say so.

Appraise, Apprise

To *appraise* is to form a judgment about the value of something. You can appraise a candidate for a job by interviewing him or her, or a race-horse from his appearance in the paddock. It is sometimes confused with *apprise*, which means inform, and is better replaced by *inform* in any case. Both the following are wrong:

> Mr Heath has been anxious to appraise himself of the developments in various Ministries since Parliament rose for the Christmas recess.
>
> Being appraised of the proposals for an oil refinery at Longhaugh . . . we wrote to the Secretary of State to express our deep concern.

Appreciate

The ordinary meaning of *appreciate*, as a transitive verb, is to form an estimate of the worth of anything, to set a value on it, and hence to acknowledge with gratitude. In this last meaning it is used, particularly in business English, in such phrases as 'I should appreciate an early reply', 'I would appreciate your asking Mr X to explain . . .', 'My class would appreciate a discussion of . . .'.

But it is sometimes used merely to make a piece of polite padding (see p. 65). And it is used far too often where it would be more suitable to use *understand*, *realise* or *recognise*. When a request has to be refused, it may be laudable to attempt to soften the refusal by such phrases as 'I appreciate how hard it is on you not to have it', and 'you will appreciate the reasons why I cannot let you have it'. But in such phrases *appreciate* is faintly pompous (some would condemn it as incorrect). The laudable intention would be better served by *realise* in the first and *understand* in the second. An effective way of curbing overuse of the word might be to resolve never to use it with a *that* clause ('I appreciate that there has been delay'), but always give it a noun to govern ('I appreciate the trouble you have taken').

'It would be appreciated if' can usually be translated into 'I shall be glad (or grateful, or obliged, or even pleased) if . . .'. 'You will appreciate that . . .' can often be better expressed by 'you will realise that', or even 'of course'.

Appropriate (adjective)

This is an irreproachable word. But so also are *right*, *suitable*, *fitting* and *proper*, and there seems to be no reason why *appropriate* should have it all its own way. In particular, the Whitehall cliché *in appropriate cases* might be confined more closely than it is now to cases in which it is appropriate.

Approximate(ly)

This means very close(ly). An approximate estimate is one that need not be exact, but should be as near as you can conveniently make it. There is no need to use *approximately* when *about* or *roughly* would do as well or even better, as in:

It is understood that Mr X spent some time in America, approximately from 1939 to 1946.

Moreover the habit of using *approximate(ly)* leads to the absurdity of saying *very approximate* when what is meant is *very rough*, that is to say, *not* very approximate, as in:

An outline should be furnished to this Branch stating the relevant circumstances and a very approximate estimate of the expenditure involved.

A priori

Do not say *a priori* when you mean *prima facie*.

Services in the bottom row of Table 2 seem *a priori* to be suited to traditional bureaucratic organization.

Several countries most advanced from a medical point of view have for the last 20 years done without this drug, 'a fact', says the Board, 'which is sufficient to show that there is an *a priori* case for its total abolition'.

No—it does not. To argue *a priori* is to argue from assumed axioms and not from experience. The argument here rests on the 20-year experience of several countries, and so is an argument *a posteriori*.

Prima facie, which is what the writer probably had in mind, means on a first impression, before hearing fully the evidence for and against. In fact you can probably get on without either phrase. In the first of the above examples *at first sight* would do very well: in the second *a strong case* or *an arguable case* would be an improvement.

Around

It is still somewhat of an Americanism to use *around* for *about* or *roughly*, as in 'around 60°'. Avoid the practice.

Ascertain

Use *find out*.

Authority

Use *right*, for that sense of the word.

Averse, Adverse

It is usual to say *averse from*, though there is good authority for *averse to*. (What cat's averse to fish?) But *adverse* is always *to*.

Aware

You can often replace 'be aware of it' by 'know it'.

Background

The word has come into great favour in metaphorical use. Up to a point its extensions have been useful. To speak of examining the background of a proposal, in the sense of trying to find out what more there is in it than meets the eye, is a reasonable metaphor. So is what is called 'background training' to distinguish it from specialised training. And it is a reasonable extension of the metaphor to write:

> Men and women with widely different backgrounds had in fact succeeded, ranging from graduates and trained social workers to a coalminer, a railway clerk and a clerk in an ironmongery store.

But, like all these new favourites, it is beginning to get out of hand, and to displace more precise words:

> From your particulars it would appear that your background is more suitable for posts in Government Departments employing quantity surveyors.

This does not seem to mean anything different from 'you are better qualified', the word *background* edging into the place of *experience* or *history*.

> The weak state of the £ provides the background of the problem.

Here it seems to be masquerading as *explanation*.

Further price increases, nevertheless, may be unavoidable against a background of rising costs.

Here the meaning seems nearer to *cause* than to *explanation*. *Against a background of* is equivalent to *because of*.

Beg the question

This does not mean, as is commonly supposed, to evade a straight answer to a question. It means to form a conclusion by making an assumption which is as much in need of proof as the conclusion itself. Logicians call this *petitio principii*. 'Thus to say that parallel lines will never meet because they are parallel is simply to assume as a fact the very thing you profess to prove' (Brewer). A single word can be used in a question-begging way. *Reactionary*, *victimisation*, *aggression*, *imperialism* and *warmonger* are examples.

Beneficial

Prefer *useful* or *helpful*, where possible.

Blueprint

This word has caught on as a picturesque substitute for *scheme* or *plan* and the shine is wearing off it. It is not reasonable to ask that metaphors should be anchored at their points of origin, but it would make for accuracy of language if writers who use this one remembered that in the engineering industries, where it comes from, the blueprint marks the final stage of paper design.

Bona fides

It means sincerity, good standing. If you use this Latin expression, use it with a singular verb, as in 'his bona fides was questioned'. *Bona fide*, which looks like the singular form, is an adjective not a noun, as in 'a bona fide query'.

Brackets, Groups

These words were put into currency by statisticians as synonyms for *class* or *category*, and they have been widely taken up. 'These are likely in the main to be bought by the lower income groups.' 'Will the Chancellor of the Exchequer move to set up a Select Committee to consider the financial hardships of the small income groups?' *Income group* has indeed become an official cliché. And we are told of what used to be called naughty children but are now juvenile delinquents:

It is some comfort to learn that the eight-to-thirteen bracket is the only one that involved more arrests.

It would be absurd to class *group* as a suspect word, but *bracket* is really rather silly as a synonym for it. The language is rich enough to do without it.

Breakdown

It is fashionable, though not always apt, to use *breakdown* in a pseudo-scientific sense vaguely connoting analysis, subdivision, or classification of statistical matter. It is certainly inept when used of things that can be physically broken down:

The houses erected should be broken down into types. (. . . classified according to type.)
The breakdown of this number of houses into varying densities per acre. (The division . . .)
The Minister wishes to avoid fragmentation of the service by breaking down the two-tier system of administration provided for in the Act into a three-tier system.

Why *breaking down* in the last example? If the word *break* must be used at all, *breaking up* would go better with *fragmentation*. But why not some ordinary word such as *changing*, *altering* or *converting*?
The fascination of this word may lead to quaint results.

Care should be taken that the breakdown of patients by the department under whose care they were immediately before discharge is strictly followed.
Unfortunately a complete breakdown of British trade is not possible.
Statistics have been issued of the population of the United States, broken down by age and sex.

Capability

This vogue word means something like feature or faculty or potential ability, as in 'nuclear capability'. Try not to overdo it.

Capitalise

Replace this vogue word by *draw upon* or *profit by* if you can, as in 'to capitalise on her legal experience'.

Casual

Like *aggressive*, *casual* has come up in the world, and can now often mean nonchalantly informal, a quality much prized today.

Catalyst

Catalyst is a metaphor borrowed from chemistry. (The dictionaries define *catalysis* as the effect produced by a substance that without undergoing change itself aids a chemical change in other bodies, and *catalyst* as the agent in catalysis.) Its popularity is growing with suspicious rapidity, and there is some danger that what can clearly be a useful and expressive metaphor will be killed or blunted by over-use. To say that a particular event was 'the catalyst of change in the attitudes' of interested parties is reasonable enough; to say that 'the Church has been the catalyst for community development' is rather more doubtful; the temptation to make the metaphor play absurd antics can be illustrated by these two extracts from politicians' speeches (one Labour, one Conservative):

. . . a traumatic catalyst for a ferment of change.
Responsibility for implementing a binding agreement would automatically act as a catalyst for bridging the gap.

Ceiling

Ceiling is a metaphor that has run wild for too long. Its respectable purpose is to provide a metaphorical equivalent to *maximum* or *limit*. But it is not a dead metaphor and it should not be used as if it were.

The advisory Committee did not apply for a general increase in the ceilings.

Any ceiling imposed under this rule may be increased or waived if the contributor agrees.

Ceiling here means *maximum prices* in the first example and *maximum benefits* in the second. The writers forgot that if one wants more headroom one does not increase the ceiling, still less perform the curious operation of waiving it; one raises it or, in the last resort, removes it.

In determining the floor-space, a ceiling of 15,000 square feet should normally be the limit.

This is indeed a complicated way of saying that floor-space should not normally exceed 15,000 square feet. Why drag down the ceiling?

There was no intention on the part of the Treasury of fixing an unrealistic ceiling which could not be held.

One wonders what sort of ceiling can. (For *unrealistic* in the sense of *unreasonable* see p. 257.)

Unless you are accustomed to thinking of a ceiling as a blunt instrument that bites you will be surprised by:

Manpower ceilings are a very blunt macro-instrument and will be either ineffective or unduly restrictive if not based on the results of management reviews and other 'micro' activities . . . ceilings are biting, but this is what they were meant to do.

Centre

Traditionally things centre on, upon or in other things, though an institution may be centred at a place. Many people still dislike the combinations *centre around* and *centre about*, as in 'many legends centre around this holy shrine'.

Chauvinism

These days, *chauvinism* nearly always means male chauvinism, the naïve sense of masculine superiority in the war between the sexes. It used to mean something like jingoism, or blind bellicose patriotism as exemplified by Nicholas Chauvin, who was one of Napoleon's veterans. The word can be used to smear the natural and even respectable emotions that are better called *nationalism* and *patriotism*. See *Beg the Question*, p. 209.

Circumstances

It used to be widely held by purists that to say 'under the circumstances' must be wrong because what is around us cannot be over us. 'In the circumstances' was the only correct expression. But these purists have not prevailed. There is good authority for *under the circumstances*, and if some of us prefer *in the circumstances*, that is a matter of taste, not of rule.

Claim

The proper meaning of *to claim* is to demand recognition of a right. But the fight to prevent it from usurping the place of *assert* has been lost in America and is probably lost here also, especially as the BBC have surrendered without a struggle. Here are some examples from this country:

The police took statements from about forty people who claimed that they had seen the gunmen in different parts of the city.

The State Department claims that discrimination is being shown against the American film industry.

There are those who claim that the Atlantic Treaty has an aggressive purpose.

I have a friend who claims to keep in his office a filing tray labelled 'Too Difficult'.

The enlargement of *claim* ought to be deplored by all those who like to treat words as tools of precision, and to keep their edges sharp. Why should *claim*, which has its own useful job to do, claim a job that is already being efficiently done by others? Perhaps the idea underlying this usage is that the writer claims credence for an improbable or unverified assertion.

Commence

Use *begin* or *start*.

Compare

There is a difference between *compare to* and *compare with*; the first is to liken one thing to another; the second is to note the resemblances and differences between two things. Thus:

Shall I compare thee to a summer's day?

If we compare the speaker's notes with the report of his speech in *The Times* . . .

Complex (noun)

As a technical term in psychology, *complex* means a collection of suppressed tendencies, or the mental abnormality caused by them; and an *inferiority complex* is a state of mind that manifests itself in self-assertiveness, not diffidence. But in common usage it is now well established as meaning a consciousness, whether well founded or not, of inferiority.

In its other meaning of a *complex whole*, the noun *complex* is increasingly misused as a showy synonym of *collection* or *group*. It should be used only where there is something complex or complicated about the group referred to.

Parliamentary control of Government expenditure depends on a complex of constitutional principles, statutory requirements and Parliamentary conventions.

The sub-committee has considered the complex of recommendations in the Fulton Report relating to the status of employment.

In the first of these, *complex* is rightly used; in the second, it means no more than *group* and there is no justification for blunting its meaning in this way.

Compound (verb)

This word is often misused. It means to *mix together* into a composite whole, or *to settle* by mutual agreement, or *to condone* for a consideration. Thus, a mixture is compounded of its ingredients; you may compound an annual liability by paying a lump sum; or you may compound a felony if you have a private motive for not wanting the felon prosecuted. It does not mean *to multiply* or *to complicate* as some people suppose (perhaps from a woolly mental association with *compound interest* or *compound fracture*). Here are two examples of misuse:

The percentage figure was wrongly calculated and applying it to the wrong total only compounded the mistake.

[A certain city's] parking problems are as serious as any in the world; and they are compounded by frequent strikes on the public transport system.

The first of these is particularly unfortunate, because *to compound a mistake* is a useful phrase in its proper meaning.

Instead of misusing *compound*, try *multiply, complicate, aggravate, increase, add to* or the like.

Comprise

A body comprises (or consists of) the elements of which it is composed (or constituted); in the first example, for instance, Op. 77 comprises the quartets, not the other way round. *Compose* or *constitute* or *form* should have been used in these examples.

The two quartets comprising Haydn's Op. 77.
The smaller Regional Hospitals which comprise a large proportion of those available to Regional Boards.
The twelve Foreign Ministers who comprise the Atlantic Treaty Council.

The *OED* now recognises *comprise* both in the sense of *compose* and of *be composed of*, but the *compose* sense still raises hackles. The difference between *comprise* and *include* is that *comprise* is correct when all the components are enumerated and *include* when only some of them are.

Concept, Conceptual

Both are overused. The first could often be replaced by *idea, design,* or *invention,* as in 'a new concept in cookware'. The second refers to the forming of concepts by generalising from particulars, which is something that psychologists and educationalists need to talk about, but that is no reason for allowing this technical word to stray outside its proper sphere.

Condition (noun)

If you mean *rule*, say so.

Confrontation

A vogue word for a direct clash between opposed forces, covering anything from unprovoked violence to passive resistance. Sit-ins and rioting are forms of student confrontation. The word is needed, but you could try sometimes using *conflict* instead.

Connection, Connexion

Both spellings are permissible, but *connection* is now commoner. Beware of the verbose *in connection with* and *in this connection*.

Consensus

The spelling *concensus* is wrong. A *consensus* is the result of common consent; it has nothing to do with censuses. This is an overused fashionable word for the moderate undisputed middle ground in politics. It can sometimes be replaced by the simpler *agreement*.

Consequence

For *as a consequence* and *in consequence*, use *so* or *therefore*.

Consequential

Consequential has now only two meanings in common use. It retains that of *self-important*, and in legal language it signifies a secondary and incidental result, especially in the phrases *consequential damages* and *consequential amendments*. For all other purposes *consequent* is the adjective of *consequence*. Thus a Minister might say, 'This amendment is consequent on a promise I gave on a second reading' and 'This amendment is consequential on one accepted yesterday'.

Consist

There is a difference between *consist of* and *consist in*. *Consist of* denotes the substance of which the subject is made; *consist in* defines the subject. .

> The writing desks consist of planks on trestles.
> The work of the branch consists in interviewing the public.

Convenience

At your convenience is better replaced by *soon* or *as soon as you can.*

Convince

Do not use *convince* like *persuade.* You may convince people of a fact, or convince them that you are right, but you cannot correctly convince them to do something.

Cosmetic

A vogue word in the metaphorical sense of superficial embellishment, as of trivial changes of policy or impermanent repairs to a house.

Crash

A fashionable vogue word for anything intended to achieve quick results. You can go on a crash diet or a crash course, or launch a crash programme. Sometimes *short* or *quick* will do instead.

Credence, Credibility, Credulity

These words are sometimes confused. *Credence* means belief or trust, *credibility* the quality of being believable and *credulity* the quality of being ready to believe anything.

In order to give some credence to the viability of the proposals made in this report an attempt has been made to . . .

Here *credence* should be *credibility* (though *plausibility* would be better). True, *credibility to the viability of* would be an ugly phrase, but the proper remedy is to omit *the viability of* altogether. The vogue word *viability* has been unnecessarily dragged in. *Credibility* has become a jargon word in the sense of power to impress, as when people speak of the credibility of the nuclear deterrent; and we hear too much these days of the *credibility gap*, the discrepancy between what is officially claimed and what is observably true.

Currently

Prefer *now* or *at present*.

Date

For *to date*, use *so far*.

Decease, Deceased

Unless the effect would be too abrupt, consider using *die, death, dead*.

Decimate

To *decimate* is to reduce *by* one-tenth, not *to* one-tenth. It meant originally to punish mutinous troops by executing one man in ten, chosen by lot. Hence by extension it means to destroy a large proportion; the suggestion it now conveys is usually of a loss much greater than 10 per cent. Because of the flavour of exactness that still hangs about it, an adverb or adverbial phrase should not be used with it. We may say 'The attacking troops were decimated', meaning that they suffered heavy losses, but we must not say 'The attacking troops were badly decimated', and still less 'decimated to the extent of 50 per cent or more'. A single creature cannot, of course, be decimated. David did not *decimate* Goliath.

Decision-making

A vogue expression in managerial jargon.

Deem

This is an old-fashioned word which starches any letter in which it is used as a synonym for *treat as* or *think*. 'This method is deemed to be contra-indicated' is an unpleasant and obscure way of saying 'This method is thought unsuitable'. But the word is still useful in its technical sense of signifying the constructive or inferential as opposed to the explicit or actual. 'Anyone who does not give notice of objection within three weeks will be deemed to have agreed'; 'Any expenditure incurred in the preparation of plans for any work . . . shall be deemed to be included in the expenditure incurred in carrying out that work.'

Definitive

This word differs from *definite* by conveying the idea of finality. A definite offer is an offer precise in its terms. A definitive offer is an offer which the person making it declares to be the last word.

Deleterious

Use *harmful*.

Depend

It is wrong in writing, though common in speech, to omit the *on* or *upon* after *depends*, as in:

It depends whether we have received another consignment by then.

Dependant

In the ordinary British usage of today *dependant* is a noun meaning 'a person who depends on another for support, etc.' (*OED*). *Dependent* is an adjective meaning relying on or subject to something else. Dependants are dependent on the person whose dependants they are.

Desire

Use *wish* or *want*.

Desist

Use *stop*.

Determine

Use *settle* or *decide*. The technical meaning of *determine* in law is better replaced by *end* or *set an end to*, since ordinary people do not understand it.

Detrimental

Use *harmful*.

Develop

The proper use of this word is to convey the idea of a gradual unfolding or building up. Do not use it as a synonym for *arise, occur, happen, take place, come*. A typical example of its misuse is 'rising prices might develop' (for 'prices might rise').

Dialogue

This is a vogue word in the sense exemplified by 'East–West dialogue'. Since it sounds a little friendlier than *negotiation*, *dialogue* has a legitimate role to play.

Dichotomy

A vogue word. *Dichotomy* is properly used of differentiation into two mutually exclusive groups, as when one speaks of the dichotomy between theory and practice. Do not use it to mean simply difference or conflict or gap, as in 'widen the dichotomy between the two wings of the party'.

Differ

In the sense of to be different, the idiom is to differ *from*. In the sense of to disagree, it is either to differ *from* or to differ *with*, whichever you please.

Different

There is good authority for *different to*, but *different from* is today the established usage. *Different than* is not unknown even in *The Times*:

> The air of the suburb has quite a different smell and feel at eleven o'clock in the morning or three o'clock in the afternoon than it has at the hours when the daily toiler is accustomed to take a few hurried sniffs of it.

But this is condemned by the grammarians, who would say that *than* in this example should have been *from what*. *Different than* is, however, common in America.

Dilemma

This word originally had a precise meaning which it would be a pity not to preserve. It should not therefore be treated as the equivalent of a difficulty, or, colloquially, of a fix or a jam. To be in a dilemma is to be faced with two (and only two) alternative courses of action, each of which is likely to have awkward results.

Dimension

This vogue word is useful enough when it suggests an increase in scope, as in 'the rise in oil prices added a new dimension to the problem'. If you are tired of *dimension*, you could say 'increased the problem'.

Direct, Directly

Direct, although an adjective, is also no less an adverb than *directly*. To avoid ambiguity, it is well to confine *directly* to its meaning of *immediately* in time, and so avoid the possibility of confusion between 'he is going to Edinburgh direct' and 'he is going to Edinburgh directly'. Here are two examples, the first of the right use of *direct* and the second of the wrong use of *directly*:

Committees should notify departments direct of the names and addresses of the banks.

He will arrange directly with the authority concerned for the recruitment and training of technicians.

In serious writing, do not use *directly* for *when*, as in 'I rang him up directly I received the letter'.

Disburse

Use *pay* or *pay out*.

Disclose

This means reveal, as when politicians are required to disclose the sources of their incomes. When *tell* or *show* will do, use them.

Disinterested

Disinterested means 'unbiased by personal interest' (*OED*). It is sometimes used wrongly for *uninterested* (i.e. not interested), as when a Minister said in Parliament:

> I hope that [what I have said] will excuse me from the charge of being disinterested in this matter.

A public figure dealing with public business can never be 'charged' with being disinterested, as if it were a crime. It is his or her elementary duty always to be so. But to avoid danger of misunderstanding, it may be safer to replace *disinterested* by *unbiased* or *impartial*.

Diverge, Divergent

If two paths diverge, they get further away from each other. *Diverge* and *divergent* do not mean the same as *differ* and *different*. Their meanings differ, but they do not diverge.

> These are all matters of considerable complexity on which BOAC and BEA held divergent views.

If this were true, there would be little hope of reconciliation. But in fact the writer only meant *different*. (You can tell that this is a bad writer, because he or she preferred *matters of considerable complexity* to *complex matters*).

> The interests of clients, administrators and the public at large may diverge, and this should be recognised in the theoretical basis of research.

If this were true, it would be hard to see how the research could ever progress from the theoretical to the practical.

Donate

Use *give*.

Doubt

British idiom requires *whether* or *if* after a positive statement and *that* or *but that* after a negative.

I doubt whether he will come today.
I have no doubt that he will come today.

But in America *I doubt that* is the common form.

Economic

There is no excuse for confusing the adjectives *economical* and *economic*, though confusion is seen sometimes in unexpected places. (For example, a Minister once prided himself on 'the more effective and economic organisation that will result from these changes'.) The first is now associated only with economy and the second only with economics. A tenant may protest with truth that what is admittedly an economic rent is not for him an economical one.

Either

Either means one or other of two or more. Its use in the sense of each of two, as in:

> On either side the river lie
> Long fields of barley and of rye

or in:

> The concert will be broadcast on either side of the nine o'clock news

is accepted idiom.

Elucidate

Use *explain*.

Emoluments

Use *earnings* or *income*.

Employ

Prefer *use* if that is what you mean.

Enable

This word means to make able, not to make possible. You may say that your courage enables you to win or makes your victory possible, but not that it enables your victory.

The following examples come from the same 'Explanatory and Financial Memorandum' published with a Parliamentary Bill:

> Clause 6 will enable reciprocal agreements with countries outside the United Kingdom to apply to . . . as well as . . .
> The provisions of the Bill are estimated to enable a net saving of about 80 staff.

The first is right, the second wrong.

An academic member of the Joint Matriculation Board should know better than to write:

> Objective testing . . . enables examination in a wide range of subjects.

Where appropriate, replace *enable* by *allow*.

Enclosed

Rephrase so as to use *inside* or *with*, if you can.

Enormity

This means great wickedness, or a very evil act. Do not use it in the sense of hugeness, as in 'I was amazed at the enormity of the compliment'.

Enquiry

Enquiry and *inquiry* have long existed together as alternative spellings of the same word. In America *inquiry* is dislodging *enquiry* for all purposes. In England a useful distinction is developing; *enquiry* is used for asking a question and *inquiry* for making an investigation. Thus you might enquire what time the inquiry begins; but it is better to replace *enquire* by *ask*.

Entail

This word is given too much work to do. Often some other word such as *need, cause, impose, necessitate, involve* might be more appropriate, or at least make a refreshing change. Sometimes *entail* intrudes where no verb is needed, a common habit of *involve*.

. . . a statement in writing that you are willing to bear the cost entailed of opening the case, withdrawing this amount and resealing.

If *entailed* must be used, the preposition should be *in*.

Enter

Use *put* or *write*, for those senses of the word.

Entitlement

Use *claim* or *right*.

Envisage

There is a place for *envisage* to indicate a mental vision of something planned but not yet created, but not nearly such a big place as is given to it. Like *anticipate*, it is used more suitably with a direct object than with a *that*-clause.

Mr X said that he envisaged that there would be no access to the school from the main road (thought).

I would refer to your letter of the 26th February in which you envisaged the repairs would be completed by the end of this month (said that you expected).

Certain items will fall to be dealt with not by transfer to the Minister but in the way envisaged in Section 60 (described).

Equally

Do not let *as* intrude between *equally* and the word it qualifies. Not *equally as good*, but *equally good*. Do not write 'This applies equally to A as to B'. *As* should be *and*.

Equivalent

You can say that something is *equivalent to* something else, or that it is *the equivalent of* it, but do not say *the equivalent to*. In any case, prefer *equal* or *the same*.

Escalate

This vogue word properly means increase step by step, and applies particularly to military strategy in which both sides counter each other's actions by progressively more drastic moves. It has been overworked in contexts where *rise* (as in 'escalating prices'), *expand* or *develop* might be at least equally appropriate:

The matter has escalated into something like a major scandal. (Use *developed*.)

Establish

Use *show* or *find out* if possible.

Ethnic

This curious word can refer to race or nationality, as when we speak of someone's ethnic origin or of ethnic minorities within a wider host community. In modern American use, and increasingly in Britain, *ethnic* has become more or less a synonym for *exotic* or *foreign*. An ethnic dress is likely to be made of handwoven Indian cotton, and an ethnic Christmas card will show a brown Virgin and Child. In America the word can be a noun too, meaning 'member of an ethnic minority', in practice someone with a whitish skin but of Central European origin. We need *ethnic*, at least as an adjective, since *race* and *racial* have become almost taboo words.

Evacuate

This means to empty, and is a technical term of the military and medical sciences. As a military term it may be used (like *empty*) either of a place (*evacuate a fortress*) or of the people in it (*evacuate a garrison*). In the latter sense it was much used during the second world war to describe the process of moving people out of dangerous places, and they were given the convenient name of *evacuees*. Its inclination to encroach on the province of the simpler word *remove* needs watching.

Event

Rephrase sentences with *in the event that* and *in the event of*, using *if*.

Eventuality

In simpler English, you could perhaps say *possible result*.

Evince

Use *show* or *display*.

Evolve

This is a useful word to denote a process of natural change or development which is gradual and perhaps self-generated. But it is sometimes used where the meaning does not require anything more than *change* or *develop*, and, like *involve*, it has a tendency to appear where nothing is needed at all, as in:

The Government accept the need for appropriate pricing policies to be evolved.

Here the last three words are either unnecessary or inappropriate, for pricing policies need to be invented, devised, or developed by conscious effort; they will not evolve or be evolved by natural selection.

Exclude, Excluding, Exclusively

Use *leave out, apart from, and only*.

Expedite

Use *hasten* or *hurry*.

Expeditiously

Use *quickly*, or *as soon as possible*.

Extend

Use *give* if that is what you mean.

Extent

You can usually replace *to the extent that* by *if* or *when*.

Facilitate

You facilitate what is being done, as in 'use torches to facilitate the search'. You do not facilitate the people who are doing something. *Help* or *assist* should be used in 'we were facilitated in our search by torches'.

Factitious

Factitious means 'engineered' in the derogatory sense of that word, i.e. not naturally or spontaneously created. It is easily confused with *fictitious*, which means sham, counterfeit, unreal. A factitious thing may be genuine; a fictitious thing cannot be.

Fail to, Failure to

Rephrase the sentence so as to use *if you do not*, if that is what you mean. Use *fail* only in the context of neglect, or of unsuccessful attempt.

Feasible

This word means *practicable, capable of being done*. It should not be used as a synonym for *probable* or *plausible*.

Feedback

In its rigorous scientific sense, *feedback* is the return to an input of part of its output, so as to provide self-corrective action. *Feedback* is a vogue word in a loose sense for which *response* would be a perfectly adequate alternative, as in 'we got a lot of valuable feedback on our advertising campaign'.

First, Firstly

There used to be a grammarians' rule that you must not write *firstly*; your enumeration must be *first, secondly, thirdly, lastly*. It was one of those arbitrary rules whose observance was supposed by a certain class of purist to be a hallmark of correct writing. This rule, unlike many of the sort, had not even logic on its side. Of late years there has been a rebellion against these rules, and probably no contemporary grammarian will mind much whether you say *first* or *firstly*. Moreover, if you have chosen *first* it is perfectly permissible to do without the *ly*-words altogether and write *first, second, third, last*.

Flaunt

To *flaunt* something is to parade it ostentatiously. Do not confuse this word with *flout*, which means to disregard a rule or law contemptuously, as in 'he has flouted my authority'.

Follows (as follows)

Do not write *as follow* for *as follows*, however numerous may be the things that follow. 'The construction in *as follows* is impersonal, and the verb should always be used in the singular' (*OED*).

Forego

To *forego* is to go before (the foregoing provision of this Act). To *forgo* is to go without, to waive (he will forgo his right).

Forenames

Use *first names* or *other names*. *Christian names* applies only to Christians, and *given names* is American.

Forthwith

Use *at once* or *now*.

Forward

Use *send* if that will do. Confine the use of *forward* to the sense of send on, as in 'forward the letters to my new address'.

Framework

Within the framework of is a cliché. For 'problems within the framework of our organisation' write simply 'within our organisation', and for 'deal with the matter within the framework of E.E.C. regulations' you could use 'in conformity with E.E.C. regulations' for a change.

Fresh

This is overused. Prefer *new* or even *renewed* if that is all you mean; or recast the sentence so as to be able to use *again*.

Function (verb)

An overused verb. You could use instead *work*, *operate* or *act*.

Furnish

Use *give* unless you are talking about furniture. To furnish particulars simply means to tell.

Future

This word gives rise to verbosity. For 'in the near future' use *soon*, and for 'in the not too distant future' use *later* or *eventually*.

Gainfully employed

This is jargon. Use *working*.

Geared to

A vogue expression, as in 'an institution geared to the needs of the handicapped'. You could perhaps say *adjusted, suited* or *satisfying*.

Got

Have got, for *possess* or *have*, says Fowler, is good colloquial but not good literary English. Others have been more lenient. Dr Johnson said:

'He has got a good estate' does not always mean that he has acquired, but barely that he possesses it. So we say 'the lady has got black eyes', merely meaning that she has them.

When such high authorities differ, what is the plain man to think? If it is true that superfluous words are an evil, we ought to condemn 'the lady has got black eyes', but not 'the lady has got a black eye'. Still, writing for those whose prose inclines more often to primness than to colloquialisms, and who are not likely to overdo the use of *got*, we advise them not to be afraid of it. The Americans have the handy practice of saying 'I have gotten' for 'I have obtained' and reserving 'I have got', if they use this word at all, for 'I possess'. But the usual way for an American to express the British 'I haven't got' is 'I don't have', which is increasingly being used in British English.

Hard, Hardly

Hard, not *hardly*, is the adverb of the adjective *hard*. *Hardly* must not be used except in the sense of *scarcely*. *Hardly earned* and *hard-earned* have quite different meanings.

Hardly, like *scarcely*, is followed by *when*, not by *than*, in such a sentence as 'I had hardly begun when I was interrupted'. *Than* sometimes intrudes from a false analogy with 'I had no sooner begun than I was interrupted'.

Headquartered

To refer to an organisation as *headquartered* in Paris verges on jargon, but the expression is a concise one. Those who dislike it may prefer to say that the organisation has its headquarters there.

Help

The expression 'more than one can help' is a literal absurdity. It means exactly the opposite of what it says. 'I won't be longer than I can help' means 'I won't be longer than is unavoidable', that is to say, longer than I *can't* help. But it is good English idiom.

They will not respect more than they can help treaties exacted from them under duress. (Winston Churchill, *The Gathering Storm*.)

Writers who find the absurdity of the phrase more than they can stomach can always write 'more than they must' instead.

Henceforth

Prefer *from now on*.

Hindsight

A vogue expression, but a useful one. It is the logical opposite of *foresight*.

Historic

Historic means noted in history; *historical* means belonging to history. This useful differentiation should not be blurred by the use of one for the other.

For largely historic reasons the bulk of new town residents are tenants.

The third word is wrong and the first two are in the wrong order. *Largely* is not intended to qualify *historic*. We need 'Largely for historical reasons'.

But we must allow accountants to continue to use *historic costs* and *historic rates of interest*. This practice may be illogical, in more senses than one, but in both senses it is hallowed by long custom.

Hopefully, Thankfully, Regretfully

A new use for *hopefully* which seems to have originated in America has become common in Britain. It can be illustrated by the following three sentences, referring to a cricket match:

> The spectators waited hopefully for the rain to stop.
> Hopefully our opponents will be dismissed before the tea interval.
> Our team will start their innings hopefully immediately after tea.

In the first sentence *hopefully* is doing the ordinary job of an adverb in qualifying the verb: it tells us how the spectators waited. In the second it is used in the new way: it does not tell us how the opponents will be dismissed but how the speaker feels about it now. 'Our opponents will (we hope) be dismissed before the tea interval.' In the third we cannot tell which way it is being used: it could be equivalent to a parenthetical *we hope*, or it could be telling us that our side will certainly start their innings immediately after tea and will do so in a state of hope (that they will make the runs or that it will not rain again). But if the new use is intended, the ambiguity could be avoided by putting a comma after *innings* or by putting *hopefully* at the beginning of the sentence.

This new use of *hopefully* has been lambasted on both sides of the Atlantic, but it continues to spread. It is of course quite illogical, but that is not fatal to its survival. Idioms are apt to be obstinately illogical (see p. 37), and it seems that the new use of *hopefully* has now established itself as a new idiom. The careful writer is now faced with a new duty: if you use *hopefully* for either purpose, make sure you avoid any ambiguity about which use you intend.

Thankfully has adopted a similar course, taking the meaning *I am thankful to say* rather than *gratefully*. Thus: *I accepted a drink thankfully* (normal use); *Thankfully some beer was still left* (new use); *Thankfully I at once quenched my thirst* (may be either).

Other adverbs may follow these examples before long. *Regretfully* is already sometimes used to mean *I regret to say*. But this is rather perverse, because *regrettably* is already available for this meaning. *Hopefully* and *thankfully* can at least claim to be filling a gap left by the absence of *hopeably* and *thankably*.

Identify with

An overused phrase. In such contexts as 'groups that are identified with conservation' it might well be replaced, now and then, by *associated with* or *closely linked with*.

Ideology

This word offends some purists, but there seems to be no reason why it should, provided that its mesmeric influence is kept in check; the old-fashioned *creed* or *faith* may sometimes serve.

I.e.

This is sometimes used (by confusion with *e.g.*) to introduce an example. It stands for *id est* ('that is') and introduces a definition, as one might say 'we are meeting on the second Tuesday of this month, i.e. the tenth'. *E.g.* (*exempli gratia*) means 'for the sake of example' and introduces an illustration, as one might say 'let us meet on a fixed day every month, e.g. the second Tuesday'.

Immediately

Use the simpler *at once*. Do not use *immediately* for *as soon as*, as in 'notify me immediately you receive it'.

Immigrant

It is both offensive and inaccurate to extend the use of this word to cover all nonwhite British citizens, since many of these families have now been here for generations.

Impact

A vogue word in the sense of effect or influence, as in 'the impact of the microchip on industry'; and in the sense of ability to impress, as in 'a marketing strategy with great dramatic impact'.

Implement

This verb, meaning to carry out or fulfil, used to be hardly known outside the Scottish Bar. In 1926 Fowler 'could not acquit of the charge of pedantry' a writer who used the expression 'implementing Labour's promises to the electorate'. It is now too firmly established to be driven out, but the occasional use of *carry out*, *keep* or *fulfil* for a change would be refreshing and sounds less technical.

Inaugurate

Except with reference to formal and ceremonious occasions, use *start* or *begin*.

Inception

Use *start* or *beginning*.

Increasingly less

Replace this logically absurd combination by the familiar idiom *less and less*.

Inculcate

One *inculcates* ideas into people, not people with ideas; *imbue* would be the right word for that. A vague association with *inoculate* may have something to do with the mistaken use of *inculcate with*.

Indicate

If possible, use *show*. *Also* *say*

Infant

If you mean *baby*, say so.

Infer

It is a common error to use *infer* for *imply*:

> Great efforts were made to write down the story, and to infer that the support was normal. . . . I felt most bitter about this attitude . . . for . . . it inferred great ignorance and stupidity on the part of the enemy.

A writer or speaker *implies* what the reader or hearer *infers*. The difference is illustrated thus by A. P. Herbert:

> If you see a man staggering along the road you may infer that he is drunk, without saying a word; but if you say 'Had one too many?' you do not infer but imply that he is drunk.

There is authority for *infer* in the sense of *imply*, as there is for *comprise* in the sense of *compose*. But here again the distinction is worth preserving in the interests of the language.

Inform

Prefer *tell* someone, or *let* someone *know*. *Inform* cannot be used with a verb in the infinitive, and the writer of this sentence has gone wrong:

> I am informing the branch to grant this application.

He or she should have said *telling*, *asking* or *instructing*.

Initiate

Prefer *begin* or *start* for that meaning. One *initiates* people into ideas, not ideas into people. Use *instil* or *inculcate* for that.

Integrate

This is a useful word in its proper place, to describe the process of combining different elements into a whole. But it has become too popular. It seems now to be the inevitable word for saying that anything has been joined, mixed, combined or amalgamated with anything else.

Interface

Interface is a metaphor that has become increasingly common in official writing. If one or two dimensions are enough for you, you can make do with a *point of contact* or a *common frontier*. If you hanker after a third dimension, you will feel the need of an *interface*. It is at present a vogue word and must be regarded as on probation. The fact that it is sometimes 'broad', sometimes 'virtual' and sometimes sat on ('I find myself sitting on a number of interfaces') suggests that it may need watching.

Internecine

This fashionable word originally meant murderous, or mutually destructive; but it now usually refers, and will be taken to refer, to conflict within a group, as in 'internecine trades union disputes'. It would be pedantic to complain about this now well-established use.

Interpersonal

Another fashionable word. Interpersonal skills are the ability to get on with people, and learning in an interpersonal situation means learning with a teacher. Sometimes you could use *face-to-face* instead.

Interval

One would not suspect this word of obscurity, but it is sometimes misused to denote merely a space or a period of time, rather than a space or a period between two things or events.

. . . the training period was still 3 years, an interval widely regarded in the industry as being unrealistically long.

This writer has more to answer for than the misuse of *interval*. He must tell us why he prefers unrealistically to *too*.

Some people object to the common phrase *at frequent intervals* on the ground that it is the frequency of the occurrences in question, not of the intervals between them, that matters. This is pedantry. But it is not pedantry to suggest that

It is expected that the Committee will meet at three or four monthly intervals, but more frequently if necessary

would have been better without the *intervals*. 'Every three or four months' or 'three or four times a year' is what is meant.

Involve

The meaning of this popular word has been diluted to a point of extreme insipidity. Originally it meant *wrap up in something, enfold*. Then it acquired the figurative meaning *entangle a person in difficulties or embarrassment*, and especially *implicate in crime*. Then it began to be used as though it meant nothing more than *include, contain* or *imply*. It has thus developed a vagueness that makes it the delight of those who dislike the effort of searching for the right word. It is consequently much used, generally where some more specific word would be better and sometimes where it is merely superfluous.

Here are a few examples:

The additonal rent involved will be £1. (Omit *involved*.)

There are certain amounts of the material available without permit, but the quantities involved are getting less. (Omit *involved*.)

It has been agreed that the capital cost involved in the installation of the works shall be included (. . . that the capital cost of installing . . .)

It has been inaccurately reported that anything from eight sheep to eight oxen were roasted at the affair. The facts are that six sheep only were involved. (*Involved* here seems to be an 'elegant variation' for *roasted*.)

Much labour has been involved in advertising. (Much labour has been expended on advertising.)

The area of dereliction involved is approximately 85 acres. (The derelict area is about 85 acres.)

Reserve *involved* for use where there is a suggestion of entanglement or complication, as when we say 'this is a most involved subject'. Here are two examples of its reasonable use:

This experience has thrown into high relief the complications and delays involved in the existing machinery for obtaining approval.

Mr Menzies protested against the Australian Government's acceptance of the invitation to the conference at Delhi on the Indonesian dispute, holding that Australia ought not to be involved.

Recently the word has undergone a further shift in meaning and it is now often used with the implication that getting involved is a desirable or a laudable thing rather than a worrying or an embarrassing one. This use is not to be objected to; it takes the word back nearer to its original meaning of *wrap up in something*. But from it has grown the current vogue of the noun *involvement*, which deserves an entry to itself.

Involvement

This is a vogue word which is becoming altogether too common for comfort. Its appeal is easy to understand: it says something that is not quite said by *co-operation, partnership, sympathy, sharing, contribution* or *responsibility*, though it is sometimes used where one of those less modish words would have done as well or better. Often it seems to be interchangeable with its fellow vogue word *participation*; indeed the two sometimes appear hand in hand. It is being reached for too often as a cosy substitute for exact meaning, and there are signs that it may before long become not merely tiresome but menacing to the language. Here are two examples:

Their involvement in, and response to, innovation is positive and refreshing.

The BBC should accept as a necessary and helpful development the [union's] policy of having more branch level participation in union decisions, in order to meet the desire of the [union's] rank and file for a greater sense of involvement in decision-making.

Irrespective of

If possible, rephrase your sentence so as to be able to say *whether or not*, or *even if*.

-Ise, -Ize

On the question whether verbs like *organise* and nouns like *organisation* should be spelt with an *s* or a *z* the authorities differ. There are some verbs (e.g. *advertise, comprise, despise, advise, exercise* and *surmise*) which are never spelt with a *z*. There are others (such as *organize*) for which the spelling with *z* is the only American form and is also a very common British one. This being so, the British writer has the advantage over the American that we may, if we wish, use an *s* all the time, for that will never be wrong, whereas *z* sometimes will be. But do not condemn those who use a *z* in its right place.

Isolation

In isolation is better replaced by *in itself*, or *alone*.

Issue (noun)

This word has a very wide range of proper meanings as a noun, and should not be made to do any more work—the work, for instance, of *subject, topic, consideration* and *dispute*.

Item

This word is a great favourite, especially in business letters. It is made to mean almost anything. It is safe to say that any sentence in which this omnibus use occurs will be improved either by omitting the word or by substituting a word of more definite meaning. The following is a typical instance; it refers to the condition of a set of batteries:

> The accessory items, stands and other parts, are satisfactory, but the sediment approximates to 1-in. in depth and . . . this item can be removed conveniently when the renewals are effected.

Accessory items should be changed to *accessories* and *this item can be removed* to *this can be removed*.

The next example is from a notice of a meeting:

> *I shall be able to attend the meeting.
> *I shall not be able to attend the meeting.
>   * Please delete item not required.

Here what meant *sediment* in the first example appears to mean *words*.

Lay, Lie

The two verbs are *lay*, *laid*, *laid* and *lie*, *lay*, *lain*, and they have been confused even by distinguished writers. Byron wrote 'There let him lay.' Most of us, however, are likelier to get into trouble with their compound forms. To *overlay* is to superimpose, to *overlie* is to be situated over. Similarly, to *underlay* is to put underneath and to *underlie* is to lie under. You *overlay* a coat of paint with another coat, and *underlay* a carpet with felt, but a layer of coal may *overlie* or *underlie* a layer of sandstone.

Leading question

This does not mean, as is widely supposed, a question difficult to answer, or the most important of a series of questions, or a question designed to embarrass the person questioned. On the contrary, it means a question designed to help the person by suggesting the answer—a type of question not permitted when a witness is being examined by the counsel who called him or her.

Less, Fewer

The following is taken from *Good and Bad English* by Whitten and Whitaker:

> *Less* appertains to degree, quantity or extent; *fewer* to number. Thus, *less* outlay, *fewer* expenses; *less* help, *fewer* helpers; *less* milk, *fewer* eggs.
>
> But although *fewer* applies to number do not join it to the word iself: a *fewer* number is incorrect; say a *smaller* number.
>
> *Less* takes a singular noun, *fewer* a plural noun; thus *less* opportunity, *fewer* opportunities.

Here is a good example of the wrong use:

> . . . including only a handful of West Indians and even less Asians.

Not only should *less* be *fewer*, but the metaphor of a handful is ill-chosen in this context; *a few* or *very few* would have been better.

Liable

Since *liable* may mean 'apt' or 'likely, replace *you are liable to* by *you have to* if that is what you mean.

Lieu

Replace *in lieu of* by the simpler *instead of*.

Limited (adjective)

It is pedantry to object to the use of *limited* in the sense of *restricted* on the ground that everything that is not unlimited must be limited. But the word should be used with discretion and should not be allowed to make a writer forget such words as *few* and *small*. To write *a limited number of* when you mean *a few* or *of limited use* when you mean *not very useful* is not perhaps a heinous crime, but if you find yourself doing it too often it is time to ask yourself whether you are forming pompous habits.

Liquidate, Liquidation

Liquidation is the process of ascertaining a debtor's liabilities and apportioning his assets to meet them—winding up his affairs in fact. The meaning has lately been enlarged so as to signify other sorts of winding-up, especially, with a sinister twist, the removal of opposition in a totalitarian state by methods possibly undisclosed but certainly unpleasant. The reason for this extension is no doubt to be found in the extension of the practices for which it stands. There are some who deprecate this enlargement of the word's meaning, but there seems to be no use in doing that; it is well established, and can justly claim to be expressive and vivid and to fill a need.

But *liquidate* is one of the words which, having once broken out, run wild. It is now apparently regarded as suitable for denoting the ending of anything, from massacring a nation to giving an employee notice. It should therefore be handled with care, and not put to such unsuitable duty as when a Local Authority writes:

> These still stand as examples of solid building construction, which will stand the test of many more years of wear and tear before their usefulness has been finally liquidated.

Literally

Do not use *literally* to intensify a metaphorical exaggeration. People in a famine relief camp may be *literally* starving, but it is not a thing to say about oneself towards lunchtime.

Livelihood

Use the more familiar *living*, if possible.

Loath, Loth

This adjective means *unwilling* and the dictionaries allow both spellings for it. But you may prefer to use *loth*, just to show that you are clear about the difference between the adjective *loth* and the verb *to loathe* (meaning to *detest*).

Locality

Use *place*.

Macro-, Micro-

These form words with a fashionably pseudo-learned ring to them. They are all very well in suitably technical combinations such as *macrofossil* and *micronucleus*, but beware of using them where *large* or *small* would do instead.

Mafia

Another vogue word in its figurative sense of a too powerful clique or network. We hear, for instance, of the mental-health mafia and the literary mafia. *Mafia* suggests the idea of a conspiracy that is out to get one.

Major

This is a harmless word, unexceptionable in such company as *major road*, *major war*, *major railway accident*. But it is so much used that it is supplanting other more serviceable ones. Do not let *major* make you forget such words as *main*, *important*, *chief*, *principal*, *great* or *big*. For instance, *important* or *significant* might have been better than *major* in:

We do not expect to see any major change in the near future.

Majority

The major part or *the majority* ought not to be used when a plain *most* would meet the case. They should be reserved for occasions when the difference between a majority and a minority is significant. Thus:

Most of the members have been slack in their attendance.
The majority of members are likely to be against the proposal.

Marginal(ly)

Marginal has a number of useful jobs to do. *Marginal notes* are notes written in the margin; *marginal cost* has an exact meaning in economics, which no other expression would convey so well; *marginal seats* provide half the excitement in a General Election. But in recent years *marginal* has come to be increasingly used to mean no more than *small*. This misuse has now reached the status of an epidemic. Here is a very small selection of passages where the epidemic has struck:

The second [point] is the marginal, but important, improvement in the detection rate of the police. (Slight)

The expenditure involved in restoring the building to its proper use was marginal. (Small)

The system is now only marginally capable of meeting the estimated demands upon it. (Barely)

The terms negotiated were marginally not as good as I could have wished. (Not quite as good)

[The building] is marginally within the danger zone. (Just)

Materialise

Do not use this showy word, or the similar word *eventuate*, when a simpler one would do as well or better, e.g. *happen*, *occur*, *come about*, *take place*, or even the colloquial *come off*.

It was thought at the time that the incoming tenant would take over the fixtures. This did not however materialise. (But he did not.)

The possibility of the boiler strike to which he had referred at the last meeting had not eventuated. (The boiler strike which he had said at the last meeting was possible had not occurred.)

Materialise has its own work to do as a transitive verb in the sense of investing something non-material with material attributes, and as an intransitive verb in the sense of appearing in bodily form.

Matrix

This is a respectable word with several exact meanings in anatomy, printing, geology, mathematics, etc. It becomes no more than would-be impressive jargon when it is used in the vague sense of situation or surrounding substance:

Folklore must be maintained in the matrix of the culture for some time before it can be accepted as genuine.

This seems to mean that a belief does not count as real folklore unless people have believed it for some time.

Maximal, Maximise; Minimal, Minimise; Optimal, Optimise

These words are all enjoying a vogue and are more often than not signs of a writer who is muddled or showy or both. Here are some extreme examples:

> Junior staff in contact with clients cannot be involved only minimally in their jobs without serious consequences for staff–client relationships.

This seems a perversely obscure way of saying that if junior staff are not much interested in their jobs they will not get on well with their clients.

> Unless the consultant's marginal productivity is greater than the sum of all his patients', the optimisation of the consultant's time is not identical to the maximisation of the community's resources.

This makes the excellent point that if a consultant keeps an outpatient clinic waiting because he is on another job, the time wasted by the patients is probably worth more in total than the time he spent on that other job: so, on the whole, the community loses. Surely a writer who can score a good mark for using *marginal* correctly should have been able to put it better.

> The likelihood of such divergence is minimised where the clientele includes all citizens at some time in their lives; it is maximised where the clientele is a small minority, especially where this minority is regarded as in some way deviant *vis-à-vis* the rest of society.

There seems no good reason why *minimised* and *maximised* should have been preferred to *smallest* and *greatest*. Perhaps it was thought that these unpretentious words would be in some way deviant *vis-à-vis* the rest of the sentence.

Maximum, Minimum

These sometimes cause confusion, leading to the use of one for the other. An example is the following sentence, which is taken from a passage deprecating the wounding of wild animals by taking too long shots at them:

> It would be impossible to attempt to regulate shooting by laying down minimum ranges and other details of that sort.

It would indeed.

A correspondent sent, as an instance of ambiguity of a similar kind,

> On the mainland of Ross the population has been more than halved in the past twenty years.

Though not actually ambiguous, this is certainly not the clearest way of saying that the population has fallen to less than half.

Methodology

This means a body of methods, or an analysis of procedures. Use *way* or *method* if that is all you mean.

Meticulous

Meticulous means, by derivation, 'full of little fears', and like its plebeian cousin *pernickety* may still retain a flavour of fussiness over trifles. It is now, however, widely used in a favourable sense like *scrupulous* or *punctilious*, so that one may speak of a meticulously spotless kitchen. There seems to be no point in objecting to this slight shift of emphasis.

Mitigate

Mitigate for *militate* is a curiously common malapropism. An example is:

> I do not think that this ought to mitigate against my chances of promotion.

More, Less

It is curiously easy to say the opposite of what one means when making comparisons of quantity, time or distance, especially if they are negative. A common type of this confusion is to be found in such statements as 'Meetings will be held at not less than monthly intervals', when what is meant is that the meetings will be not less frequent than once a month, that is to say, at not more than monthly intervals. A similar confusion led during the second world war to the issue of a Control of Maps Order prohibiting the sale of maps drawn to a scale greater than one mile to the inch, instead of greater than one inch to the mile, as was intended.

Much more and *much less* sometimes get transposed, as do *most of all* and *least of all*. Short sentences present little difficulty.

He cannot walk, much less run.
I dislike cats, most of all Siamese.

But in longer sentences the writer sometimes goes astray, as in:

He finds it difficult to walk slowly on level ground, much less run up a hill with a pack on his back.
I do not approve of cats treating me as an intruder in my own house, most of all those horrible Siamese.

Moreover

If appropriate, replace it by *and* or *also*, or simply leave it out.

Name

Replace *by the name of* by *called*.

Nature

In the nature of can usually be replaced by *like*.

Necessitate

It may necessitate could become, in simpler English, *you may have to*.

Negative

An answer *in the negative* is 'no', and that is the better way to express the idea.

Normalise

Those who feel that we have altogether too many new verbs ending in -ise may prefer to write *restore to normal*.

Notify

Prefer the simpler *tell*. To *notify* people is to *let them know*.

Office

Consider replacing the somewhat starchy *this office* by *I*, *me*, *we*, *us*. It is more human.

Ongoing

An overused vogue word, particularly in the phrase *ongoing situation*. You could replace it by *continuing* or *in progress*.

Opinion

This word gives rise to verbosity. 'In my opinion' and 'I am of the opinion that . . .' mean merely 'I think . . .'.

Optimistic

Optimism is the quality of being disposed in all circumstances to hope for the best. The edge of the meaning of *optimistic* is being blunted by its being habitually used for *sanguine* or *hopeful*, when what is referred to is not a habit of mind, but an attitude towards particular circumstances.

Examples of its unsuitable use are:

The negotiations are making good progress, but it is too early to be either optimistic or pessimistic about them.

When an offender has shown positive interest in improving his skills ready for discharge, this is an optimistic sign.

Optimum (adjective)

Do not treat *optimum* as a showy synonym for *best*. It should only be used of the product of conflicting forces. The optimum speed of a car is not the fastest it is capable of, but that which reconciles in the most satisfactory way the conflicting desires of its owner to move quickly, to economise petrol and to avoid needless wear and tear.

There is no great harm in preferring *optimal* to *optimum* as an adjective. But where *optimum* is wrong, *optimal* will be wrong too.

Oral, Verbal

Oral has to do with the mouth; *verbal* has to do with words. To use *verbal* where *oral* is meant is another surprisingly common mistake. It is not very helpful to describe a message or an agreement as *verbal*; most messages and agreements are in words rather than, say, figures or smoke-signals. But an *oral* message or agreement is one expressed by word of mouth, not in writing. A *verbal* misunderstanding or argument is one about words rather than substance, and the words may have been either written or spoken: an *oral* misunderstanding is due, as like as not, to a faulty telephone line.

One need not know Latin to remember which is which. No one chooses wrong in *oral contraceptive* or *verbal diarrhoea*.

Order (in order that)

May or *might* are the words to follow 'in order that'. It is incorrect to write 'in order that no further delay will occur' or 'in order that we can have a talk on the subject'. And it is stilted to write *in order to* where *to* will serve equally well. Jack and Jill did not go up the hill in order to fetch a pail of water. English idiom recognises *so as to* and *so that they might* as alternative ways of expressing purpose. *So* without *that* ('so they could fetch a pail of water') is heard in conversation but is not yet established in written English.

Otherwise

This word, though an adverb, has had the odd experience of being used more and more as an adjective, a noun or a verb.

The adjective that *otherwise* dispossesses is *other*. This is exemplified in such a sentence as 'There are many difficulties, legal and otherwise, about doing what you ask'.

The noun or verb that *otherwise* displaces is whatever noun or verb had the contrary meaning to the one just mentioned. In

I have had one case which turned on the validity or otherwise of a Nigerian customary marriage.

We shall be glad if you will now confirm or otherwise your desire to avail yourself of our offer.

the words replaced are *invalidity* and *deny*.

All these uses can be condemned as ungrammatical, and since it is just as easy in the first case to write *other* and in the others either to omit *or otherwise* or to substitute the appropriate noun or verb, there is no reason why one should not do the grammatical thing.

Sometimes *other* gets its revenge, and supplants *otherwise*.

It is news to me that a sheep improves the land other than by the food fed through it.

Overall (adjective)

The favour that this word has won is astonishing. It is an egregious example of the process we have described as boring out a weapon of precision into a blunderbuss. Indeed the word seems to have a quality that impels people to use it in settings in which it has no meaning at all.

Examples of its meaningless use are:

The overall growth of London should be restrained.

Radical changes will be necessary in the general scheme of Exchequer grants in aid of local authorities, therefore, to secure that overall the policy of the Government in concentrating those grants as far as possible where the need is greatest is further developed. (Here, it will be observed, *overall* is an adverb.)

It looks as if the yield for the first fortnight . . . will be fewer than forty fresh orders, representing an overall annual output of no more than a thousand.

When *overall* is not meaningless, it is commonly used as a synonym for some more familiar word, especially *average, total* and *aggregate*.

For *aggregate*:

Compared with the same week a year ago, overall production of coal showed an increase of more than 100,000 tons [i.e. deep-mined plus opencast.]

For *in all* or *altogether*:

Overall the broadcasting of 'Faust' will cover eight hours.

For *total*:

I have made a note of the overall demand of this company for the next year. We must be realistic in terms of recruitment possibilities in determining the overall manpower figure for the Civil Service.

For *average*:

The houses here are built to an overall density of three to the acre.

For *on balance*:

The purpose of the plan is to enable a larger initial payment to be made and correspondingly lower payments subsequently, entailing an overall saving to the customer.

Overall, according to the dictionaries, means 'including everything between the extreme points', as one speaks of the overall length of a ship. For this purpose it is useful, and it is so used in a trader's announcement:

Overall floor space taken up by the machine is 24 by 24 inches.

But it is high time that its excursions into the fields of other words were checked.

Overlook

This can correctly mean either 'fail to notice' or 'supervise'. To avoid possible confusion between these two almost opposite senses, you may sometimes have to use *neglect* or *disregard* for the one, and *oversee* for the other.

Parameter

Parameter is a mathematical term with a precise meaning which, it is safe to say, not one in ten of those who use it understands. It is becoming increasingly common as a grand and showy synonym for *boundary*, *limit*, *framework* or *condition*. Sometimes one even suspects its users of confusing it with *perimeter*. The wise writer's attitude to *parameter*, as to *interface*, must at present be 'watch it'.

Participate, Participation

These, like *involvement*, are vogue words for the process of sharing in a communal experience or enterprise. There seems to be no reason against replacing *participate*, in such contexts as 'participate in the election', by *take part*.

Pending

It can mean 'not yet dealt with', as in 'decisions still pending'. *Pending* is there an adjective. It is also used as a preposition meaning 'while awaiting':

> They delayed their decision pending further information.

As a preposition, *pending* is a starchy word. Try to recast your sentence so as to be able to use *until*.

Per annum, Per diem, Per capita

Use *a year, a day, a head*.

Percentage, Proportion, Fraction

Do not use the expression *a percentage* or *a proportion* when what you mean is *some*, as in:

> This drug has proved of much value in a percentage of cases.
> The London Branch of the National Association of Fire Officers, which includes a proportion of station officers . . .

Here *percentage* and *proportion* pretend to mean something more than *some*, but do not really do so. They do not give the reader any idea of the number or proportion of the successful cases or station officers. One per cent is just as much 'a percentage' as 99 per cent. So, for that matter, is 200 per cent.

Use *percentage* or *proportion* only if you want to express not an absolute number but the relation of one number to another, and can give at least an approximate degree of exactitude; so that, though you may not be able to put an actual figure on the percentage or proportion, you can at any rate say 'a high percentage', 'a large proportion', 'a low percentage', 'a small proportion'. But never use such phrases merely for the sake of their impressive appearance. Remember the simple words *many*, *few* and *some* and do not desert them for proportions and percentages unless your meaning compels you to.

Fraction is different. It has become so common to use 'only a fraction' in the sense of 'only a small fraction' that it would be pedantry to object that $^{999}/_{1000}$ is as much a fraction as $^{1}/_{1000}$, just as it would certainly be pedantry to point out to anyone who says 'He has got a temperature' that 37 degrees is just as much 'a temperature' as 40.

Perform

To many people this means 'give a performance'. If you mean no more than *do*, then that is a less misleading word to use.

Period

This word leads to verbosity. A period of ten years and a short period of time are no more than ten years and a short time. Apart from its technical senses, a period is chiefly a length of time rather than a point in time. If you want to know the *date* when something happened, it is misleading to ask for the *period* of its happening.

Persons

Except in very formal contexts, use *people* or *anyone*.

Position, Situation

These words have a great fascination for those who are given to blurring the sharp outlines of what they have to say. A debate takes place in the House of Commons about a rise in unemployment. A speaker wants to say that he does not see how it would have been possible for the Government to make sure of there being enough work. Does he say so? No; the miasma of abstract words envelops him and he says, 'In view of all the circumstances I do not see how this situation could have been in any way warded off'. Later the spokesman for the Government wants to strike a reassuring note, and express his confidence that the rise is only temporary. He too takes refuge in vague abstractions. 'We shall', he says, 'ease through this position without any deleterious effect on the long-term situation.' On an historic occasion it fell to a master of words to make an announcement at a time of even graver crisis. Winston Churchill did not begin his broadcast on the 17th June 1940: 'The position in regard to France is extremely serious.' He began: 'The news from France is very bad.' He did not end it: 'We have absolute confidence that eventually the situation will be restored.' He ended: 'We are sure that in the end all will come right.'

Position and *situation*, besides replacing more precise words, have a way of intruding into sentences that can do better without them:

> It may be useful for inspectors to be informed about the present situation on this matter. (. . . to know how this matter now stands.)
>
> Unless these wagons can be moved the position will soon be reached where there will be no more wagons to be filled. (. . . there will soon be no more. . . .)

Position in regard to is an ugly expression, not always easy to avoid, but used more often than it need be. 'The position in regard to invisible exports has deteriorated' seems to come more naturally to the pen than 'invisible exports have dropped'. Come to that, *I am in a position to* is a pompous way of saying that I *can*.

Practical, Practicable

Practical, with its implied antithesis of *theoretical*, means useful in practice. *Practicable* means capable of being carried out in action.

> That which is practicable is often not practical. Anything that is possible of accomplishment by available means may be called practicable. Only that which can be accomplished successfully or profitably under given circumstances may be called practical.
>
> (Weseen, *Words Confused and Misused*)

Practically

Use *almost*, *nearly* or *all but* to make a change from this overused word. Since it can also mean 'in a practical way', avoid using *practically* in such phrases as 'practically trained engineers', which might be ambiguous.

Preceding

Use *last*, or *before*.

Prescribed

Prefer *set* or *fixed*.

Presently

This means 'soon'. The use of *presently* for 'now' has always been current in Scotland, is common in American use, and is being revived in Britain, but it may still cause offence. Do not write things like 'he is presently giving a course of lectures'.

Prevent

You may choose any one of three constructions with *prevent*: *prevent him from coming*, *prevent him coming* and *prevent his coming*. The first usually sounds the most natural, the second is somewhat informal.

Pristine

The first meaning of *pristine* was original and primitive. It then came to mean uncorrupted by civilisation and free from impurity, as in 'pristine innocence'. The word is now often used to mean fresh and clean:

the pristine, air-conditioned building.

Many reputable writers use *pristine* in this latest sense, but the usage has not yet won total acceptance.

Productive

Is productive of is a longwinded way of saying *produces*.

Provisions

Use *rules* or *terms*, if that is what you mean.

Purport

The ordinary meaning of the verb *purport* is 'to profess or claim by its tenor', e.g. 'this letter purports to be written by you'. The use of the verb in the passive is an objectionable and unnecessary innovation. 'Statements which were purported to have been official confirmed the rumours' should be 'statements which purported to be official confirmed the rumours'. The noun *purport* may be more simply paraphrased by *upshot*, *gist*, or *substance*.

Pursuant to

This is legal jargon:

> pursuant to the terms of this agreement.

Use *under* or *according to*.

Qua

This Latin word means in the capacity of. To be interested in money qua money is, in plain English, to be interested in money as such. Prefer the plain English alternative.

Question (noun)

Alternatives to this somewhat overworked word are *subject*, *topic*, *matter* and *problem*. Note that *no question that* is ambiguous. 'There's no question that children are involved' might be taken to mean either that they certainly are, or that they certainly are not. To make matters clear use *no question but that* for the first, and *no question of* for the second.

Reaction

Reaction may be properly used as a technical term of chemistry (the response of a substance to a reagent), of biology (the response of an organ of the body to an external stimulus), or of mechanics ('to every action there is an equal and opposite reaction'). In its figurative sense ('What is your reaction?') it really ought to connote an automatic rather than an intellectual response. Yet it is increasingly used to replace such words as *opinion, view* or *impression*, whether or not reflection has preceded reaction. This offends many lovers of the language; they would say that though an *immediate reaction*, a *market reaction* and even *popular reaction* are admissible, a *considered reaction* is nonsense. *Reaction*'s extension of meaning may now be so firmly settled that to condemn it would be to risk a charge of pedantry. If so it is a pity, for exactitude of meaning has been blunted. But you need not fear such a charge if you choose yourself to use *reaction* only where you mean something automatic or 'off-the-cuff'. In its extended meaning it has plenty of natural synonyms.

In scientific use a stimulus has a *reaction on* something, so that in such contexts *reaction* means *effect*. In general use, however, the preposition must be *to*. It is permissible to say 'His reaction to your letter was unfavourable'. But it is not permissible to say 'Your letter had an unfavourable reaction on him'.

Realistic

This word has become exceeding popular, perhaps because it has a question-begging flavour. What is realistic is what the writer agrees with.

Realistic is ousting words like *sensible, reasonable, practical, feasible, workmanlike, probable, likely, frank*. In some contexts it seems to mean merely *big*. For that is what a trade union official really means when he says that he will not start negotiations until he gets a 'realistic offer' from the employers. Here are a few examples to illustrate the versatility of the word:

The Corporation was morally bound to take up underwriting so long as the terms were realistic at the time of issue. (Reasonable)

Lord X made a most realistic observation when he suggested that the House of Lords should meet later. (Sensible)

This was a realistic speech which pulled no punches. (Frank)

We do not see as realistic any major expansion in the direct teaching of research methods. (Likely)

Grants towards the cost should be realistic. (Generous, *or* big enough)

We must be realistic in terms of recruitment possibilities in determining the overall manpower figure for the Civil Service. (We must not overestimate recruitment possibilities . . .)

Reason is because

It is redundant to write 'the reason for this is because . . .' instead of either 'this is because' or 'the reason for this is that . . .' as in these examples:

> The Ministry say that the reason for the higher price of the biscuits is because the cost of chocolate has increased.
>
> The reason for the long delay appears to be due to the fact that the medical certificates went astray. (A confusion between 'the reason is that the certificates went astray' and 'the delay is due to the fact that the certificates went astray'.)

Something equally repetitious seems to have happened here:

> The cause of the delay is due to the shortage of materials. (A confusion between 'the cause of the delay is the shortage' and 'the delay is due to the shortage'.)
>
> By far the greater majority. . . . (A confusion between 'the great majority' and 'by far the greater part'.)
>
> He did not say that all actions for libel or slander were never properly brought. (A confusion between 'that all actions . . . were improperly brought' and 'that actions . . . were never properly brought'.)
>
> An attempt will be made this morning to try to avert the threatened strike. (Those who were going to do this might have attempted to do it or tried to do it. But merely to attempt to try seems rather half-hearted.)
>
> Save only in exceptional circumstances will any further development be contemplated. (A confusion between 'only in exceptional circumstances will any further development be contemplated' and 'save in exceptional circumstances no further development will be contemplated'.)

Redundant

This is an imposing word and, no doubt for that reason, is used in senses that it will not bear. The idea of *too much* is inseparable from it; 'superabundant, superfluous, excessive', is what the dictionary says. To treat it as meaning merely *inappropriate* is wrong. *Redundancy* now has a special meaning in relation to employment, when some of the present work-force becomes unnecessary either because the work is being reduced or because new methods or machinery enable it to be done by fewer people. But when a trade union official insists that there must be 'no redundancy' he does not necessarily mean that no steps must be taken which will make any of the work-force redundant: he means rather that no one must be dismissed as a result.

Reference

To *have reference to* something is to *be about* it or to *mean* it. You could perhaps use these shorter forms.

Refrain from

Try to rephrase your injunction so as to use the more direct *do not.*

Refute

Refute should be confined to the sense of proving falsity or error, and not used loosely as a synonym for *deny* or *repudiate,* as in:

The local authority refute the suggestion that their proposal is extravagant, but their arguments are wholly unconvincing.

Regard (verb)

Unlike *consider*, *count* and *deem*, *regard* requires an *as* in such a sentence as 'I regard it as an honour'.

Reimburse

Use *repay*, or *pay back.*

Remittance

Use *payment* or *money.*

Render

In such contexts as 'to render irrigation unnecessary' you could use *make.*

Rendition

The word is less common in England than in America, where it is freely

Relate (to)

used in the sense of translation or version, and of musical or dramatic performance. For these we in Britain still prefer *rendering*, though, with our usual disposition to imitate things American, we are giving *rendition* a run.

Represent

Use *show*, *be*, or *stand for* (as in 'the red lines represent railways') if that is what you mean.

Require

Require should not be used as an intransitive verb in the sense of *need* as it is in:

You do not require to do any stamping unless you wish (you need not).
Special arrangements require to be worked out in the light of local circumstances (special arrangements will have to be. . .).

In general, prefer *want* or *need* rather than *require*, as in 'Will you be requiring breakfast?'

Resource

There is much pardonable confusion between *resource*, *recourse* and *resort*. The most common mistake is to write 'have resource to' instead of 'have recourse to' or 'have resort to'. The correct usage can be illustrated thus:

They had recourse (or had resort, or resorted) to their reserves; it was their last resource (or resort); they had no other resources.

Responsibility

'You have a *responsibility* to notify your landlord' may be more clearly expressed as 'You must'.

Result

As a result of can be shortened to *because of*, and *with the result that* to *so that*.

Rewarding

As variations on this overused word, you could use *satisfying*, *gratifying*, or *valuable*.

Said

Do not use *said* as an adjective, as in 'the said shop'; it is legal jargon. *The*, *this*, or *those* will almost always make your meaning perfectly clear.

Scenario

This is a cliché word in the sense of an outline of an imagined chain of events:

On this scenario, our supplies will be exhausted in two years.

You could use instead *scheme*, *plan*, *programme*, or *prediction*, as appropriate.

Seasonable, Seasonal

Seasonable means suitable for the season. Snow is seasonable at Christmas. *Seasonal* means depending on the season. Hotel work at a ski resort is seasonal.

Short supply

Things that are in short supply are *scarce*. Prefer the shorter form.

Sibling

This jargon word is a necessary technical term for those sociologists and educationalists who need to refer to a brother or sister irrespective of sex. Unless you really need to say this, use the more human words *brother*, *brothers*, *brother and sister*, etc.

Significant(ly)

This is a good and useful word, but it has a special flavour of its own and it should not be thoughtlessly used as a mere variant of *important, considerable, appreciable,* or *quite large* when one is dealing with numbers or quantities or other mathematical concepts. For one thing it has a special and precise meaning for mathematicians and statisticians which they are entitled to keep inviolate. For another, it ought to be used only where there is a ready answer to the reader's unspoken question 'Significant, is it? And what does it signify?' In 'A significant number of Government supporters abstained', 'There was no significant loss of power when the engine was tested with lower-octane fuel', this question can clearly be answered; but the writers of the following had no such significance in mind:

> Even after this . . . reduction the size of our labour force in [a particular factory] will remain significantly larger than it was a year ago. (Appreciably)
>
> A significantly higher level of expenditure must be expected on libraries etc. (Considerably)
>
> After the low proportion of commitments in respect of new dwellings during the fourth quarter there was a significant upturn in January. (Marked)

In the last example the upturn (or increase) might, it is true, have been significant; but the context shows that it was not, and no one is going to give the benefit of the doubt to anyone who writes of a *low proportion of commitments in respect of new dwellings.*

Spearhead (verb)

This word is popular in managerial contexts, where to *spearhead* a new marketing programme presumably sounds more dashing than merely to *head, lead,* or *direct* it. *Spearhead* is not yet quite at home in other sorts of serious writing.

Spectrum

This is another vogue word; not, of course, in its technical sense in the field of optics, but as it is used in such phrases as 'a wide spectrum of interests'. You could use *range* instead.

Subsequent(ly)

Use *then, after, afterwards, later.*

Substitute

To *substitute* means to put a person or thing in the place of another; it does not mean to take the place of another. When *A* is removed and *B* is put in its place, *B* is substituted for *A* and *A* is replaced by *B*. *Substitute* is wrongly used in:

The Minister said he hoped to substitute coarse grain with home-grown barley.

The Minister ought either to have used the verb *replace*, or, if he insisted on the verb *substitute*, to have said 'to substitute home-grown barley for coarse grain'.

Suffice

Prefer *be enough*, or *do*.

Supplementary

The word is familiar in the combination *supplementary benefit*. Elsewhere, prefer *extra* or *more*.

Syndrome

Syndrome is another fairly new metaphor which is in danger of overuse. The medical meaning of the word is a group of symptoms or malfunctions which together suggest a particular disease or state of imbalance, either physical or mental. A syndrome is not itself a disease and the metaphor is wrongly used in such a sentence as 'His latest speeches suggest that on this topic he is suffering from an unfortunate syndrome'.

Target

Target has been a favourite metaphor for so long that it might have been expected by now to be almost dead. But it is not, and there is still an air of absurdity about its use in ways unsuitable to its literal meaning. We cannot yet use it as if it were the same as *objective*, *goal*, *ambition*, or *purpose*. We must still remember that to hit a target is to be successful and that to overshoot it is not. Yet we still find ourselves being urged, as we have been for years, not only to reach and attain our targets, but also to fight for them, to achieve them and to obtain them. We must not be lulled by a near target. It is discouraging to be a long way short of our target and (what seems to amount to the same thing) to be a long way behind it, but it is splendid to be a long way beyond it. The headline 'Target in danger' means that it is in no danger of being hit, and 'Target in sight' is intended to be exceptionally encouraging to those who are trying to hit it. A lecturer has recorded that when he read in a speech by one of our Ministers of a 'global target' which, to the Minister's regret, could not be 'broken down', the picture that came into his mind was of a drunken reveller attacking a Belisha beacon. Nor should journalists say that only so many tons of coal are needed to 'top the year's bull's-eye', forgetting that bull's-eyes, like golf balls, give more satisfaction when hit in the middle than when topped. Nor can even the exigencies of headline language excuse the headline 'Export Target Hit' to introduce the news that, owing to a dock strike, the export target is unlikely to be hit.

Terminate

Prefer *end*.

Thus

Where suitable, use the less formal *so* or *therefore*.

Times more

We learn at an early age that if we want to declare one figure to be a multiple of another the proper way of doing so is to say that the first is so many times the second. 'Nine is three times three.' But in later life some of us seem to forget this and to say 'Nine is three times greater (or three times more) than three'. Not only is this an unnecessary distortion of a simple idiom, but a stickler for accuracy might say even that it was misleading: the figure that is three times greater (or more) than three is not nine but twelve. Consider the following passage:

The figure set for the production of iron ore in 1955 is 3,500,000 tons, more than twelve times greater than in 1936; for pig-iron it is 2,000,000 tons, ten times greater than in 1936; for cement 4,000,000 tons, twice as much as in 1936.

The writer of this seems to have forgotten the formula of the multiplication tables until reminded of it by the awkwardness of having to say 'twice greater'. Confusion is even more likely to be caused if percentages are used. 'Production was 250 per cent greater than in 1928' leaves the reader guessing whether it was 2½ times or 3½ times as great.

Transpire

Do not use *transpire* for *happen* or *occur*, but in the sense of *become known*, as in the following:

It transpired that he was not qualified for the position.

Try

Try and is well established in conversational use. *Try to* is to be preferred in serious writing.

Ultimately

Prefer *at last* or *in the end*.

Undersigned

Instead of referring to yourself as *the undersigned*, use the more human *I* or *we*.

Undertake

Prefer *promise*, or *agree*, or *say you will*.

Unequal

The idiom is unequal *to* a task; not *for* a task, and not *to* perform it.

Usage

This word is increasingly employed where *use* would be the right word. *Usage* does not mean *use*; it means either a manner of use (e.g. rough usage) or a habitual practice creating a standard (e.g. modern English usage). An example of *usage* wrongly employed for *use* is

There is a serious world shortage of X-ray films due to increasing usage in all countries. In this country usage during the first six months of 1951 was 16 per cent greater than in the corresponding period of 1950.

An academic authority wrote that certain words

come into usage, are gradually made meaningless by constant repetition and then suddenly drop out of usage altogether.

One of the words which will so drop out is, we must hope, the word *usage*, in contexts where *use* is meant.

Utilise, Utilisation

These words are rarely needed, for the simple word *use* will almost always serve. The official (not a Government official) who wrote 'This document is forwarded herewith for the favour of your utilisation' might have written 'please use this form'. That says what needed to be said in four syllables instead of 21.

Nor is there any reason for preferring the longer word in

The sum so released may, upon receipt of same, be utilised to reimburse you for expenses.

Certainly *use* and *utilise* should not be employed merely by way of 'elegant variation' as they apparently are in

It is expected that Boards will be able to utilise the accommodation now being used by the existing governing bodies.

Valid, Validate, Validity

These vogue words can often be replaced, in the interest of variety, by *sound* or *relevant* ('a valid theory, or argument'), by *confirm* ('validate a hypothesis'), and by *standing* or *merit*.

Very

One of the most popular objects of the chase among amateur hunters of so-called grammatical mistakes used to be *very* with a past participle—'very pleased', for instance. It is true that *very* cannot be used grammatically with a past participle—that one cannot, for instance, say 'The effect was very enhanced'; we must say *much* or *greatly*. But when the participle is no longer serving as a verb, and has become in effect an adjective, it is legitimate to use *very* with it as with most other adjectives. There can be no objection to 'very pleased', which means no more than 'very glad', or to 'very tired', which means no more than 'very weary'. But it will not do to say 'very disliked' or 'very removed', and in between are doubtful cases where it will be as well to be on the safe side and refrain from *very*.

Viable

Viable is a biological term denoting the capacity of a newly created organism to maintain its separate existence. Its present vogue rivals that of *realistic*; its victims include *durable, lasting, workable, effective, practicable* and many others.

What is the alternative? I do not pretend to know the answer but who can doubt that no viable answer is possible unless and until the Commonwealth is strong and united within itself.

Here 'no viable answer is possible' seems to be merely a confused way of saying 'no alternative will work'.

It is legitimate to wonder whether a new business venture will prove economically viable (though some may prefer to wonder whether it will pay). But if one is considering how best to subject Zetland school teachers to Aberdeen University lectures there is no excuse for

It may well be more economically viable to send a team of lecturers to Lerwick than to bring a group of teachers from Zetland to Aberdeen.

Here *more economically viable* merely means *cheaper*.

View

You can replace *with a view to* by *to* alone.

Voluntary

Prefer something like *by choice* if that is what you mean. *Voluntary* might be taken to mean unpaid, as in 'voluntary workers'.

Wastage

There is a difference that ought to be preserved between *waste* and *wastage*; *wastage* should not be used as a more dignified alternative to *waste*. The ordinary meaning of *waste* is 'useless expenditure or consumption, squandering (of money, time, etc.)'. The ordinary meaning of *wastage* is 'loss by use, decay, evaporation, leakage, or the like'. You may, for instance, properly say that the daily wastage of a reservoir is so many gallons. But you must not say that a contributory factor is the wastage of water by householders if what you mean is that householders waste it.

Waste has recently come to be used as a verb, signifying 'convert into waste paper'. This is quite unnecessary (*destroy* or *throw away* will generally do) and may be misleading. One hopes, at least, that *waste* does not carry its normal meaning in the following official instructions.

Departments are asked to ensure that as many documents as possible are wasted at the earliest possible date.

On receipt of [this leaflet] previous prints are to be wasted.

Whensoever

Use *when*.

-Wise

This is overused in such contexts as 'an impossible proposition resources-wise'. It certainly makes for conciseness, since *taxwise* and *saleswise* are shorter than 'from the tax point of view' and 'when it comes to sales', but the device has not yet established itself in good writing.

Worth

Worth has a prepositional force, and needs an object. This object may be either *while* (i.e. the spending of time) or something else. It is therefore correct to say 'this job is worth while'; it is also correct to say 'this job is worth doing'. But one object is enough, and so it is wrong to say 'this job is worth while doing'.

Worthwhile as an adjective ('a worthwhile job') is written either as one word or with a hyphen.

18
Epilogue

He that will write well in any tongue, must follow this counsel of Aristotle, to speak as the common people do, to think as wise men do; and so should every man understand him, and the judgment of wise men allow him.

Roger Ascham

A book designed as a guide to officials in the use of English runs the risk of giving a false impression. It cannot help being concerned mainly with faults to be corrected, and so may make the picture look blacker than it is. The true justification for such a book is not so much that official English is specially bad as that it is specially important for it to be good. The efficiency of government, central and local, depends to an ever-increasing extent on the ability of a large number of officials to express themselves clearly. At present there is a popular idea that most of them cannot—or will not—do so. The term *officialese* has been invented for what is supposed to be their ineffective way of trying.

It is not true that officials write a language of their own of a uniquely deplorable kind. Undoubtedly they have their peculiarities of style. So have journalists theirs. It is reasonable to attribute those of officials in the main to the peculiar difficulties with which official writers have to contend. As we have seen, much of what they write has to be devoted to the almost impossible task of translating the language of the law, which is obscure in order that it may be unambiguous, into terms that are simple and yet free from ambiguity. And our system of government imposes on officials the need always of being cautious and often of avoiding a precision of statement that might be politically dangerous. Moreover, they do not easily shake off the idea that dignity of position demands dignity of diction. But it is certainly wrong to imagine that official writing, as an instrument for conveying thought, is generally inferior to the lamentably low standard now prevalent except among professional writers. It is not only officials who yield to the lure of the pompous or meretricious word, and overwork it; it is not they alone who sometimes fail to think clearly what meaning they want to convey by what they are about to write, or fail to revise and prune what they have written so as to make sure that they have conveyed it. From some common faults officials are comparatively free. Most of them write grammatically correct English. Their style is untainted by the silly jargon of commercialese, the catchpenny tricks of the worst sort of journalism, the more nebulous nebulosities of politicians, or the recondite abstractions of Greek or Latin origin in which men of science, philosophers and economists often wrap their thoughts. Sometimes it is very good, but then no one notices it. Occasionally it reaches a level of rare excellence.

The fact is not that officials do uniquely badly but that they are uniquely vulnerable. Making fun of them has always been one of the diversions of the British public. The fun sometimes has a touch of malice in it, but the habit springs from qualities in the British character that no one would like to see atrophied. The field for its exercise and the temptation to indulge in it are constantly growing. *De facto* executive power, which during the seventeenth and eighteenth centuries moved from the King to Ministers, is being diffused lower still by the growth of social legislation. The theory that every act of every official is the act of a Minister is wearing thin. The 'fierce light that beats upon a throne and blackens every blot' is no longer focused on the apex; it shines on the whole pyramid. So many people have to read so many official instructions. These offer a bigger target for possible criticism than any other class of writing except journalism, and they are more likely to get it than any other class, because our readers' critical faculty is sharpened by being told—as we all so often have to be nowadays—that they cannot do something they want to, or must do something they do not want to, or that they can only do something they want to by going through a lot of tiresome formalities.

So it is natural enough that official writing, with its undeniable tendency to certain idiosyncrasies of style, should have been worked up into a stock joke. The professional humorist, in print or on the stage or on the air, can always be sure of a laugh by quoting or inventing bits of it. It is a way of getting one's own back. It is pleasantly flattering to the critics' sense of superiority. Bagehot once pictured the public of his day as saying to themselves with unction:

Thank God *I* am not as that man; *I* did not send green coffee to the Crimea;

I did not send patent cartridge to the common guns and common cartridge to the breech-loaders. *I* make money; that miserable public functionary only wastes it.

So we may imagine the critic of today saying: 'Thank God *I* am not as that man; when *I* write a letter I make my meaning plain; this miserable public functionary only obscures his, if indeed he ever had any'. He may be right about the functionary, but he is probably wrong about himself.

Though the spirit that still moves us to mock our officials may be healthy, the amusement can be overdone. Some critics of so-called officialese have indulged in it to excess, deriding without discrimination, putting in their pillory good as well as bad, sometimes even mistaking the inventions of other scoffers for monstrosities actually committed. That is regrettable. It is a curious fact that attempts to teach 'good English' often meet with resistance. Probably the explanation is that an exaggerated importance was for so long given to things that do not greatly matter; the conviction still lingers that instruction in good English means having to learn highbrow rules of no practical usefulness. It will take a long time to put the truth across that 'good English' consists less in observance of grammatical pedantries than in a capacity to express oneself simply and neatly. Unfair criticism arouses reasonable resentment, and increases the difficulty of creating an atmosphere receptive to the new ideas. Even the notion that *officialese* in its derogatory sense is encouraged by authority has not wholly disappeared. The truth is, on the contrary, that great pains are now taken to train staffs to write clear and straightforward English—greater pains, probably, than are taken by any employer outside the Civil Service.

It does not seem to be true to say that the language itself is in decay. Its grammatical and syntactical usages are carefully preserved, perhaps too carefully. It is constantly being invited to assimilate new words, and seems capable of digesting many of them without any great harm, some indeed with profit. Some of the changes that have taken place in the meaning of words have weakened the language, but others have strengthened it, and on the whole there is no great cause for disquiet here. The language remains as fine and flexible an instrument as it was when used by Shakespeare and Bacon; in some respects it has been enriched. There are some alive today, and some recently dead, whose exact and delicate English would bear comparison with the outstanding writers of any generation. What is wrong is not the instrument itself but the way we use it. That should encourage us to hope that we may do better. When we are tempted to say that we have fallen away from the high standard of our forefathers, we must not forget the vast increase in the part played by the written word in our affairs. With such an increase in quantity it would be surprising if there were not some deterioration in quality. The field in which these faults are most readily noticed—the writings of officials for the guidance of the public—is almost wholly new. We cannot say whether the crop that grows there is better or worse than it was a hundred years ago, for no crop then grew there.

However unfair it may be that official English should have been singled out for derision, the fact has a significance that the official must not forget. Readers are on the look-out for the tricks of style that they have been taught to expect from official writing. Shortcomings are magnified, and the difficulties that all writers have in affecting their readers precisely as they wish are for the official wantonly increased. All the greater is our duty to try to convert *officialese* into a term of praise by cultivating unremittingly that clarity of thought and simplicity of expression which have always been preached by those who have studied the art of writing. Thus we may learn, in the words of the 400-year-old advice that heads this chapter, by thinking as wise men do, and speaking as the common people do, to make everyone understand us.

References

ALFORD, Henry, *The Queen's English*. George Bell & Co., 1889.

ALLBUTT, Sir T. Clifford, *Notes on the Composition of Scientific Papers*. Macmillan, 1925.

CAREY, G. V., *Mind the Stop*. Cambridge University Press, 1939. 2nd edition, Penguin 1971.

COBBETT, William, *A Grammar of the English Language*. Oxford University Press, 1906. New edition, with introduction by Robert Burchfield, 1984.

FOWLER, H. W., *Modern English Usage*. Oxford University Press. 2nd edition, revised by Sir Ernest Gowers, 1968.

HERBERT, Sir A. P., *What a Word!* Methuen, 1949.

MENCKEN, H. L., *The American Language*. 3 volumes. Routledge, 1948.

OGDEN, C. K. and I. A. Richards, *The Meaning of Meaning*. Kegan Paul, 1946.

Oxford English Dictionary (= *OED*). Clarendon Press. 2nd edition, 1953.

PARTRIDGE, E., *Dictionary of Clichés*. Routledge and Kegan Paul, 4th edition, 1950.

PERRIN, P. G., *Writer's Guide and Index to English*. New York. Scott, 1942.

SMITH, Logan Pearsall, *The English Language*. Williams and Norgate, 1912.

TREBLE, H. A. and G. H. Vallins, *An ABC of English Usage*. Oxford University Press, 1936.

WESEEN, Maurice H., *Words Confused and Misused*. Pitman, 1952.

WHITTEN, W. and F. Whitaker, *Good and Bad English*. Newnes. 2nd edition, 1950.

For further reading

BURCHFIELD, Robert, *The Spoken Word*. BBC, 1981.

COPPERUD, R. H., *American Usage and Style: The Consensus*. Van Nostrand Reinhold, 1980.

CRYSTAL, David, *Who Cares about English Usage?* Penguin, 1984.

GREENBAUM, Sidney (ed.), *The English Language Today*. Pergamon, 1984.

HOWARD, Philip, *New Words for Old*. Unwin Paperbacks, 1980.

HUDSON, Kenneth, *The Dictionary of Diseased English*. Macmillan, 1977.

MICHAELS, Leonard and Christopher Ricks (eds), *The State of the Language*. University of California Press, 1980.

MITTINS, W. H., Mary Salu, Mary Edminson and Sheila Coyne, *Attitudes to English Usage*. Oxford University Press, 1970.

QUIRK, Randolph, *The Use of English*. Longman. 2nd edition, 1968.

QUIRK, Randolph, Sidney Greenbaum, Geoffrey Leech, and Jan Svartvik, *A Comprehensive Grammar of the English Language*. Longman, 1985.

ROOM, Adrian, *The Penguin Dictionary of Confusibles*. Penguin, 1980.

The Right Word at the Right Time. Reader's Digest, 1985.

See also Carey and Fowler in the References list opposite.

Index

Words and phrases discussed in the text are indexed in *italics*; topics discussed are in roman type. Main page-references are in **bold** type.

Printed for Her Majesty's Stationery Office by Hazell Watson & Viney Ltd. C500 4/86